R Projects

by Joseph Schmuller, PhD

R Projects For Dummies®

Published by: **John Wiley & Sons, Inc.**, 111 River Street, Hoboken, NJ 07030-5774, www.wiley.com

Copyright © 2018 by John Wiley & Sons, Inc., Hoboken, New Jersey

Published simultaneously in Canada

No part of this publication may be reproduced, stored in a retrieval system or transmitted in any form or by any means, electronic, mechanical, photocopying, recording, scanning or otherwise, except as permitted under Sections 107 or 108 of the 1976 United States Copyright Act, without the prior written permission of the Publisher. Requests to the Publisher for permission should be addressed to the Permissions Department, John Wiley & Sons, Inc., 111 River Street, Hoboken, NJ 07030, (201) 748-6011, fax (201) 748-6008, or online at http://www.wiley.com/go/permissions.

Trademarks: Wiley, For Dummies, the Dummies Man logo, Dummies.com, Making Everything Easier, and related trade dress are trademarks or registered trademarks of John Wiley & Sons, Inc. and may not be used without written permission. All other trademarks are the property of their respective owners. John Wiley & Sons, Inc. is not associated with any product or vendor mentioned in this book.

LIMIT OF LIABILITY/DISCLAIMER OF WARRANTY: THE PUBLISHER AND THE AUTHOR MAKE NO REPRESENTATIONS OR WARRANTIES WITH RESPECT TO THE ACCURACY OR COMPLETENESS OF THE CONTENTS OF THIS WORK AND SPECIFICALLY DISCLAIM ALL WARRANTIES, INCLUDING WITHOUT LIMITATION WARRANTIES OF FITNESS FOR A PARTICULAR PURPOSE. NO WARRANTY MAY BE CREATED OR EXTENDED BY SALES OR PROMOTIONAL MATERIALS. THE ADVICE AND STRATEGIES CONTAINED HEREIN MAY NOT BE SUITABLE FOR EVERY SITUATION. THIS WORK IS SOLD WITH THE UNDERSTANDING THAT THE PUBLISHER IS NOT ENGAGED IN RENDERING LEGAL, ACCOUNTING, OR OTHER PROFESSIONAL SERVICES. IF PROFESSIONAL ASSISTANCE IS REQUIRED, THE SERVICES OF A COMPETENT PROFESSIONAL PERSON SHOULD BE SOUGHT. NEITHER THE PUBLISHER NOR THE AUTHOR SHALL BE LIABLE FOR DAMAGES ARISING HEREFROM. THE FACT THAT AN ORGANIZATION OR WEBSITE IS REFERRED TO IN THIS WORK AS A CITATION AND/OR A POTENTIAL SOURCE OF FURTHER INFORMATION DOES NOT MEAN THAT THE AUTHOR OR THE PUBLISHER ENDORSES THE INFORMATION THE ORGANIZATION OR WEBSITE MAY PROVIDE OR RECOMMENDATIONS IT MAY MAKE. FURTHER, READERS SHOULD BE AWARE THAT INTERNET WEBSITES LISTED IN THIS WORK MAY HAVE CHANGED OR DISAPPEARED BETWEEN WHEN THIS WORK WAS WRITTEN AND WHEN IT IS READ.

For general information on our other products and services, please contact our Customer Care Department within the U.S. at 877-762-2974, outside the U.S. at 317-572-3993, or fax 317-572-4002. For technical support, please visit https://hub.wiley.com/community/support/dummies.

Wiley publishes in a variety of print and electronic formats and by print-on-demand. Some material included with standard print versions of this book may not be included in e-books or in print-on-demand. If this book refers to media such as a CD or DVD that is not included in the version you purchased, you may download this material at http://booksupport.wiley.com. For more information about Wiley products, visit www.wiley.com.

Library of Congress Control Number: 2017964027

ISBN: 978-1-119-44618-7; 978-1-119-44617-0 (ebk); 978-1-119-44616-3 (ebk)

Manufactured in the United States of America

10 9 8 7 6 5 4 3 2 1

Contents at a Glance

Table of Contents

Introduction

If you're like me, you think the best way to learn is by doing. Don't just read about something — practice it! If you want to be a builder, then build. If you want to be a writer, then write. If you want to be a carpenter, then carpenter. (Yes, that noun and verb are the same. *Carpent* is not a word.)

I based this book on that learning-by-doing philosophy. My objective is for you to expand your R skill set by using R to complete projects in a variety of areas, and to learn something about those areas, too.

Even with those noble intentions, a book like this one can fall into a trap. It can quickly become a cookbook: Use this package, use these functions, create a graphic — and presto, you've finished a project and it's time to move on.

I didn't want to write that book. Instead, beginning in Part 2 (which is where the projects start), each chapter does more than just walk you through a project. First, I show you some background material about the subject area, and then (in most chapters) you work through a scaled-down project in that area to get your feet wet, and then you complete a larger project.

But a chapter doesn't end there. At the end of each chapter, you'll find a Suggested Project that challenges you to apply your newly minted skills. For each of those, I supply just enough information to get you started. (Wherever necessary, I include tips about potential pitfalls.)

Along the way, you'll also encounter Quick Suggested Projects. These are based on tweaks to projects you've already completed, and they present additional challenges to your growing skill set.

One more thing: Every subject area could be the basis for an entire book, so I can only scratch the surface of each one. Chapter 17 directs you toward resources that provide more information.

About This Book

I've organized this book into six parts.

Part 1: The Tools of the Trade

Part 1 is all about R and RStudio. I discuss R functions, structures, and packages, and I show you how to create a variety of graphics.

Part 2: Interacting with a User

The projects begin in Part 2, where you learn to create applications that respond to users. I discuss the `shiny` package for working with web browsers, and the `shinydashboard` package for creating dashboards.

Part 3: Machine Learning

This is the longest part of the book. I begin by telling you about the University of California–Irvine Machine Learning Repository, which provides the data sets for the projects. I also discuss the `rattle` package for creating machine learning applications. The projects cover decision trees, random forests, support vector machines, k-means clustering, and neural networks.

Part 4: Large(ish) Data Sets

The two projects in Part 4 deal with larger data sets than you encounter earlier in the book. The first project is a customer segmentation analysis of over 300,000 customers of an online retailer. A follow-up analysis applies machine learning. The second project analyzes a data set of more than 500,000 airline flights.

Part 5: Maps and Images

Two projects are in Part 5. The first is to plot the location (along with other information) of airports in one of the US states. The second shows you how to combine an animated image with a stationary one.

Part 6: The Part of Tens

The first chapter in Part 6 provides information about useful packages that can help you with future projects. The second tells you where to learn more about the subject areas of this book.

What You Can Safely Skip

Any reference book throws a lot of information at you, and this one is no exception. I intended it all to be useful, but I didn't aim it all at the same level. So if you're not deeply into the subject matter, you can avoid paragraphs marked with the Technical Stuff icon, and you can also skip the sidebars.

Foolish Assumptions

I'm assuming that you

- Know how to work with Windows or the Mac. I don't spell out the details of pointing, clicking, selecting, and other actions.
- Can install R and RStudio (I show you how in Chapter 1), and follow along with the examples. I use the Windows version of RStudio, but you should have no problem if you're working on a Mac.

Icons Used in This Book

You'll find icons in all *For Dummies* books, and this one is no exception. Each one is a little picture in the margin that lets you know something special about the paragraph it sits next to.

TIP

This icon points out a hint or a shortcut that helps you in your work and makes you an all-around better person.

REMEMBER

This one points out timeless wisdom to take with you as you continue on the path to enlightenment.

Pay attention to this icon. It's a reminder to avoid something that might gum up the works for you.

As I mention in the earlier section "What You Can Safely Skip," this icon indicates material you can blow past if it's just too technical. (I've kept this information to a minimum.)

Beyond the Book

In addition to what you're reading right now, this product comes with a free access-anywhere Cheat Sheet that presents a selected list of R functions and describes what they do. To get this Cheat Sheet, visit `www.dummies.com` and type **R Projects For Dummies Cheat Sheet** in the Search box.

Where to Go from Here

You can start the book anywhere, but here are a couple of hints. Want to introduce yourself to R and packages? You'll find the info in Chapters 1 and 2. Want to start with graphics? Hit Chapter 3. For anything else, find it in the table of contents or in the index and go for it.

If you're a cover-to-cover reader, turn the page. . . .

1

The Tools of the Trade

IN THIS PART . . .

Learn about R and RStudio

Understand R Functions and Structures

Create your own R Functions

Examine data

Use base R graphics

Graduate to `ggplot2` graphics

IN THIS CHAPTER

» **Getting R and RStudio on your computer**

» **Plunging into a session with R**

» **Working with R functions**

» **Working with R structures**

Chapter 1

R: What It Does and How It Does It

So you're ready to journey into the wonderful world of R! Designed by and for statisticians and data scientists, R has a short but illustrious history.

In the 1990s, Ross Ihaka and Robert Gentleman developed R at the University of Auckland, New Zealand. The Foundation for Statistical Computing supports R, which is growing more popular by the day.

Getting R

If you don't already have R on your computer, the first thing to do is to download R and install it.

You'll find the appropriate software on the website of the Comprehensive R Archive Network (CRAN). In your browser, type this web address if you work in Windows:

```
cran.r-project.org/bin/windows/base
```

Type this one if you work on the Mac:

```
cran.r-project.org/bin/macosx
```

Click the link to download R. This puts a `win.exe` file in your Windows computer or a `pkg` file in your Mac. In either case, follow the usual installation procedures. When installation is complete, Windows users see two R icons on their desktop, one for 32-bit processors and one for 64-bit processors (pick the one that's right for you). Mac users see an R icon in their `Application` folder.

Both addresses provide helpful links to FAQs. The windows-related one also has the link Installation and Other Instructions.

Getting RStudio

Working with R is a lot easier if you do it through an application called RStudio. Computer honchos refer to RStudio as an IDE (*I*ntegrated *D*evelopment *E*nvironment). Think of it as a tool that helps you write, edit, run, and keep track of your R code, and as an environment that connects you to a world of helpful hints about R.

Here's the web address for this terrific tool:

```
www.rstudio.com/products/rstudio/download
```

Click the link for the installer for your computer's operating system — Windows, Mac, or a flavor of Linux — and again follow the usual installation procedures.

In this book, I work with R version 3.4.0 and RStudio version 1.0.143. By the time you read this, later versions of both might be available.

After you finish installing R and RStudio, click on your brand-new RStudio icon to open the window shown in Figure 1-1.

The large Console pane on the left runs R code. One way to run R code is to type it directly into the Console pane. I show you another in a moment.

The other two panes provide helpful information as you work with R. The Environment/History pane is in the upper right. The Environment tab keeps track of the things you create (which R calls objects) as you work with R. The History tab tracks R code that you enter.

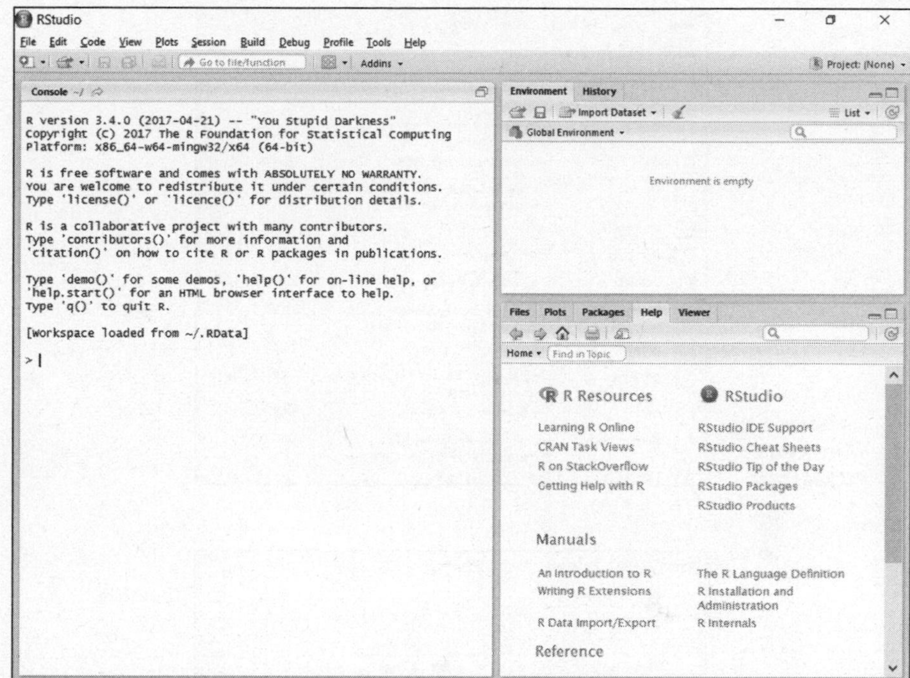

FIGURE 1-1: RStudio, immediately after you install it and click on its icon.

TIP

Get used to the word *object.* Everything in R is an object.The Files/Plots/Packages/Help pane is in the lower right. The Files tab shows files you create. The Plots tab holds graphs you create from your data. The Packages tab shows add-ons (called *packages*) that have downloaded with R. Bear in mind that *downloaded* doesn't mean "ready to use." To use a package's capabilities, one more step is necessary, and trust me — you'll want to use packages.

Figure 1-2 shows the Packages tab. I discuss packages later in this chapter.

The Help tab, shown in Figure 1-3, links you to a wealth of information about R and RStudio.

To tap into the full power of RStudio as an IDE, click the icon in the upper right corner of the Console pane. That changes the appearance of RStudio so that it looks like Figure 1-4.

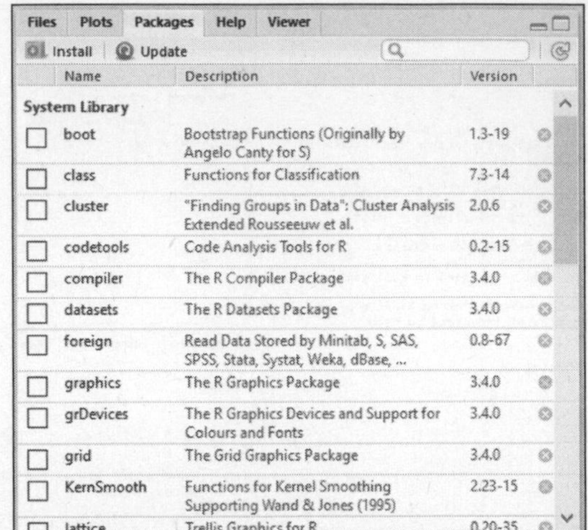

FIGURE 1-2: The RStudio Packages tab.

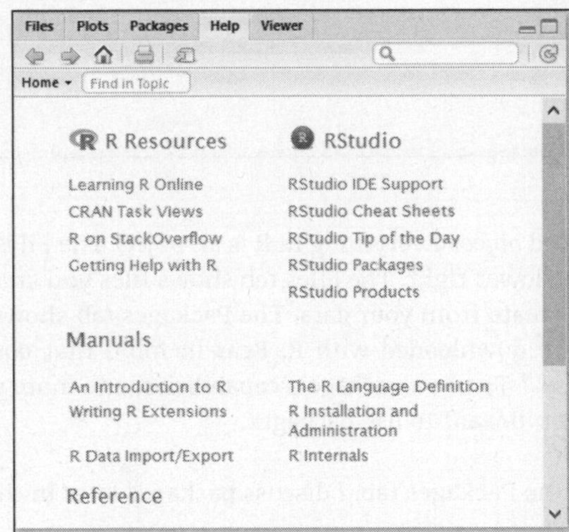

FIGURE 1-3: The RStudio Help tab.

The Console pane relocates to the lower left. The new pane in the upper left is the Scripts pane. You type and edit code in the Scripts pane by pressing Ctrl+R (Command+Enter on the Mac), and then the code executes in the Console pane.

TIP

Ctrl+Enter works just like Ctrl+R. You can also highlight lines of code in the Scripts pane and select Code ⇨ Run Selected Line(s) from RStudio's main menu.

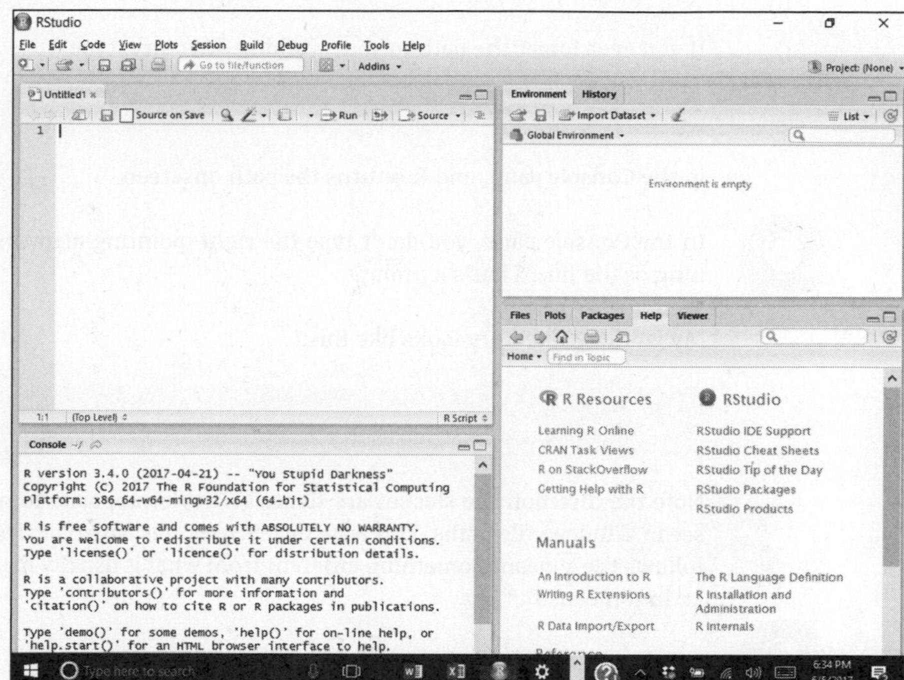

FIGURE 1-4: RStudio after you click the icon in the upper right corner of the Console pane.

A Session with R

Before you start working, select File ➪ Save As from the main menu and then save your work file as My First R Session. This relabels the tab in the Scripts pane with the name of the file and adds the `.R` extension. This also causes the filename (along with the `.R` extension) to appear on the Files tab.

The working directory

What exactly does R save, and where does R save it? What R saves is called the *workspace*, which is the environment you're working in. R saves the workspace in the *working directory*. In Windows, the default working directory is

```
C:\Users\<User Name>\Documents
```

On a Mac, it's

```
/Users/<User Name>
```

If you ever forget the path to your working directory, type

```
> getwd()
```

in the Console pane, and R returns the path onscreen.

TIP

In the Console pane, you don't type the right-pointing arrowhead at the beginning of the line. That's a prompt.

My working directory looks like this:

```
> getwd()
[1] "C:/Users/Joseph Schmuller/Documents
```

Note the direction the slashes are slanted. They're opposite to what you typically see in Windows file paths. This is because R uses \ as an *escape character* — whatever follows the \ means something different from what it usually means. For example, `\t` in R means *Tab key.*

TIP

You can also write a Windows file path in R as

```
C:\\Users\\<User Name>\\Documents
```

If you like, you can change the working directory:

```
> setwd(<file path>)
```

Another way to change the working directory is to select Session⇨Set Working Directory⇨Choose Directory from the main menu.

Getting started

Let's get down to business and start writing R code. In the Scripts pane, type

```
x <- c(5,10,15,20,25,30,35,40)
```

and then press Ctrl+R.

That puts this line into the Console pane:

```
> x <- c(5,10,15,20,25,30,35,40)
```

As I say in an earlier Tip paragraph, the right-pointing arrowhead (the greater-than sign) is a prompt that R puts in the Console pane. You don't see it in the Scripts pane.

Here's what R just did: The arrow-sign says that x gets assigned whatever is to the right of the arrow-sign. Think of the arrow-sign as R's *assignment operator.* So the set of numbers 5, 10, 15, 20 . . . 40 is now assigned to x.

REMEMBER

In R-speak, a set of numbers like this is a *vector.* I tell you more about this concept in the later section "R Structures."

You can read that line of code as "x gets the vector 5, 10, 15, 20."

Type **x** into the Scripts pane and press Ctrl+R, and here's what you see in the Console pane:

```
> x
[1]  5 10 15 20 25 30 35 40
```

The 1 in square brackets is the label for the first line of output. So this signifies that 5 is the first value.

Here you have only one line, of course. What happens when R outputs many values over many lines? Each line gets a bracketed numeric label, and the number corresponds to the first value in the line. For example, if the output consists of 23 values and the eighteenth value is the first one on the second line, the second line begins with [18].

Creating the vector x causes the Environment tab to look like Figure 1-5.

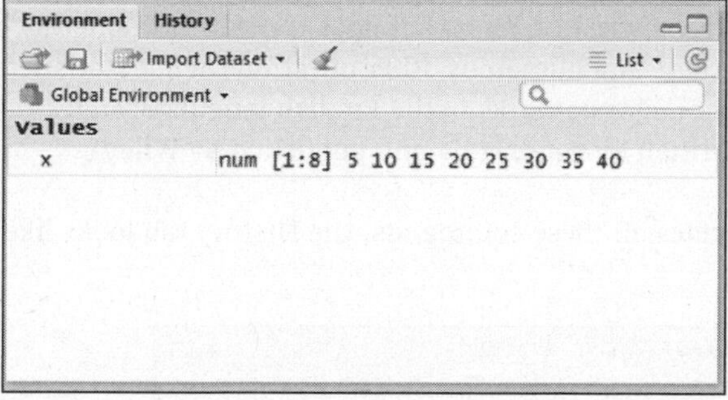

FIGURE 1-5: The RStudio Environment tab after creating the vector x.

TIP

Another way to see the objects in the environment is to type **ls()** into the Scripts pane and then press Ctrl+R. Or you can type **> ls()** directly into the Console pane and press Enter. Either way, the result in the Console pane is

```
[1] "x"
```

Now you can work with x. First, add all numbers in the vector. Typing **sum(x)** in the Scripts pane (be sure to follow with Ctrl+R) executes the following line in the Console pane:

```
> sum(x)
[1] 180
```

How about the average of the numbers in vector x?

That would involve typing **mean(x)** in the Scripts pane, which (when followed by Ctrl+R) executes

```
> mean(x)
[1] 22.5
```

in the Console pane.

TIP

As you type in the Scripts pane or in the Console pane, you see that helpful information pops up. As you become experienced with RStudio, you learn how to use that information.

Variance is a measure of how much a set of numbers differ from their mean. Here's how to use R to calculate variance:

```
> var(x)
[1] 150
```

What, exactly, is variance and what does it mean? (Shameless plug alert.) For the answers to these and numerous other questions about statistics and analysis, read one of the most classic works in the English language: *Statistical Analysis with R For Dummies* (written by yours truly and published by Wiley).

After R executes all these commands, the History tab looks like Figure 1-6.

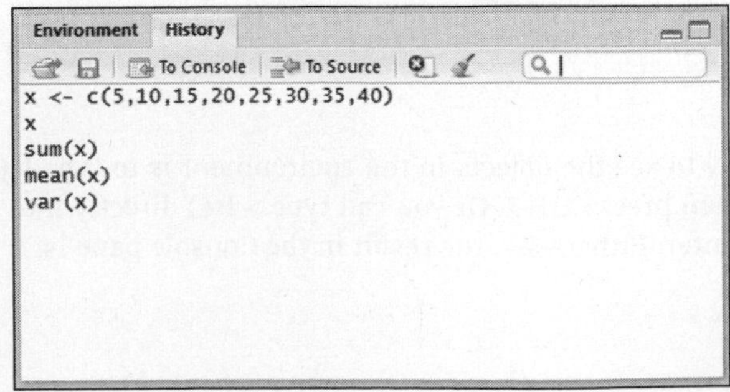

FIGURE 1-6: The History tab, after creating and working with a vector.

To end a session, select File ⇨ Quit Session from the main menu or press Ctrl+Q. As Figure 1-7 shows, a dialog box opens and asks what you want to save from the session. Saving the selections enables you to reopen the session where you left off the next time you open RStudio (although the Console pane doesn't save your work).

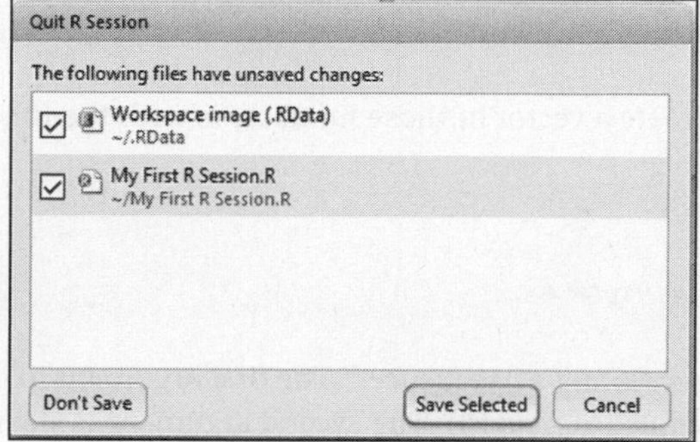

FIGURE 1-7: The Quit R Session dialog box.

REMEMBER

Moving forward, most of the time I don't say "Type this code into the Scripts pane and press Ctrl+Enter" whenever I take you through an example. I just show you the code and its output, as in the `var()` example.

REMEMBER

Also, sometimes I show code with the > prompt, and sometimes without. Generally, I show the prompt when I want you to see R code and its results. I don't show the prompt when I just want you to see R code that I create in the Scripts pane.

R Functions

The examples in the preceding section use `c()`, `sum()`, and `var()`. These are three *functions* built into R. Each one consists of a function name immediately followed by parentheses. Inside the parentheses are *arguments*. In the context of a function, *argument* doesn't mean "debate" or "disagreement" or anything like that. It's the math name for whatever a function operates on.

REMEMBER

Sometimes a function takes no arguments (as is the case with `ls()`). You still include the parentheses.

The functions in the examples I showed you are pretty simple: Supply an argument, and each one gives you a result. Some R functions, however, take more than one argument.

R has a couple of ways for you to deal with multi-argument functions. One way is to list the arguments in the order that they appear in the function's definition. R calls this *positional mapping*.

Here's an example. Remember when I created the vector x?

```
x <- c(5,10,15,20,25,30,35,40)
```

Another way to create a vector of those numbers is with the function seq():

```
> y <- seq(5,40,5)
> y
[1]  5 10 15 20 25 30 35 40
```

Think of seq() as creating a "sequence." The first argument to seq() is the number to start the sequence *from* (5). The second argument is the number that ends the sequence — the number the sequence goes *to* (40). The third argument is the increment of the sequence — the amount the sequence increases *by* (5).

If you *name* the arguments, it doesn't matter how you order them:

```
> z <- seq(to=40,by=5,from=5)
> z
[1]  5 10 15 20 25 30 35 40
```

So when you use a function, you can place its arguments out of order, if you name them. R calls this *keyword matching*. This comes in handy when you use an R function that has many arguments. If you can't remember their order, use their names, and the function works.

TIP

For help on a particular function — seq(), for example — type **?seq**. When you run that code, helpful information appears on the Help tab and useful information pops up in a little window right next to where you're typing.

User-Defined Functions

R enables you to create your own functions, and here are the fundamentals on how to do it.

The form of an R function is

```
myfunction <- function(argument1, argument2, ...){
  statements
  return(object)
}
```

Here's a function for dealing with right triangles. Remember them? A right triangle has two sides that form a right angle, and a third side called a *hypotenuse*. You might also remember that a guy named Pythagoras showed that if one side has length *a* and the other side has length *b*, the length of the hypotenuse, *c*, is

$$c = \sqrt{a^2 + b^2}$$

So here's a simple function called `hypotenuse()` that takes two numbers `a` and `b`, (the lengths of the two sides of a right triangle) and returns `c`, the length of the hypotenuse:

```
hypotenuse <- function(a,b){
  hyp <- sqrt(a^2+b^2)
  return(hyp)
}
```

Type that code snippet into the Scripts pane and highlight it. Then press Ctrl+Enter. Here's what appears in the Console pane:

```
> hypotenuse <- function(a,b){
+   hyp <- sqrt(a^2+b^2)
+   return(hyp)
+ }
```

Each plus sign is a *continuation prompt*. It just indicates that a line continues from the preceding line.

And here's how to use the function:

```
> hypotenuse(3,4)
[1] 5
```

TIP

Writing R functions can encompass *way* more than I've shown you here. To learn more, take a look at *R For Dummies*, by Andrie de Vries and Joris Meys (Wiley).

Comments

A *comment* is a way of annotating code. Begin a comment with the # symbol, which, as everyone knows, is called an *octothorpe*. (Wait. What? "Hashtag?" Get atta here!) This symbol tells R to ignore everything to the right of it.

Comments help someone who has to read the code you've written. For example:

```
hypotenuse <- function(a,b){ # list the arguments
  hyp <- sqrt(a^2+b^2) # perform the computation
  return(hyp) # return the value
}
```

Here's a heads-up: I don't typically add comments to lines of code in this book. Instead, I provide detailed descriptions. In a book like this, I feel it's the best way to get the message across.

R Structures

As I mention in the "R Functions" section, earlier in this chapter, an R function can have many arguments. An R function can also have many outputs. To understand the possible inputs and outputs, you must understand the structures that R works with.

Vectors

The *vector* is the fundamental structure in R. I show it to you in earlier examples. It's an array of elements of the same type. The data elements in a vector are called *components*.

To create a vector, use the function `c()`, as I do in the earlier example:

```
x <- c(5,10,15,20,25,30,35,40)
```

In the vector `x`, of course, the components are numbers.

In a *character vector*, the components are quoted text strings:

```
> beatles <- c("john","paul","george","ringo")
```

It's also possible to have a *logical vector*, whose components are TRUE and FALSE, or the abbreviations T and F:

```
> w <- c(T,F,F,T,T,F)
```

To refer to a specific component of a vector, follow the vector name with a bracketed number:

```
> beatles[2]
[1] "paul"
```

Within the brackets, you can use a colon (:) to refer to two consecutive components:

```
> beatles[2:3]
[1] "paul"   "george"
```

Want to refer to nonconsecutive components? That's a bit more complicated, but doable via c():

```
> beatles[c(2,4)]
[1] "paul"  "ringo"
```

Numerical vectors

In addition to c(), R provides two shortcut functions for creating numerical vectors. One, seq(), I showed you earlier:

```
> y <- seq(5,40,5)
> y
[1]  5 10 15 20 25 30 35 40
```

Without the third argument, the sequence increases by 1:

```
> y <- seq(5,40)
> y
 [1]  5  6  7  8  9 10 11 12 13 14 15 16 17 18 19 20 21 22 23
[20] 24 25 26 27 28 29 30 31 32 33 34 35 36 37 38 39 40
```

REMEMBER

On my screen, and probably on yours too, all the elements in y appear on one line. The printed page, however, is not as wide as the Console pane. Accordingly, I separated the output into two lines and added the R-style bracketed number [20] to the beginning of the second line.

TIP

R has a special syntax for creating a numerical vector whose elements increase by 1:

```
> y <- 5:40
> y
 [1]  5  6  7  8  9 10 11 12 13 14 15 16 17 18 19 20 21 22 23
[20] 24 25 26 27 28 29 30 31 32 33 34 35 36 37 38 39 40
```

Another function, `rep()`, creates a vector of repeating values:

```
> quadrifecta <- c(7,8,4,3)
> repeated_quadrifecta <- rep(quadrifecta,3)
> repeated_quadrifecta
 [1] 7 8 4 3 7 8 4 3 7 8 4 3
```

You can also supply a vector as the second argument:

```
> rep_vector <-c(1,2,3,4)
> repeated_quadrifecta <- rep(quadrifecta,rep_vector)
```

The vector specifies the number of repetitions for each element. So here's what happens:

```
> repeated_quadrifecta
 [1] 7 8 8 4 4 4 3 3 3 3
```

The first element repeats once; the second, twice; the third, three times; and the fourth, four times.

You can use `append()` to add an item at the end of a vector:

```
> xx <- c(3,4,5)
> xx
[1] 3 4 5
> xx <- append(xx,6)
> xx
[1] 3 4 5 6
```

and you can use `prepend()` to add an item at the beginning of a vector:

```
> xx <- prepend(xx,2)
> xx
[1] 2 3 4 5 6
```

How many items are in a vector? That's

```
> length(xx)
[1] 5
```

Matrices

A *matrix* is a 2-dimensional array of data elements of the same type. You can have a matrix of numbers:

5	30	55	80
10	35	60	85
15	40	65	90
20	45	70	95
25	50	75	100

or a matrix of character strings:

"john"	"paul"	"george"	"ringo"
"groucho"	"harpo"	"chico"	"zeppo"
"levi"	"duke"	"larry"	"obie"

The numbers are a 5 (rows) X 4 (columns) matrix. The character strings matrix is 3 X 4.

To create this particular 5 X 4 numerical matrix, first create the vector of numbers from 5 to 100 in steps of 5:

```
> num_matrix <- seq(5,100,5)
```

Then you use R's `dim()` function to turn the vector into a 2-dimensional matrix:

```
> dim(num_matrix) <- c(5,4)
> num_matrix
     [,1] [,2] [,3] [,4]
[1,]    5   30   55   80
[2,]   10   35   60   85
[3,]   15   40   65   90
[4,]   20   45   70   95
[5,]   25   50   75  100
```

Note how R displays the bracketed row numbers along the side, and the bracketed column numbers along the top.

Transposing a matrix interchanges the rows with the columns. The `t()` function takes care of that:

```
> t(num_matrix)
     [,1] [,2] [,3] [,4] [,5]
[1,]    5   10   15   20   25
[2,]   30   35   40   45   50
[3,]   55   60   65   70   75
[4,]   80   85   90   95  100
```

The function `matrix()` gives you another way to create matrices:

```
> num_matrix <- matrix(seq(5,100,5),nrow=5)
> num_matrix
     [,1] [,2] [,3] [,4]
[1,]    5   30   55   80
[2,]   10   35   60   85
[3,]   15   40   65   90
[4,]   20   45   70   95
[5,]   25   50   75  100
```

If you add the argument `byrow=T`, R fills the matrix by rows, like this:

```
> num_matrix <- matrix(seq(5,100,5),nrow=5,byrow=T)
> num_matrix
     [,1] [,2] [,3] [,4]
[1,]    5   10   15   20
[2,]   25   30   35   40
[3,]   45   50   55   60
[4,]   65   70   75   80
[5,]   85   90   95  100
```

How do you refer to a specific matrix component? You type the matrix name and then, in brackets, the row number, a comma, and the column number:

```
> num_matrix[5,4]
[1] 100
```

To refer to a whole row (like the third one):

```
> num_matrix[3,]
[1] 45 50 55 60
```

and to a whole column (like the second one):

```
> num_matrix[,2]
[1] 10 30 50 70 90
```

Although it's a column, R displays it as a row in the Console pane.

BUT BEAR IN MIND . . .

As I mention, a matrix is a 2-dimensional array. In R, however, an array can have more than two dimensions. One well-known set of data (which I use as an example in Chapter 3) has three dimensions: Hair Color (Black, Brown, Red, Blond), Eye Color (Brown, Blue, Hazel, Green), and Gender (Male, Female). So this particular array is 4 X 4 X 2. It's called `HairEycColor` and it looks like this:

```
> HairEyeColor
, , Sex = Male

       Eye
Hair    Brown Blue Hazel Green
  Black    32   11    10     3
  Brown    53   50    25    15
  Rcd      10   10     7     7
  Blond     3   30     5     8

, , Sex = Female

       Eye
Hair    Brown Blue Hazel Green
  Black    36    9     5     2
  Brown    66   34    29    14
  Red      16    7     7     7
  Blond     4   64     5     8
```

Each number represents the number of people in this group who have a particular combination of hair color, eye color, and gender — 16 brown-eyed, red-haired females, for example. (Why did I choose brown-eyed, red-haired females? Because I have the pleasure of looking at an extremely beautiful one every day!)

How would I refer to all the females? That's

```
HairEyeColor[,,2]
```

Lists

In R, a *list* is a collection of objects that aren't necessarily the same type. Suppose you're putting together some information on the Beatles:

```
> beatles <- c("john","paul","george","ringo")
```

One piece of important information might be each Beatle's age when he joined the group. John and Paul started singing together when they were 17 and 15, respectively, and 14-year-old George joined them soon after. Ringo, a late arrival, became a Beatle when he was 22. So

```
> ages <- c(17,15,14,22)
```

To combine the information into a list, you use the `list()` function:

```
> beatles_info <-list(names=beatles,age_joined=ages)
```

Naming each argument (`names, age_joined`) causes R to use those names as the names of the list components.

And here's what the list looks like:

```
> beatles_info
$names
[1] "john"   "paul"   "george" "ringo"

$age_joined
[1] 17 15 14 22
```

R uses the dollar sign ($) to indicate each component of the list. If you want to refer to a list component, you type the name of the list, the dollar sign, and the component name:

```
> beatles_info$names
[1] "john"   "paul"   "george" "ringo"
```

And to zero in on a particular Beatle, like the fourth one? You can probably figure out that it's

```
> beatles_info$names[4]
[1] "ringo"
```

R also allows you to use criteria inside the brackets. For example, to refer to members of the Fab Four who were older than 16 when they joined:

```
> beatles_info$names[beatles_info$age_joined > 16]
[1] "john"  "ringo"
```

Data frames

A list is a good way to collect data. A *data frame* is even better. Why? When you think about data for a group of individuals, you typically think in terms of rows that represent the individuals and columns that represent the data variables. And that's a data frame. If the terms *data set* or *data matrix* come to mind, you've got the right idea.

Here's an example. Suppose I have a set of six people:

> name <- c("al","barbara","charles","donna","ellen","fred") and that I have each person's height (in inches) and weight (in pounds):

```
> height <- c(72,64,73,65,66,71)
> weight <- c(195,117,205,122,125,199)
```

I also tabulate each person's gender:

```
> gender <- c("M","F","M","F","F","M")
```

Before I show you how to combine all these vectors into a data frame, I have to show you one more thing. The components of the `gender` vector are character strings. For purposes of data summary and analysis, it's a good idea to turn them into categories — the Male category and the Female category. To do this, I use the `factor()` function:

```
> factor_gender <-factor(gender)
> factor_gender
[1] M F M F F M
Levels: F M
```

In the last line of output, `Levels` is the term that R uses for "categories."

The function `data.frame()` works with the vectors to create a data frame:

```
> d <- data.frame(name,factor_gender,height,weight)
> d
     name factor_gender height weight
```

```
1       al          M    72    195
2 barbara           M    64    117
3 charles           M    73    205
4   donna           F    65    122
5   ellen           F    66    125
6    fred           M    71    199
```

Want to know the height of the third person?

```
> d[3,3]
[1] 73
```

How about all the information for the fifth person:

```
> d[5,]
   name factor_gender height weight
5 ellen             F     66    125
```

Like lists, data frames use the dollar sign. In this context, the dollar sign identifies a column:

```
> d$height
[1] 72 64 73 65 66 71
```

You can calculate statistics, like the average height:

```
> mean(d$height)
[1] 68.5
```

As is the case with lists, you can put criteria inside the brackets. This is often done with data frames, to summarize and analyze data within categories. To find the average height of the females:

```
> mean(d$height[d$factor_gender == "F"])
[1] 65
```

The double equal sign (==) in the brackets is a *logical operator*. Think of it as "if d$factor_gender is equal to "F".

REMEMBER

The double equal sign (a == b) distinguishes the logical operator ("if a equals b") from the assignment operator (a=b; "set a equal to b").

TIP

Yes, I know — I went through an involved explanation about `factor()` and how it's better to have categories (levels) than character strings, and then I had to put quote marks around `F` inside the brackets. R is quirky that way.

TIP

If you'd like to eliminate $ signs from your R code, you can use the function `with()`. You put your code inside the parentheses after the first argument, which is the data you're using.

For example,

```
> with(d,mean(height[factor_gender == "F"]))
```

is equivalent to

```
> mean(d$height[d$factor_gender == "F"])
```

How many rows are in a data frame?

```
> nrow(d)
[1] 6
```

And how many columns?

```
> ncol(d)
[1] 4
```

To add a column to a data frame, I use `cbind()`. Begin with a vector of scores:

```
> aptitude <- c(35,20,32,22,18,15)
```

Then add that vector as a column:

```
> d.apt <- cbind(d,aptitude)
> d.apt
     name factor_gender height weight aptitude
1      al             M     72    195       35
2 barbara             F     64    117       20
3 charles             M     73    205       32
4   donna             F     65    122       22
5   ellen             F     66    125       18
6    fred             M     71    199       15
```

Of for Loops and if Statements

Like many programming languages, R provides a way to iterate through its structures to get things done. R's way is called the *for loop*. And, like many languages, R gives you a way to test against a criterion: the *if* statement.

The general format of a `for` loop is

```
for counter in start:end{
            statement 1
                                                              .
                                                              .
                                                              .
statement n
}
```

As you might imagine, `counter` tracks the iterations.

The simplest general format of an `if` statement is

```
if(test){statement to execute if test is TRUE}
else{statement to execute if test is FALSE}
```

Here's an example that incorporates both. I have one vector `xx`:

```
> xx
[1] 2 3 4 5 6
```

And another vector `yy` with nothing in it at the moment:

```
> yy <-NULL
```

I want the components of `yy` to reflect the components of `xx`: If a number in `xx` is an odd number, I want the corresponding component of `yy` to be `"ODD"`, and if the `xx` number is even, I want the `yy` component to be `"EVEN"`.

How do I test a number to see whether it's odd or even? Mathematicians have developed *modular arithmetic*, which is concerned with the remainder of a division operation. If you divide *a* by *b* and the result has a remainder of *r*, mathematicians say that "a *modulo* b is r." So 10 divided by 3 leaves a remainder of 1, and 10 modulo 3 is 1. Typically, *modulo* gets shortened to *mod*, so that would be "10 mod 3 = 1."

Most computer languages write 10 mod 3 as `mod(10,3)`. (Excel does that, in fact.). R does it differently: R uses the double percent sign (`%%`) as its *mod operator:*

```
> 10 %% 3
[1] 1
> 5 %% 2
[1] 1
> 4 %% 2
[1] 0
```

I think you're getting the picture: `if xx[i] %% 2 == 0`, then `xx[i]` is even. Otherwise, it's odd.

Here, then, is the `for` loop and the `if` statement:

```
for(i in 1:length(xx)){
if(xx[i] %% 2 == 0){yy[i]<- "EVEN"}
else{yy[i] <- "ODD"}
}

> yy
[1] "EVEN" "ODD"  "EVEN" "ODD"  "EVEN"
```

IN THIS CHAPTER

» Installing packages

» Examining data

» Exploring a tidy little universe

Chapter 2

Working with Packages

A *package* is a collection of functions and data that augments R. If you're looking for data to work with, you'll find many data frames in R packages. If you're looking for a specialized function that's not in the basic R installation, you can probably find it in a package.

Installing Packages

As the Packages tab (in the Files/Plots/Packages/Help/Viewer pane of RStudio) shows, many packages come with the basic R installation, but if you want to work with them, you have to install them. This means putting them in a directory called the *library*. To get one of these comes-with-basic-R packages into the library, you click the Packages tab. Figure 2-1 shows this tab.

Scroll down until you find the package you're looking for. For this example, I work with the `datasets` package.

I click the check box next to `datasets`, and this line appears in the Console pane:

```
> library("datasets", lib.loc="C:/Program Files/R/R-3.4.0/library")
```

This tells you the `datasets` package is installed. For information on what's in this package, click on `datasets` in the Packages tab. (You can do this before you install or after.) Information about the package appears on the Help tab, as Figure 2-2 shows.

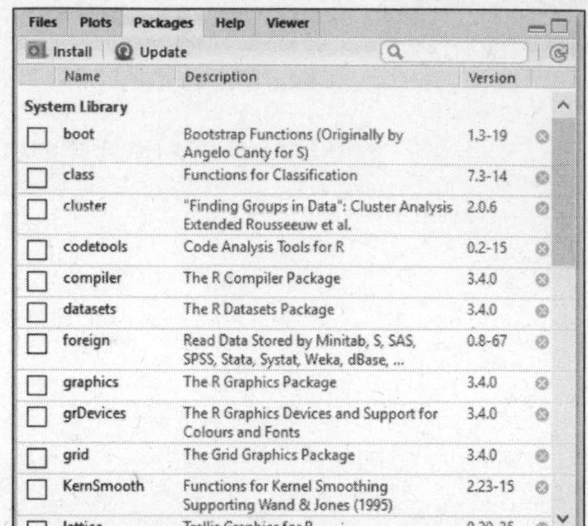

FIGURE 2-1: The Packages tab in RStudio.

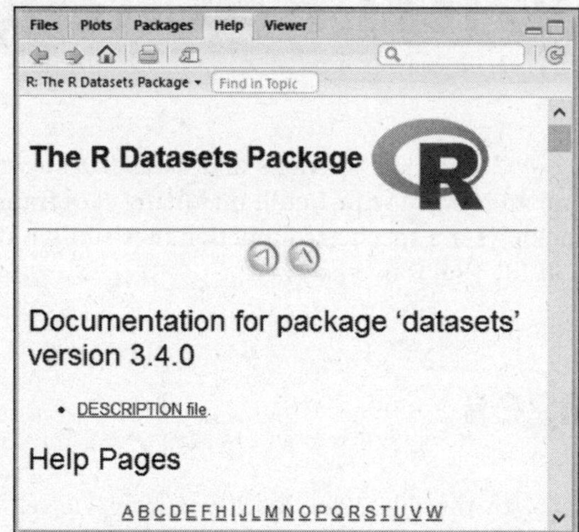

FIGURE 2-2: The Help tab, after clicking `datasets` on the Packages tab.

TIP

If you have a package downloaded but not installed, you can use `library()` to put it in the library:

```
> library(MASS)
```

This is also called *attaching* the package, and it's equivalent to checking the check box on the Packages tab.

Examining Data

Let's take a look at one of the data frames in `datasets`. The data frame `airquality` provides measurements of four aspects of air quality (ozone, solar radiation, temperature, and velocity) in New York City over the 153 days from May 1, 1973, to September 30, 1973.

Heads and tails

To get an idea of what the data look like, I can use the function `head()` to show the first six rows of the data frame:

```
> head(airquality)
  Ozone Solar.R Wind Temp Month Day
1    41     190  7.4   67     5   1
2    36     118  8.0   72     5   2
3    12     149 12.6   74     5   3
4    18     313 11.5   62     5   4
5    NA      NA 14.3   56     5   5
6    28      NA 14.9   66     5   6
```

and `tail()` to show the final six:

```
> tail(airquality)
    Ozone Solar.R Wind Temp Month Day
148    14      20 16.6   63     9  25
149    30     193  6.9   70     9  26
150    NA     145 13.2   77     9  27
151    14     191 14.3   75     9  28
152    18     131  8.0   76     9  29
153    20     223 11.5   68     9  30
```

Missing data

Notice the `NA` in each output. This means that a particular data entry is missing, a common occurrence in data frames. If you try to find the average of, say, Ozone, here's what happens:

```
> mean(airquality$Ozone)
[1] NA
```

You have to remove the NAs before you calculate, and you do that by adding an argument to `mean()`:

```
> mean(airquality$Ozone, na.rm=TRUE)
[1] 42.12931
```

The `rm` in `na.rm` means "remove," and `= TRUE` means "get it done."

Subsets

Sometimes you're interested in part of a data frame. For example, in `airquality`, you might want to work only with `Month`, `Day`, and `Ozone`. To isolate those columns into a data frame, use `subset()`:

```
> Month.Day.Ozone <- subset(airquality,
                            select = c(Month,Day,Ozone))
> head(Month.Day.Ozone)
  Month Day Ozone
1     5   1    41
2     5   2    36
3     5   3    12
4     5   4    18
5     5   5    NA
6     5   6    28
```

The second argument, `select`, is the vector of columns you want to work with. You have to name that argument because it's not the second argument in the definition of `subset()`.

The `subset()` function also allows you to select rows. To work with the ozone data from August, add as the second argument the criterion for selecting the rows:

```
> August.Ozone <- subset(airquality, Month == 8, select =  c(Month,Day,Ozone))
> head(August.Ozone)
   Month Day Ozone
93     8   1    39
94     8   2     9
95     8   3    16
96     8   4    78
97     8   5    35
98     8   6    66
```

R Formulas

Suppose I'm interested in how the temperature varies with the month. Having lived through many Mays through Septembers in my hometown, my guess is that the temperature generally increases in this data frame from month to month. Is that the case?

This gets into the area of statistical analysis, and at a fairly esoteric level. This book, strictly speaking, is not about statistics, so I'll just touch on the basics here to show you another R capability — the *formula*.

In this example, we would say that Temperature depends on Month. Another way to say this is that Temperature is the *dependent variable* and Month is the *independent variable*.

An R formula incorporates these concepts and serves as the basis for many of R's statistical functions and graphing functions. This is the basic structure of an R formula:

```
function(dependent_var ~ independent_var, data = data.frame)
```

Read the tilde operator (~) as "depends on."

Here's how I address the relationship between `Temp` and `Month`:

```
> analysis <- lm(Temp ~ Month, data=airquality)
```

The name of the function `lm()` is an abbreviation for *l*inear *m*odel. This means that I expect the temperature to increase linearly (at a constant rate) from month to month. To see the results of the analysis, I use `summary()`:

```
> summary(analysis)

Call:
lm(formula = Temp ~ Month, data = airquality)

Residuals:
     Min       1Q   Median       3Q      Max
-20.5263  -6.2752   0.9121   6.2865  17.9121

Coefficients:
            Estimate Std. Error t value Pr(>|t|)
(Intercept)  58.2112     3.5191  16.541  < 2e-16 ***
```

```
Month          2.8128     0.4933   5.703 6.03e-08 ***
---
Signif. codes:  0 '***' 0.001 '**' 0.01 '*' 0.05 '.' 0.1 ' ' 1

Residual standard error: 8.614 on 151 degrees of freedom
Multiple R-squared:  0.1772, Adjusted R-squared:  0.1717
F-statistic: 32.52 on 1 and 151 DF,  p-value: 6.026e-08
```

Whoa! What does all that mean? For the complete answer, see the book shamelessly plugged in Chapter 1. Right now, I'll just tell you that the `Estimate` for `Month` indicates that temperature increases at a rate of 2.8128 degrees per month between May and September. Along with the `Estimate` for `(Intercept)`, I can summarize the relationship between `Temp` and `Month` as

$$Temp = 58.2112 + (2.8128 \times Month)$$

where *Month* is a number from 5 to 9.

You might remember from algebra class that when you graph this kind of equation, you get a straight line — hence the term *linear model*. Is the linear model a good way to summarize these data? The numbers in the bottom line of the output say that it is, but I won't go into the details.

REMEMBER

The output of `summary()` (and other statistical functions in R) is a list. (See Chapter 1.) So if you want to refer to the `Estimate` for `Month`, that's

```
> s <- summary(analysis)
> s$coefficients[2,1]
[1] 2.812789
```

More Packages

Members of the R community create and contribute useful new packages to the Comprehensive R Archive Network (CRAN) all the time. So you won't find every R package on the RStudio Packages tab.

When you find out about a package that you think might be helpful, it's easy to install it in your library. I illustrate by installing `tidyverse`, a package (consisting of other packages!) created by R megastar Hadley Wickham to help you manage your data.

One way to install it is via the Packages tab. (Refer to Figure 2-1.) Click the Install icon in the upper left corner of the tab. This opens the Install Packages dialog box, shown in Figure 2-3.

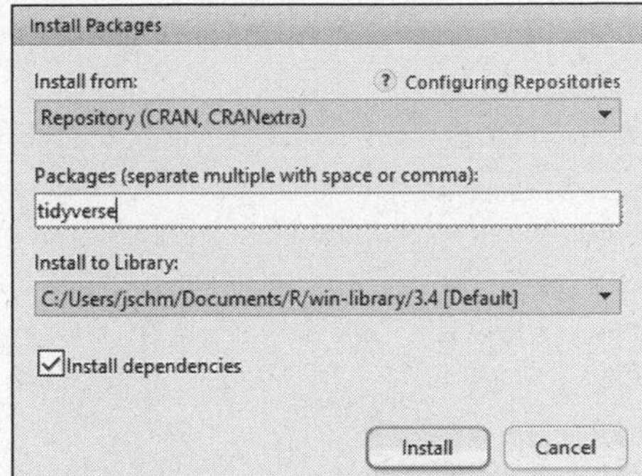

FIGURE 2-3: The Install Packages dialog box.

In the Packages field, I've typed `tidyverse`. Click Install, and the following line appears in the Console pane:

```
> install.packages("tidyverse")
```

It's difficult to see this line because lots and lots of other things happen immediately in the Console pane and in onscreen status bars. The process might seem to stall temporarily, but be patient.

When the downloading is finished, `tidyverse` and a number of other packages appear on the Packages tab. Click the check box next to `tidyverse`, and R installs most of them in the library.

Exploring the tidyverse

Let's take a look at some of the wonders of the `tidyverse`. One of the component packages is `tidyr`. One of its extremely useful functions is called `drop_na()`. The name tells you it deletes data frame rows that have missing data.

Here, I'll show you:

```
> aq.no.missing <-drop_na(airquality)
> head(aq.no.missing)
  Ozone Solar.R Wind Temp Month Day
1    41     190  7.4   67     5   1
2    36     118  8.0   72     5   2
3    12     149 12.6   74     5   3
4    18     313 11.5   62     5   4
7    23     299  8.6   65     5   7
8    19      99 13.8   59     5   8
```

Compare this with

```
> head(airquality)
  Ozone Solar.R Wind Temp Month Day
1    41     190  7.4   67     5   1
2    36     118  8.0   72     5   2
3    12     149 12.6   74     5   3
4    18     313 11.5   62     5   4
5    NA      NA 14.3   56     5   5
6    28      NA 14.9   66     5   6
```

Another `tidyverse` package is called `tibble`. This package has functions that help you modify data frames. For example, I have a data frame that shows the revenue in millions of dollars for five industries connected with outer space. The data are for the years 1990–1994:

```
> space.revenues
                                1990 1991 1992 1993 1994
Commercial Satellites Delivered 1000 1300 1300 1100 1400
Satellite Services               800 1200 1500 1850 2330
Satellite Ground Equipment       860 1300 1400 1600 1970
Commercial Launches              570  380  450  465  580
Remote Sensing Data              155  190  210  250  300
```

The first column has the row names (rather than row numbers) as the identifiers for the rows. You can do something like this:

```
> space.revenues["Satellite Services",2]
[1] 1200
```

which is equivalent to this:

```
> space.revenues[2,2]
[1] 1200
```

But it's more productive (for analysis and graphing) to turn those identifiers into a named column. The `tibble` function `rownames_to_column()` does just that:

```
> revenues.industry <- rownames_to_column(space.revenues, var="Industry")
```

Now I have a column called `Industry`:

```
> revenues.industry
                         Industry 1990 1991 1992 1993 1994
1 Commercial Satellites Delivered 1000 1300 1300 1100 1400
```

```
2            Satellite Services  800 1200 1500 1850 2330
3     Satellite Ground Equipment  860 1300 1400 1600 1970
4           Commercial Launches  570  380  450  465  580
5           Remote Sensing Data  155  190  210  250  300
```

Why did I do that? Glad you asked. That little trick enables me to *reshape* the data.

Here's what I mean. The `revenues.industry` data frame is in *wide format*. The revenues are in multiple columns. Many R analysis and graphics functions prefer to see the data in *long format*, in which all revenues are stacked into one column.

Think of revenue as a dependent variable. If the revenue values are stacked into one column, it's easy to see how each revenue value depends on the combination of the other variables (`Industry` and `Year`) in its row. Long format looks like this:

```
> long.revenues
                         Industry Year Million_Dollars
1  Commercial Satellites Delivered 1990            1000
2               Satellite Services 1990             800
3       Satellite Ground Equipment 1990             860
4              Commercial Launches 1990             570
5              Remote Sensing Data 1990             155
6  Commercial Satellites Delivered 1991            1300
7               Satellite Services 1991            1200
8       Satellite Ground Equipment 1991            1300
9              Commercial Launches 1991             380
10             Remote Sensing Data 1991             190
11 Commercial Satellites Delivered 1992            1300
12              Satellite Services 1992            1500
13      Satellite Ground Equipment 1992            1400
14             Commercial Launches 1992             450
15             Remote Sensing Data 1992             210
16 Commercial Satellites Delivered 1993            1100
17              Satellite Services 1993            1850
18      Satellite Ground Equipment 1993            1600
19             Commercial Launches 1993             465
20             Remote Sensing Data 1993             250
21 Commercial Satellites Delivered 1994            1400
22              Satellite Services 1994            2330
23      Satellite Ground Equipment 1994            1970
24             Commercial Launches 1994             580
25             Remote Sensing Data 1994             300
```

How do I accomplish this format change? A `tidyr` function called `gather()` does the trick. Here's how to reshape `revenues.industry` into `long.revenues`:

```
long.revenues <- gather(revenues.industry,Year,Million_Dollars,2:6)
```

The first argument to `gather()` is the data frame to reshape, the second is the name of the new column in which to *gather* existing columns, the third is the new name for the dependent variable, and the fourth is the sequence of columns to gather from.

Had I not used `rownames_to_column()` earlier, all of this would have been difficult to do.

If it's ever necessary to go in the opposite direction (from long format to wide format), the `tidyr` function `spread()` handles it:

```
> spread(long.revenues,Year,Million_Dollars)
                       Industry 1990 1991 1992 1993 1994
1           Commercial Launches  570  380  450  465  580
2 Commercial Satellites Delivered 1000 1300 1300 1100 1400
3           Remote Sensing Data  155  190  210  250  300
4      Satellite Ground Equipment  860 1300 1400 1600 1970
5            Satellite Services  800 1200 1500 1850 2330
```

Another prominent package in the `tidyverse` is called `dplyr`. This one is also for data manipulation. One of its functions, `filter()`, returns rows that meet a condition or a set of conditions. For example, if I want to have just the rows in `long.revenue` that hold information for `Satellite Services`, I write:

```
> filter(long.revenues,Industry == "Satellite Services")
            Industry Year Million_Dollars
1 Satellite Services 1990             800
2 Satellite Services 1991            1200
3 Satellite Services 1992            1500
4 Satellite Services 1993            1850
5 Satellite Services 1994            2330
```

Suppose I want the data for the first day of each month in the `airquality` data frame:

```
  Ozone Solar.R Wind Temp Month Day
1    41     190  7.4   67     5   1
2    NA     286  8.6   78     6   1
3   135     269  4.1   84     7   1
```

```
4    39      83  6.9   81     8   1
5    96     167  6.9   91     9   1
```

How would I do that?

I've given you only a taste of the tidyverse. Possibly the most widely used tidyverse package is ggplot2, and I tell you about that one in Chapter 3.

TIP

To search for R packages and functions that might suit your needs, visit www.rdocumentation.org. How many packages are available? As I write this, over 14,000! By the time you read this, that number will surely be higher.

IN THIS CHAPTER . . .

» R Base graphics

» Kicking it up a notch with ggplot2

Chapter 3 Getting Graphic

From its very beginnings, R has been about data visualization as much as data analysis. That's because a good graph enables an analyst to spot trends and make predictions. Graphics also help you present your ideas to others. And as you'll see, graphics are the lifeblood of the projects in this book.

The R community has developed a considerable number of graphics packages. In this chapter, I introduce you to the two most widely used ones: the base graphics package that comes with your R installation and `ggplot2`, which is part of the `tidyverse` package I discuss in Chapter 2. As we get into the projects, I use other packages as necessary.

Touching Base

Base R enables you to develop a wide variety of graphs. Its general format for creating (most) graphics is

```
graphics_function(data, argument1, argument2, ...)
```

That's pretty much it!

TIP

After you create a graph in RStudio, click the Zoom icon on the RStudio Plots tab to open the graph in a larger window. The graph is clearer in the Zoom window than it is on the Plots tab.

Histograms

One way of finding trends in data is to examine the frequencies of values. A *histogram* — a plot that shows values of a variable and how many times each one occurs in a data frame — is a quick and easy way to do this. For example, one of the variables (columns) in the `airquality` data frame in the `datasets` package (see Chapter 2) presents daily temperatures from May 1 to September 30, 1973, in New York City.

```
> library(datasets)
> head(airquality)
  Ozone Solar.R Wind Temp Month Day
1    41     190  7.4   67     5   1
2    36     118  8.0   72     5   2
3    12     149 12.6   74     5   3
4    18     313 11.5   62     5   4
5    NA      NA 14.3   56     5   5
6    28      NA 14.9   66     5   6
```

I create a histogram to show the frequencies of the temperatures. To do this, I use the `hist()` function:

```
> hist(airquality$Temp)
```

The result is the graph in Figure 3-1.

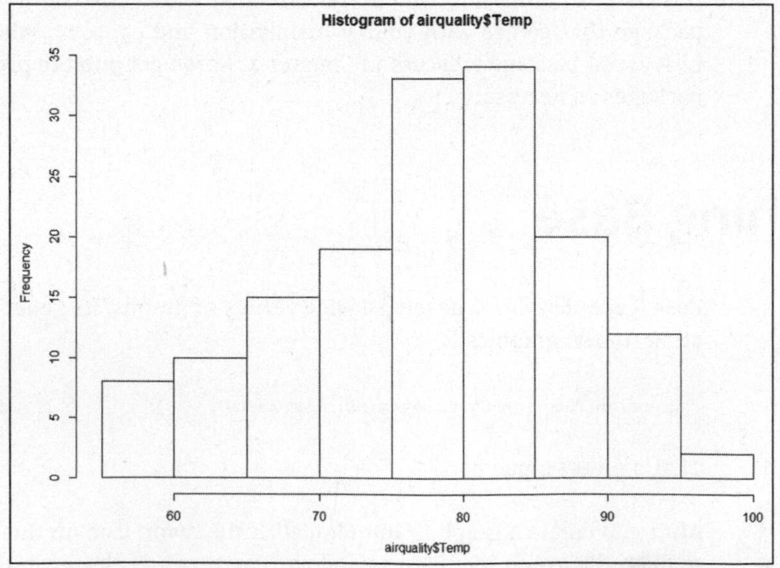

FIGURE 3-1: Histogram of temperatures in the airquality data frame.

I can make the graph a bit more viewer friendly by changing the x-axis to "Temperature (Degrees Fahrenheit)" and the title to "Temperatures in New York City May 1 – September 30, 1973." To do that, I add arguments to `hist()`. To change the x-axis, I add the `xlab` argument; to change the title, I add the `main` argument:

```
> hist(airquality$Temp,xlab="Temperature (Degrees
  Fahrenheit)",main="Temperatures in New York City May 1 - September 30, 1973")
```

This produces Figure 3-2.

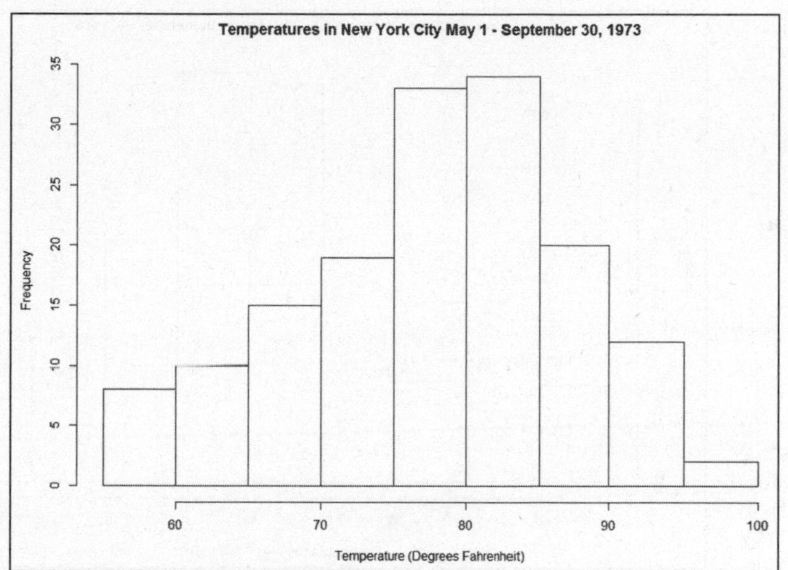

FIGURE 3-2: The histogram, with a friendlier title and an x-axis.

TIP

When you're creating a histogram, R figures out the optimum number of columns for a nice-looking appearance. In this example, R decided that 9 is a good number. You can vary the number of columns by adding an argument called `breaks` and setting its value. R doesn't always give you the value you set. Instead, it produces something close to that value and tries to maintain a good appearance. Add this argument, set its value (`breaks = 4`, for example), and you'll see what I mean.

Density plots

Another way to show histogram information is to think in terms of probabilities rather than frequencies. So instead of the frequency of temperatures between 60 and 70 degrees, you graph the probability that a temperature selected from the data is in that range. To make this happen, add

```
probability = TRUE
```

to the arguments. Now the R code looks like this:

```
> hist(airquality$Temp,xlab="Temperature (Degrees
  Fahrenheit)",main="Temperatures in New York City May 1 - September 30, 1973",
  probability = TRUE)
```

The result appears in Figure 3-3. The y-axis shows *Density* — a concept related to probability — and the graph is called a *density plot*. Think of density as the height of a rectangle whose area represents probability.

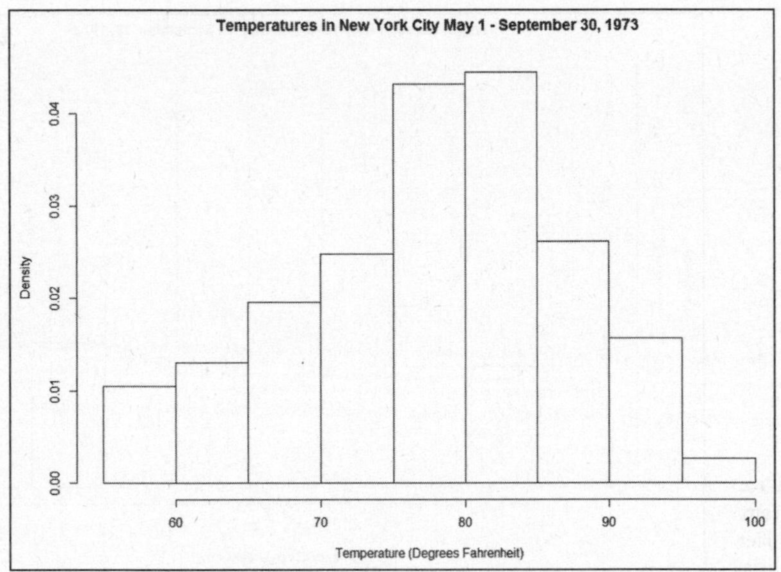

FIGURE 3-3: Density plot of temperatures in the `airquality` data frame.

After you create the graph, you can use an additional function called `lines()` to add a line to the density plot:

```
> lines(density(airquality$Temp))
```

The graph now looks like Figure 3-4. (Adding a line is a great way to summarize information and possibly spot trends.)

REMEMBER

In base R graphics, you can create a graph and then start adding to it after you see what the initial graph looks like. If you ever watched the old TV show *The Joy of Painting*, you'll remember that Bob Ross would paint a picture of a lake and then start adding trees and mountains. It's something like that.

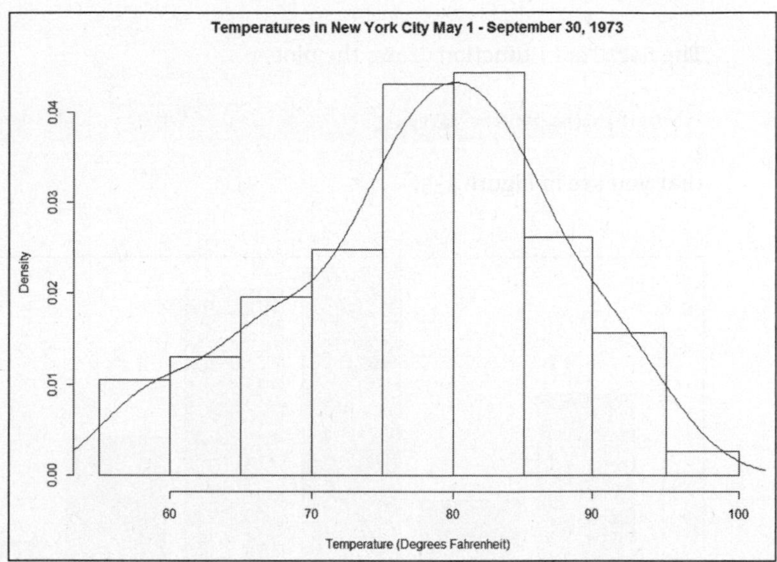

FIGURE 3-4: Density plot with an added line.

Bar plots

A histogram shows frequencies when the variable on the x-axis is numerical (like temperature). When the entries on the x-axis are categories, the appropriate way to present frequencies is called a *bar plot.*

Illustrative data come from Cars93, a data frame in the MASS package presenting data on 93 models of 1993 cars. It has 27 columns. I won't show you all the data, but here are the first three columns in the first six rows:

```
> library(MASS)
> head(Cars93[1:3])
  Manufacturer   Model    Type
1        Acura Integra   Small
2        Acura  Legend Midsize
3         Audi      90 Compact
4         Audi     100 Midsize
5          BMW    535i Midsize
6        Buick Century Midsize
```

To show the frequency of each Type of car, I create a bar plot. I first have to create a table of the frequencies. The table() function does that:

```
> table(Cars93$Type)

Compact   Large Midsize   Small  Sporty     Van
     16      11      22      21      14       9
```

The barplot() function draws the plot

```
> barplot(table(Cars93$Type))
```

that you see in Figure 3-5.

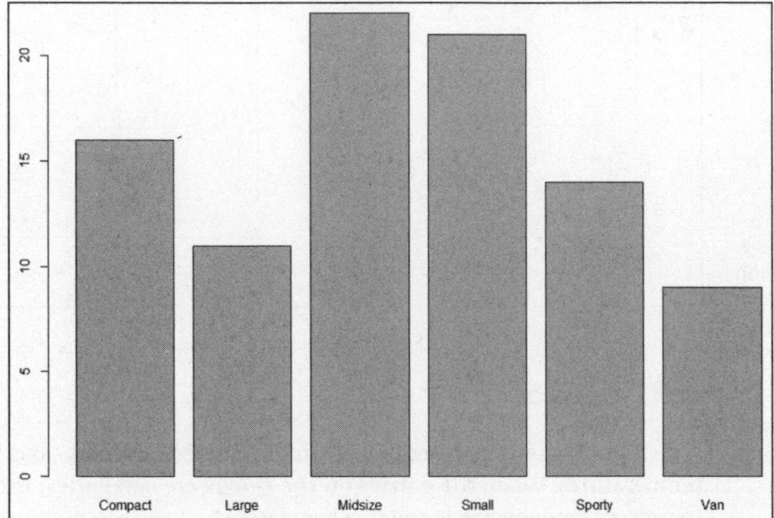

FIGURE 3-5: Initial bar plot of Type in the Cars93 data frame.

I can add some arguments to barplot() to augment the plot. Notice that the bar for Midsize extends beyond the y-axis upper limit (20). To correct for this, I add this argument:

```
ylim = c(0,25)
```

And to add labels for the axes, I add

```
xlab = "Type"
ylab = "Frequency"
```

On graphs like this, I prefer a solid x-axis. To draw one, the argument is

```
axis.lty = "solid"
```

Finally, I can increase the spacing between bars by adding

```
space = .5
```

So the function

```
> barplot(table(Cars93$Type),ylim=c(0,25),xlab="Type", ylab="Frequency", axis.
   lty="solid",space=.5)
```

produces the graph in Figure 3-6.

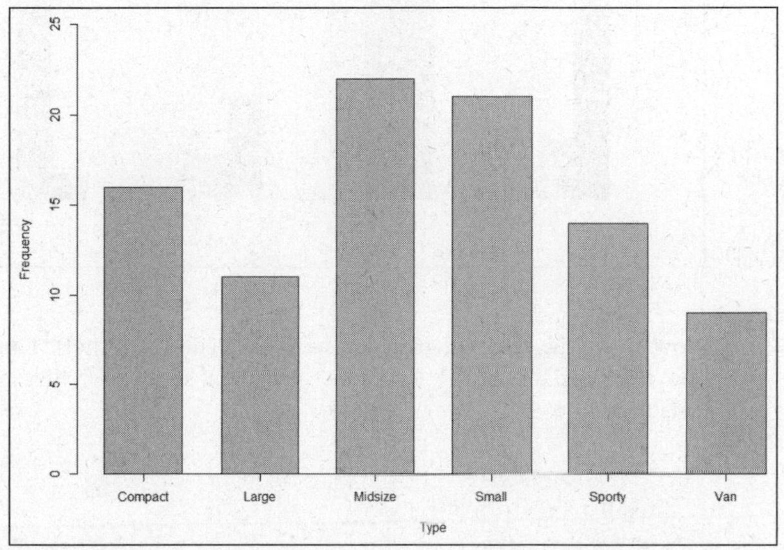

FIGURE 3-6: Augmented bar plot of Type in the `Cars93` data frame.

As an exercise, make a bar plot that shows these data for cars made in the USA. Begin with the `filter()` function I describe in Chapter 2:

```
> library(dplyr)
> USA.Cars93 <- filter(Cars93,Origin == "USA")
```

and then create a bar plot. Next, complete the same steps for non-USA cars, and compare. You might also try to create some bar plots for `Cylinders`.

Grouping the bars

You've probably seen bar plots where each point on the x-axis has more than one bar. Figure 3-7 shows an example. The bar plot shows the frequency of eye color for four hair colors in 313 female students. The data is from the `HairEyeColor` data set I mention in the sidebar in Chapter 1. This type of plot is called a *grouped bar plot*.

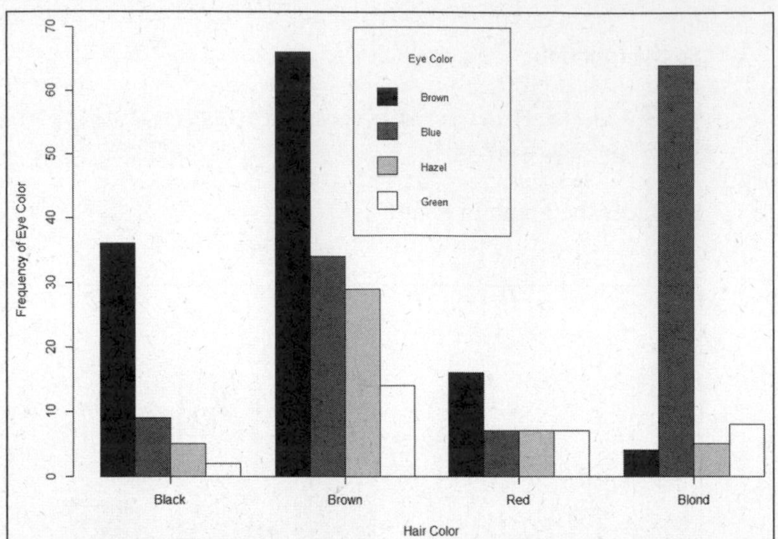

FIGURE 3-7: Grouped bar plot of Eye Color and Hair Color in 313 female students.

How does the base R graphics package deal with that? I begin by isolating the female data in the `HairEyeColor` data set, which lives in the `datasets` package:

```
> library(datasets)
> females <- HairEyeColor[,,2]
> females
       Eye
Hair    Brown Blue Hazel Green
  Black    36    9     5     2
  Brown    66   34    29    14
  Red      16    7     7     7
  Blond     4   64     5     8
```

To begin producing Figure 3-7, I have to specify the colors in the bars and in the legend:

```
> color.names = c("black","grey40","grey80","white")
```

A word about those names: You can combine `grey` with any number from 0 to 100 to create a color — `"grey0"` is equivalent to `"black"` and `"grey100"` is equivalent to `"white"`.

Now I turn once again to the barplot() function. Interestingly, if I use females as the first argument for barplot(), R draws a plot with Eye Color on the x-axis (rather than Hair Color, as in Figure 3-7). To reverse that, I use t() to interchange (*transpose*, in other words) the rows and columns (see Chapter 1):

```
> t(females)
       Hair
Eye     Black Brown Red Blond
  Brown    36    66  16     4
  Blue      9    34   7    64
  Hazel     5    29   7     5
  Green     2    14   7     8
```

The function that produces the bar plot is

```
> barplot(t(females),beside=T,ylim=c(0,70),xlab="Hair Color",ylab="Frequency of
  Eye Color", col=color.names,axis.lty="solid")
```

beside=T tells R to plot the bars, well, beside each other. (Try it without this argument and watch what happens.) ylim insures that no bar will rise above the highest value on the y-axis. col=color.names supplies the colors named in the vector.

The plot isn't complete without the legend (the box that tells you which plot colors correspond to which eye colors):

```
> legend("top",rownames(t(females)),cex =0.8,fill=color.names,title="Eye Color")
```

The first argument puts the legend at the top of the plot, and the second argument provides the names. The third argument specifies the size of the characters in the legend — .08 means "80% of the normal size." The fourth argument gives the colors for the color swatches, and the fifth, of course, provides the title.

Quick Suggested Project

Think you've got it? Try completing the same steps for the Males data.

LEGENDARY COLORS

I use shades of gray for the colors because the book you're holding is in black-and-white. It would be cool if the colors in the plot and the legend (at least somewhat) matched the actual eye colors.

Try making this happen. Set up a vector with the names of those colors.

Warning: As wonderful as hazel eyes are (and I know, because I have a pair of them), "hazel" is not a color name in R. You'll probably have to use a shade of green instead. You can look through all 657 color names in R:

```
> colors()
```

Or you can make it easy on yourself by using the search function `grep()` to find just the colors with *green* in their names:

```
> colors()[grep("green",colors())]
```

QUICK SUGGESTED PROJECT: GROUPING REVISITED

At the end of the preceding section, I suggest that you look at the `Cars93` data frame and create a bar plot for the `Type` of USA cars and another for non-USA cars and then compare the two.

This comparison is a natural for a grouped bar plot. So here's another quick suggested project for you. You won't need the whole `Cars93` data frame, so use `subset()` to create a data frame consisting of just `Type` and `Origin`. (For a refresher on `subset()`, see Chapter 2.). The subset data frame (I called it `Type.Origin`) should look like this:

```
> head(Type.Origin)
     Type  Origin
1   Small non-USA
2 Midsize non-USA
3 Compact non-USA
4 Midsize non-USA
5 Midsize non-USA
6 Midsize     USA
```

Your final bar plot should look like this figure:

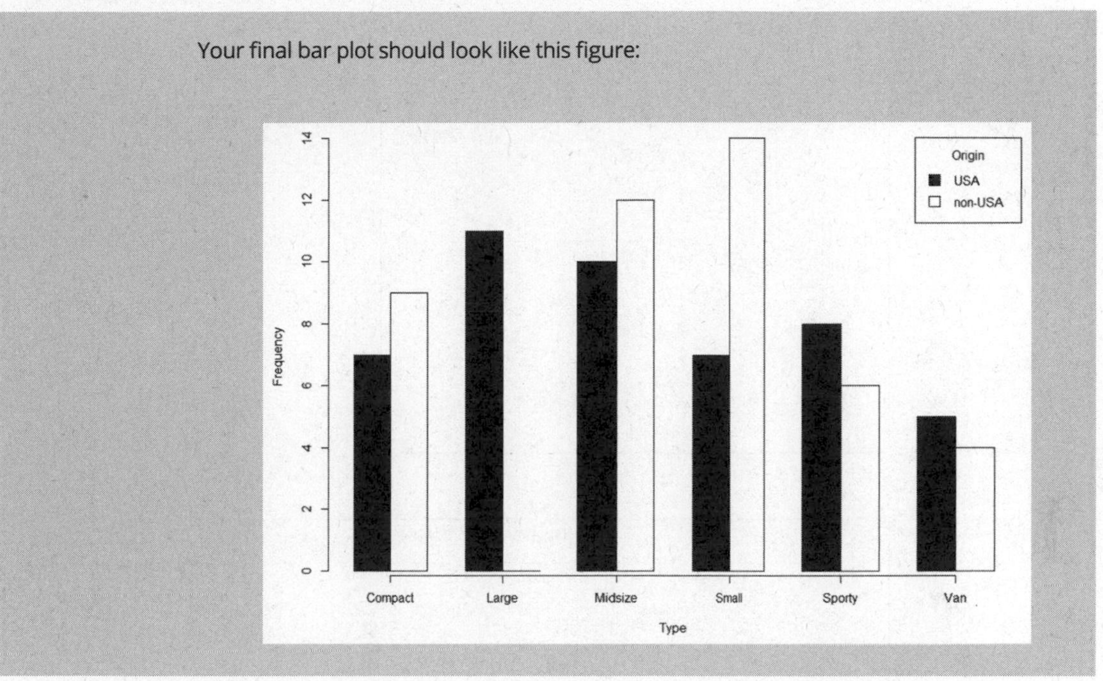

Pie graphs

Another way to show frequency information is to represent the whole set of data as a pie, and the categories as slices of the pie. The size of a slice represents the proportion of the pie associated with that category. Going back to `Cars93`,

```
> library(MASS)
> pie(table(Cars93$Type))
```

draws Figure 3-8.

Scatterplots

It's often the case that you want to visualize the relationship between two variables, like `Wind` and `Temp` in `airquality`. The *scatterplot* is the graph for that, as Figure 3-9 shows.

The `plot()` function draws this graph:

```
> library(datasets)
> plot(airquality$Wind,airquality$Temp, pch=16,xlab = "Wind Velocity (MPH)",
  ylab ="Temperature (Fahrenheit)", main = "Temperature vs Wind Velocity")
```

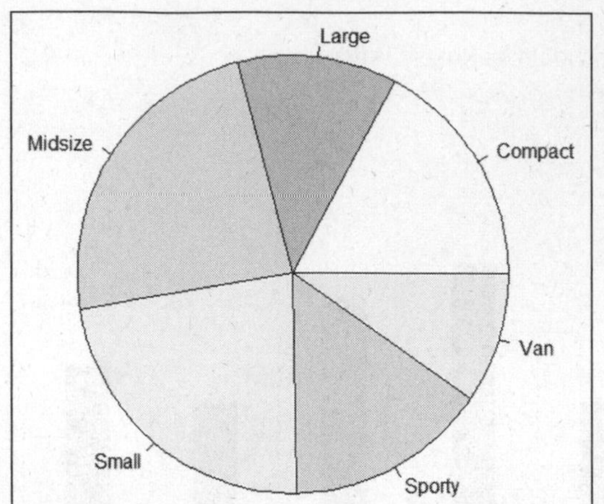

FIGURE 3-8: Pie chart for Type in the `Cars93` data frame.

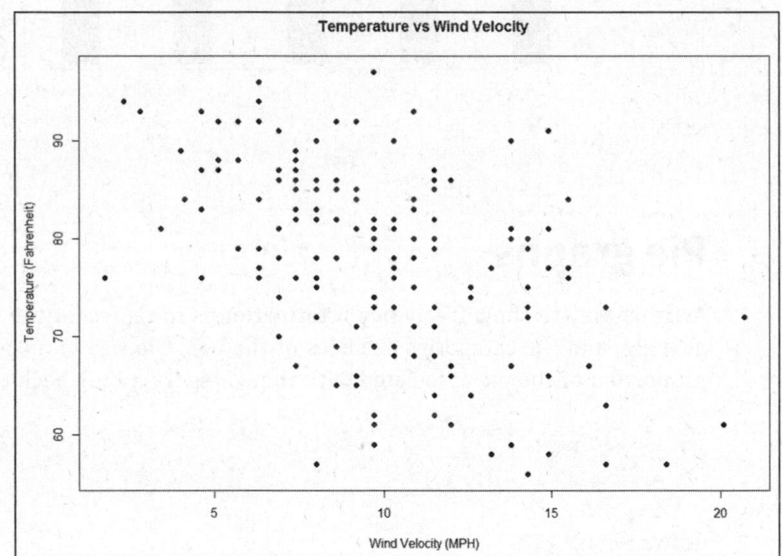

FIGURE 3-9: Temperature versus Wind Velocity in the `airquality` data frame.

The first two arguments are the variables. The third argument, `pch = 16`, specifies black as the color of the little circles that represent the data points. Omitting this argument leaves the circles open (like little *o*'s). Think of `pch` as *plot character.* The remaining arguments add the axis labels and the title.

If you prefer to use a formula that shows `Temp` dependent on `Wind`, here's how to code it (and draw the same scatterplot):

```
> plot(airquality$Temp ~ airquality$Wind, pch=16,xlab = "Wind Velocity
  (MPH)",ylab ="Temperature (Fahrenheit)", main = "Temperature vs Wind
  Velocity")
```

By the way, if you like, take another look at the analysis in the "R Formulas" section in Chapter 2, and do that same analysis on the relationship between `Temp` and `Wind`. That Chapter 2 analysis is on the relationship between `Temp` and `Month`. What would a scatterplot of that relationship look like?

Scatterplot matrix

Base R provides a nice way to show relationships among more than two variables. For example, I might want to examine how `Ozone`, `Temp`, and `Wind` are related in `airquality`. "Examining how they are related" means looking at all the pairwise relationships among the three.

The scatterplot matrix, as shown in Figure 3-10, shows all this.

The names of the variables, of course, are in the boxes along the main diagonal. The other boxes show scatterplots. Each scatterplot shows the relationship between the variable in its row (on the x-axis) and the variable in its column (on the y-axis). For example, in the first row and second column, the scatterplot shows `Ozone` on the x-axis and `Temp` on the y-axis. In the second row and first column, it's `Temp` on the x-axis and `Ozone` on the y-axis.

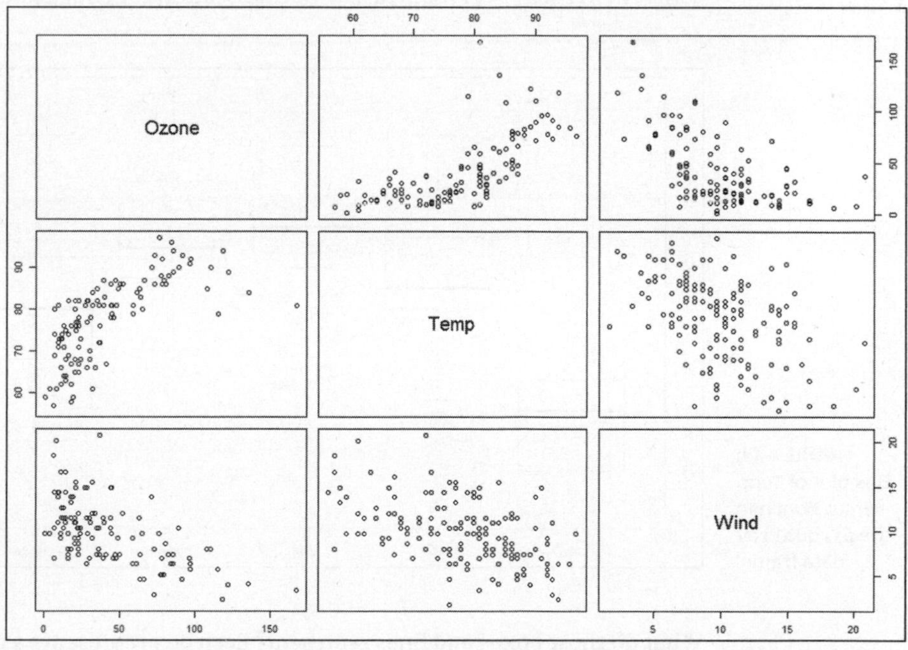

FIGURE 3-10: Scatterplot matrix of `Ozone`, `Wind`, and `Temp` in the `airquality` data frame.

To create the matrix, I begin by taking a subset of `airquality` that holds the data only for the variables I'm interested in:

```
> Ozone.Temp.Wind <- subset(airquality,select = c(Ozone,Temp,Wind))
> head(Ozone.Temp.Wind)
  Ozone Temp Wind
1    41   67  7.4
2    36   72  8.0
3    12   74 12.6
4    18   62 11.5
5    NA   56 14.3
6    28   66 14.9
```

Then I use the `pairs()` function to draw the matrix:

```
> pairs(Ozone.Temp.Wind)
```

Box plots

Brainchild of famed statistician John Tukey, the *box plot* is a quick and easy way to visualize data. Figure 3-11 shows a box plot of the relationship between `Temp` and `Month` in `airquality`. (Compare with that scatterplot I suggested you try.)

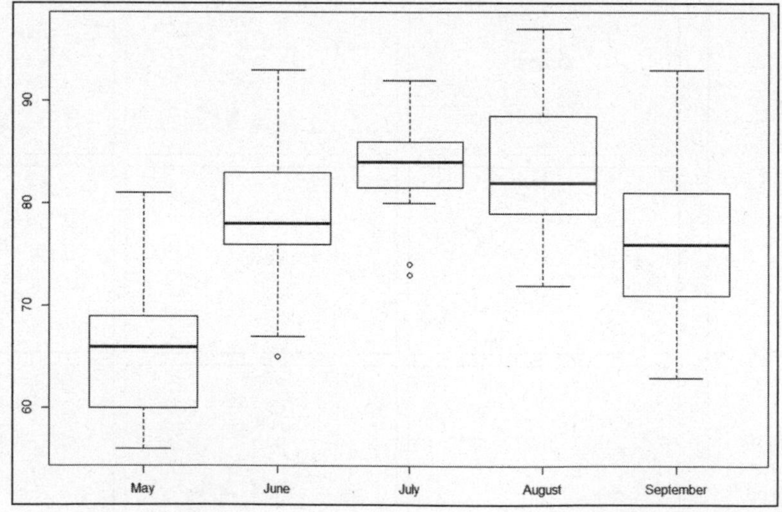

FIGURE 3-11: Box plot of `Temp` versus `Month` in the `airquality` data frame.

What do those boxes and lines represent? Each box represents a group of numbers. The leftmost box, for example, represents temperatures in May. The black solid line inside the box is the *median*, the temperature that divides the lower half of the temperatures from the upper half. The lower and upper edges of each box are called *hinges*. The lower hinge represents the *lower quartile*, the temperature below which 25 percent of the temperatures fall. The upper hinge represents the *upper quartile*, the temperature that exceeds 75% of the temperatures.

The dotted lines sticking out of the hinges are called *whiskers*. (Some refer to this type of graph as a *box-and-whiskers* plot.) The whiskers include data values outside the hinges. The upper whisker boundary is either the maximum value or the upper hinge plus 1.5 times the length of the box, whichever is *smaller*. The lower whisker boundary is either the minimum value or the lower hinge minus 1.5 times the length of the box, whichever is *larger*. Data points outside the whiskers are *outliers*. Figure 3-11 shows one outlier for June and two for July.

For this box plot, I use a formula to show that `Temp` is the dependent variable and `Month` is the independent variable:

```
> boxplot(Temp ~ Month, data=airquality, xaxt = "n")
```

The third argument, `xaxt = n`, suppresses the labels that would ordinarily appear on the x-axis (5, 6, 7, 8, and 9, which represent the months in the data frame). Instead, I use the function `axis()`:

```
> axis(1, at=1:5,labels=c("May","June","July","August", "September"))
```

to have the month names be the x-axis labels.

Graduating to ggplot2

Though the base R graphics toolset offers a nice variety of plots, `ggplot2` provides many more possibilities. A component of Hadley Wickham's `tidyverse` package, `ggplot2` is based on a concept called *grammar of graphics* (represented by the *gg* in the package name). This is also the title of a book by graphics guru Leland Wilkinson that is the source of the concepts for this package.

First, some background: A *grammar* is a set of rules for combining things. In English grammar, the things are words, phrases, and clauses. English grammar tells you how to combine these components to produce valid (*grammatical*, in other words) sentences.

In the same way, a "grammar of graphics" is a set of rules for combining graphics components to produce graphs. Wilkinson proposed that all graphs have underlying common components — like data, a coordinate system (the familiar x- and y- axes, for example), statistical transformations (like frequency counts), and objects within the graph (dots, bars, lines, or pie slices, for example), to name a few.

Just as combining words and phrases produces grammatical sentences, combining graphics components produces graphs. And just as some sentences are grammatical but make no sense ("Courageous bananas dream extraterrestrial paradigms."), some ggplot2 creations are beautiful graphs that might not be useful. It's up to the writer/speaker to make sense for an audience, and it's up to the graphics developer to create useful graphs for people who use them.

How it works

In ggplot2, Wickham's implementation of Wilkinson's grammar is an easy-to-learn structure for R graphics code.

A graph starts with the function ggplot(), which takes two arguments. The first argument is the source of the data. The second argument maps the data components of interest into components of the graph. That argument is a function called aes(), which stands for *aes*thetic mapping. Each argument to aes() is called an *aesthetic*.

For example, if I'm creating a histogram of Temp in the airquality data frame, I want Type on the x-axis. The code looks like this:

```
ggplot(airquality, aes(x=Temp))
```

All that does is specify the foundation for the graph — the data source and the mapping. If I type that code into the Scripts window and press Ctrl+R, all I would have is a blank grid with Temp on the x-axis.

Well, what about the histogram? To add it to the foundation, I add another function that tells R to plot the histogram and take care of all the details. The function I add is called a geom function (*geom* is short for *geom*etric object).

These geom functions come in a variety of types: ggplot2 supplies one for almost every graphing need, and provides the flexibility to work with special cases. For a histogram, the geom function is geom_histogram(). For a bar plot, it's geom_bar(). For a point, it's geom_point().

To add a geom to ggplot, I use a plus sign:

```
ggplot(airquality, aes(x=Temp)) +
   geom_histogram()
```

That's just about it, except for any finishing touches to the graph's appearance. To modify the appearance of the geom, I add arguments to the geom() function. To modify the background color scheme, I can add one or more `theme()` functions. To add labels to the axes and a title to the graph, I add the function `labs()`.

So, the overall structure for a `ggplot` graph is

```
ggplot(data_source, aes(map data components to graph components)) +
  geom_xxx(arguments to modify the appearance of the geom) +
  theme_xxx(arguments to change the overall appearance) +
  labs(add axis-labels and a title)
```

It's like building a house: The `ggplot()` function is the foundation, the `geom()` function is the house, `theme()` is the landscaping, and `labs()` puts the address on the door. Additional functions are available for modifying the graph.

Still another way to look at `ggplot` (and more in line with mainstream thinking) is to imagine a graph as a set of layers. The `ggplot()` function provides the first layer, the `geom` function the next, and so on.

Make sure you have ggplot2 installed (see Chapter 2 for more on that) so that you can follow along, and let's move on.

Histograms

In this section, I give you the example I hinted at in the preceding section — a histogram for `Temp` in the `airquality` data frame. When it's done, it will look like Figure 3-12.

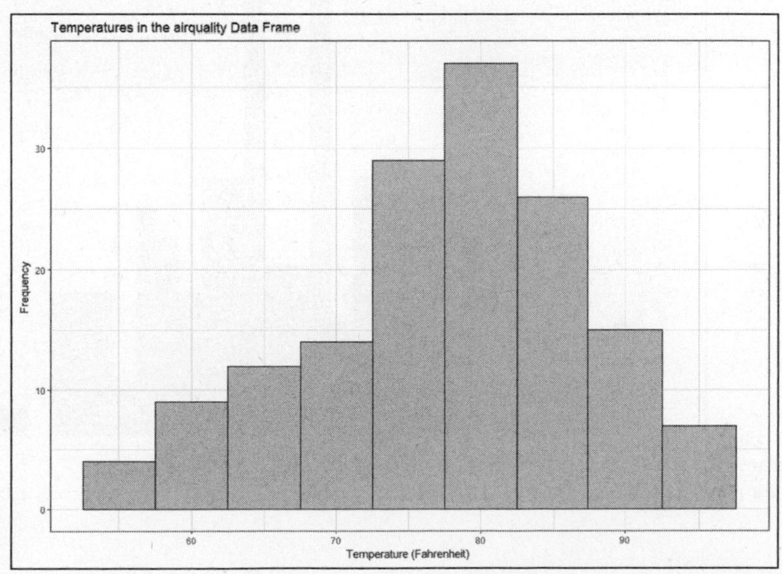

FIGURE 3-12: Histogram of Temp in the `airquality` data frame, plotted in `ggplot`.

I begin with the foundation:

```
ggplot(airquality,aes(x=Temp)) +
```

As I say in the preceding section, aes() maps Temp in the data frame to the x-axis in the graph. Wait a minute. Doesn't anything map to the y-axis? Nope. That's because this is a histogram and nothing in the data explicitly provides a y-value for each x. So I can't say "y =" in aes(). Instead, I let R do the work to calculate the heights of the bars in the histogram.

Now for the house:

```
geom_histogram()
```

These two lines of code produce Figure 3-13 — a far cry from the finished product.

The first thing to do is modify the appearance of the bars. Each bar is called a *bin*, and by default, ggplot uses 30 of them. After plotting the histogram, ggplot displays in the Console window a message that advises experimenting with binwidth (which, unsurprisingly, specifies the width of each bin). So I add binwidth = 5 as an argument to geom_histogram():

```
geom_histogram(binwidth = 5)
```

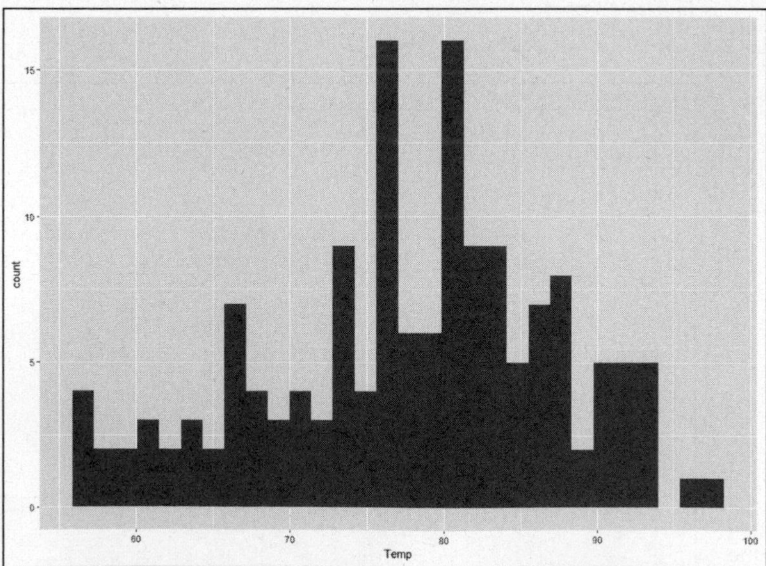

FIGURE 3-13: Initial histogram of Temp.

How do I get the bars to have the same colors as in Figure 3-13? Add two more arguments — one for the color of the bar boundaries (`color`) and one for the color inside the bars (`fill`):

```
geom_histogram(binwidth=5,color = "black",fill="grey80")
```

What about the background? That's landscaping. Adding a `theme` function called `theme_bw()` makes the background white:

```
theme_bw()
```

And `labs()` adds the axis labels and the title:

```
labs(x = "Temperature (Fahrenheit)",y="Frequency", title= "Temperatures in the
  airquality Data Frame")
```

Putting all these lines together (with the plus signs!):

```
ggplot(airquality,aes(x=Temp)) +
 geom_histogram(binwidth=5,color = "black",fill="grey80") +
 theme_bw() +
 labs(x = "Temperature (Fahrenheit)",y="Frequency", title= "Temperatures in the
   airquality Data Frame")
```

produces Figure 3-12.

Bar plots

Drawing a bar plot in `ggplot2` is a bit easier than drawing one in base R: It's not necessary to create a table of frequencies in order to draw the graph.

As in the example in the preceding section, I don't specify an aesthetic mapping for `y`. This time, the `geom` function is `geom_bar()`, and `ggplot2` works with the data to draw the plot:

```
library(MASS)
ggplot(Cars93,aes(x=Type)) +
  geom_bar()+
  labs(y="Frequency",title="Car Type and Frequency in Cars93")
```

The result is Figure 3-14. Try a little landscaping, if you like. (You can add `theme` functions to the end of the code.)

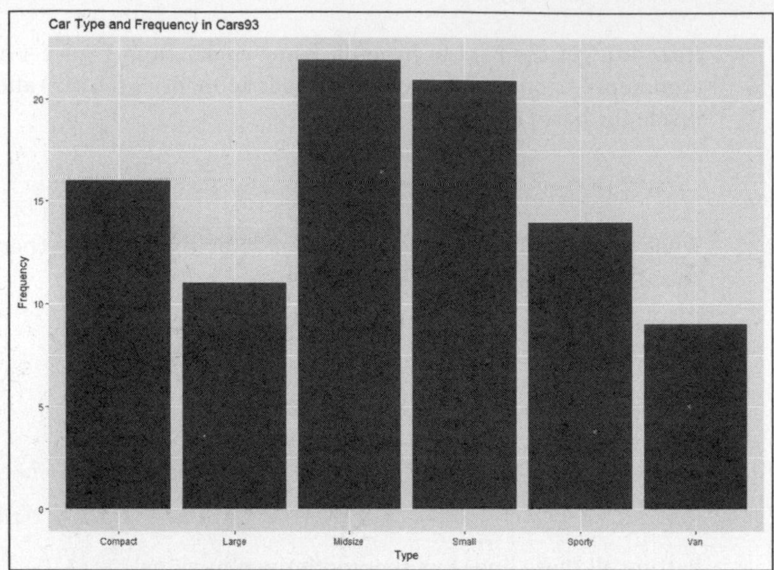

FIGURE 3-14: Bar plot for Type in the Cars93 data frame.

Grouped bar plots

Taking the plot from the preceding example and splitting the data into `Origin` (USA versus non-USA) is what I suggest you do in the earlier sidebar "Grouping revisited." This, remember, is called a *grouped bar plot,* and it's fairly straightforward in `ggplot2`. Here's how to do it.

First, for convenience I created `Type.Origin`:

```
> Type.Origin <- subset(Cars93,select=c("Type","Origin"))
> head(Type.Origin)
     Type  Origin
1   Small non-USA
2 Midsize non-USA
3 Compact non-USA
4 Midsize non-USA
5 Midsize non-USA
6 Midsize     USA
```

I begin the graphing with `ggplot()`, and this time I add a second aesthetic to `aes()`:

```
ggplot(Type.Origin,aes(x=Type,fill=Origin))
```

As before, `aes()` maps `Type` into the x-axis. The second argument to `aes()`, `fill`, maps `Origin` into the colors that will fill the bars. Now, you might be thinking, "Wait a second. Shouldn't a mapping that specifies the colors of the bars go into geom_bar()?" And you'd be right: Another way to specify the color inside the bar is to add aes(fill=Origin) as an argument to geom_bar().

But I have other arguments to add to geom_bar():

```
geom_bar(position="dodge",color="black")
```

The value for the first argument is a cute name that means the bars "dodge" each other and line up side by side. It's analogous to "beside=T" in base R. The second argument sets the color for the borders of each bar.

I still have to specify the range of colors for the bars, and the function scale_fill_grey() handles that task:

```
scale_fill_grey(start=0,end=1)
```

The two arguments indicate that the colors start with black and end with white.

Here's the whole thing:

```
ggplot(Type.Origin, aes(x=Type, fill=Origin))+
  geom_bar(position="dodge",color="black")+
  scale_fill_grey(start=0,end=1)
```

And that code results in Figure 3-15. Feel free to add axis labels and a title, and to use theme functions to modify the graph's appearance.

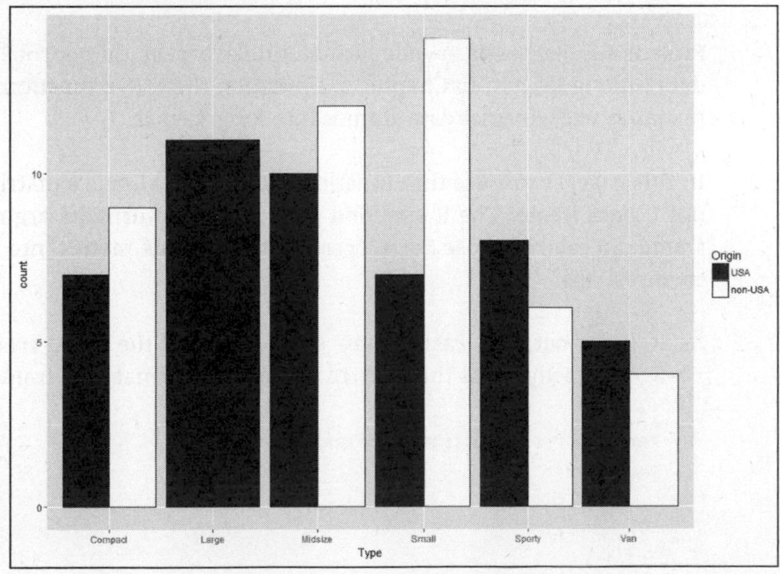

FIGURE 3-15: Grouped bar plot of Type and Origin in the Cars93 data frame.

Two things to note in Figure 3-15: First, ggplot2 kindly supplies the legend. Second, compare Figure 3-15 with the base R version shown in the figure in the earlier "Grouping revisited" sidebar. Base R and ggplot have different ways of dealing with a frequency of zero (Large non-USA cars). For the Large cars, the base R version shows a bar for the USA and no bar for the non-USA, and the USA bar for Large is the same width as all the others. Not so in the ggplot version: With no non-USA bar to take up any space, the USA bar for Large is twice as wide as the others.

Grouping yet again

In each of the preceding examples, it hasn't been necessary to map anything to the y-axis. The data are instances of each category, and ggplot() counts the frequency of each instance as it does its work.

But sometimes the frequencies have already been counted. Earlier in this chapter, I used:

```
> females
       Eye
Hair     Brown Blue Hazel Green
  Black     36    9     5     2
  Brown     66   34    29    14
  Red       16    7     7     7
  Blond      4   64     5     8
```

What happens then?

First of all, females is in wide format. Unlike base R, the ggplot2 package requires data in long format. In Chapter 2, I mention the tidyr function gather(), which reshapes wide-format data frames into long format.

In this case, I can't use that function because females is a matrix (see Chapter 1), not a data frame. The R function data.frame() turns its argument into a data frame. So can I just use data.frame() to turn this matrix into a data frame and then reshape?

As it turns out, it's easier than that. Applying the data.frame() function to females directly turns this matrix into a long-format data frame:

```
> females.df <- data.frame(females)
> females.df
    Hair   Eye Freq
1  Black Brown   36
```

```
2  Brown Brown   66
3    Red Brown   16
4  Blond Brown    4
5  Black  Blue    9
6  Brown  Blue   34
7    Red  Blue    7
8  Blond  Blue   64
9  Black Hazel    5
10 Brown Hazel   29
11   Red Hazel    7
12 Blond Hazel    5
13 Black Green    2
14 Brown Green   14
15   Red Green    7
16 Blond Green    8
```

Now I'm ready to roll. Here's the code for the stacked bar plot:

```
ggplot(females.df, aes(x=Hair,y = Freq, fill=Eye))+
  geom_bar(position="dodge",color="black",stat="identity")+
  scale_fill_grey(start=0,end=1)
```

It looks just like the code in the preceding section, except for two important additions:

In `ggplot()`, I've added an aesthetic for the y-axis. It's the second argument:

```
ggplot(females.df, aes(x=Hair,y = Freq, fill=Eye))
```

And in `geom_bar()`, I've added the argument `stat = "identity"`:

```
  geom_bar(position="dodge",color="black",stat="identity")
```

This lets `ggplot()` know that this graph is based on explicit data values. So `stat= "identity"` means, "Use the given numbers as the data, and don't bother to tally the frequencies of the instances."

The result is shown in Figure 3-16.

TIP

With all the info I've given you about using bar plots for frequency data in `ggplot2`, you might be wondering, "Where's the scoop on how to draw pie charts?" I purposely left that out. It's way easier in base R. Trust me.

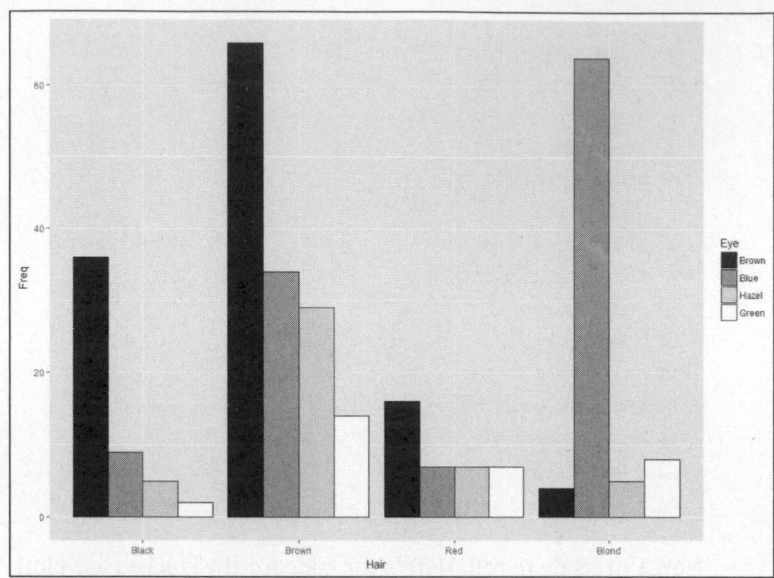

FIGURE 3-16: Stacked bar plot of `females.df`.

SUGGESTED PROJECT: GROUPING ONE MORE TIME

Here's a project that incorporates knowledge from Chapters 1, 2, and 3. The objective is to produce a grouped bar plot that looks like this:

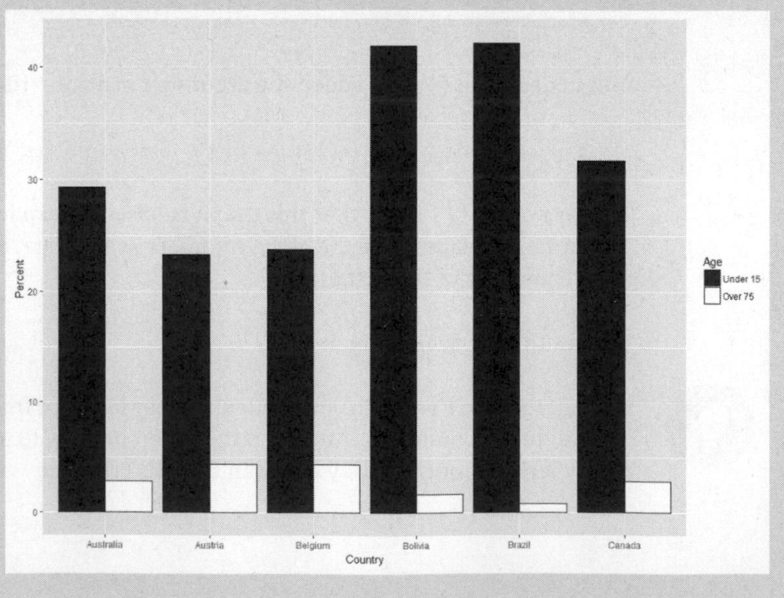

The data come from LifeCycleSavings, a data frame in the datasets package. This data frame contains data for 55 countries. Use head() and subset() to create this data frame:

```
          pop15 pop75
Australia 29.35  2.87
Austria   23.32  4.41
Belgium   23.80  4.43
Bolivia   41.89  1.67
Brazil    42.19  0.83
Canada    31.72  2.85
```

Then use row_names_to_column() to create

```
    Country pop15 pop75
1 Australia 29.35  2.87
2   Austria 23.32  4.41
3   Belgium 23.80  4.43
4   Bolivia 41.89  1.67
5    Brazil 42.19  0.83
6    Canada 31.72  2.85
```

Here, pop15 means "Percent of population under 15 years old," and pop75 means "Percent of population over 75 years old."

Before you start plotting, use gather() to put the data into long format, and use Percent as the name of the dependent variable. Then use ggplot(), geom_bar(), and scale_fill_grey() as in the bar plot examples. ***Hint:*** To make the labels in the legend look like the ones in the figure, add the argument labels =c("Under 15", "Over 75") to scale_fill_grey().

Scatterplots

As I mention earlier in this chapter, a scatterplot is a great way to show the relationship between two variables, like Wind and Temp in the airquality data frame.

If you've been following along, the grammar of this will be easy for you:

```
ggplot(airquality, aes(x=Wind,y=Temp))+
  geom_point()
```

Figure 3-17 shows the scatterplot.

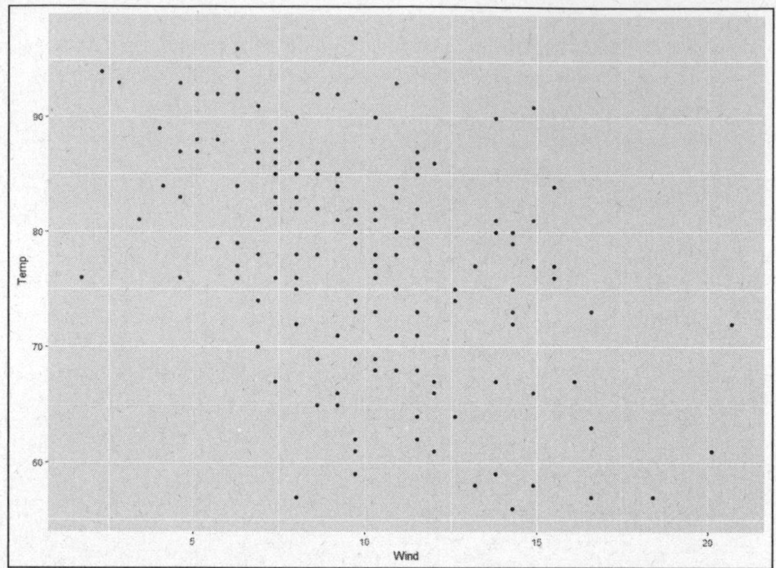

FIGURE 3-17: `Wind` versus `Temp` in the `airquality` data frame.

The plot thickens . . .

I can use the color of the points in the scatterplot to represent a third variable. In addition to `Wind` and `Temp`, I want to represent `Ozone`. If an ozone level for a particular day is less than or equal to the median ozone level, I'll call that level "Low". Otherwise, I'll call it "High". One point-color will represent "High", and another will represent "Low". Figure 3-18 shows what I'm talking about.

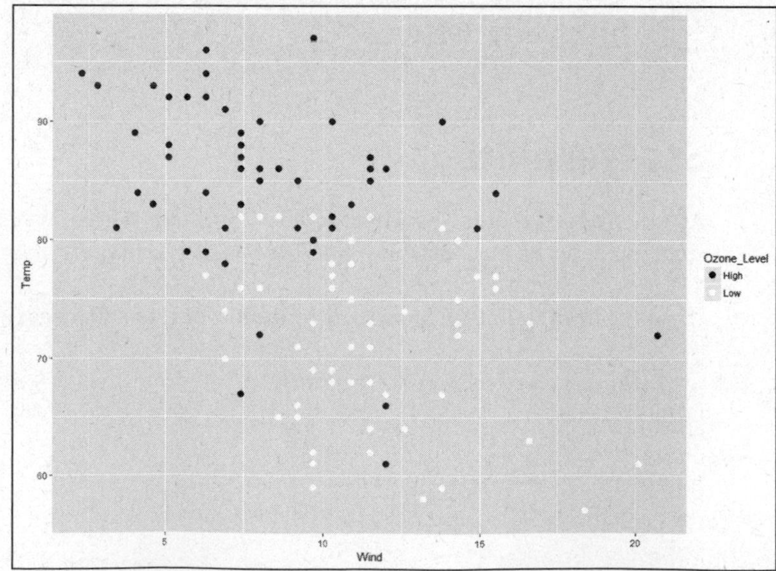

FIGURE 3-18: Scatterplot of `Wind` versus `Temp`, with the dot color representing `Ozone_Level`.

I begin by using the `tidyr` function `drop.na()` to eliminate all `NA` values:

```
> library(tidyr)
> aq.no.NA <- drop_na(airquality)
```

Next, I calculate the median ozone level:

```
> median.Ozone <- median(aq.no.NA$Ozone)
```

My next objective is to add a column called `Ozone_Level` to the `aq.no.NA` data frame. Each entry in this column will be either `High` or `Low`. I start that off by creating an `Ozone_Level` vector:

```
> Ozone_Level <- NULL
```

And then I use an `if` statement inside a `for` loop (see Chapter 1) to populate that vector:

```
for(i in 1:nrow(aq.no.NA)){
 if (aq.no.NA$Ozone[i] <= median.Ozone){
   Ozone_Level[i] <- "Low"}
   else{Ozone_Level[i] <- "High"}
}
```

Finally, I use `cbind()` (see Chapter 1) to add the `Ozone_Level` vector as a column to `aq.no.NA`:

```
aq.Ozone.Level <- cbind(aq.no.NA, Ozone_Level)
```

The first six rows of the new `aq.Ozone.Level` data frame look like this:

```
> head(aq.Ozone.Level)
  Ozone Solar.R Wind Temp Month Day Ozone_Level
1    41     190  7.4   67     5   1        High
2    36     118  8.0   72     5   2        High
3    12     149 12.6   74     5   3         Low
4    18     313 11.5   62     5   4         Low
7    23     299  8.6   65     5   7         Low
8    19      99 13.8   59     5   8         Low
```

This is the data frame I use in the scatterplot. The first statement, as always, involves `ggplot()` and `aes()`:

```
ggplot(aq.Ozone.Level, aes(x=Wind,y=Temp,color=Ozone_Level))
```

That last argument to aes() maps Ozone_Level to the color of the points in the plot.

In the next statement:

```
geom_point(size=3)
```

I add size=3 to make the points larger and easier to see. Experiment with other values for size to see what happens.

The final statement

```
scale_color_grey(start=0,end=1)
```

makes the point colors black and white.

Here's the code that produces Figure 3-18:

```
ggplot(aq.Ozone.Level, aes(x=Wind,y=Temp,color=Ozone_Level))+
  geom_point(size=3)+
  scale_color_grey(start=0,end=1)
```

TEMPERATURE, WIND, AND OZONE

The pattern in the scatterplot in Figure 3-18 strongly suggests a relationship among the three variables. The black points are predominantly in the upper left; the white points, in the lower right. How would we analyze this relationship without transforming Ozone into Ozone_Level? In Chapter 2, I show how to analyze the relationship between Temp (a dependent variable) and Month (an independent variable). Here, I extend the analysis to two independent variables (Wind and Ozone) rather than one:

```
> aq.analysis <- lm(Temp ~ Wind + Ozone, data= aq.Ozone.Level)
```

If you run that code and then this:

```
> summary(aq.analysis)
```

you see a table much like the one in Chapter 2, in the section about R formulas. If the last number in the bottom line (it's called p-value) is smaller than .05, statisticians would say the relationship is *statistically significant,* which is another way of saying that the observed relationship among the variables is probably not due to chance. Try it and see what happens.

What's that? You want to plot all those variables on a 3-dimensional scatterplot? Okay. Just because you asked, here's how to create one that looks like the scatterplot in this figure:

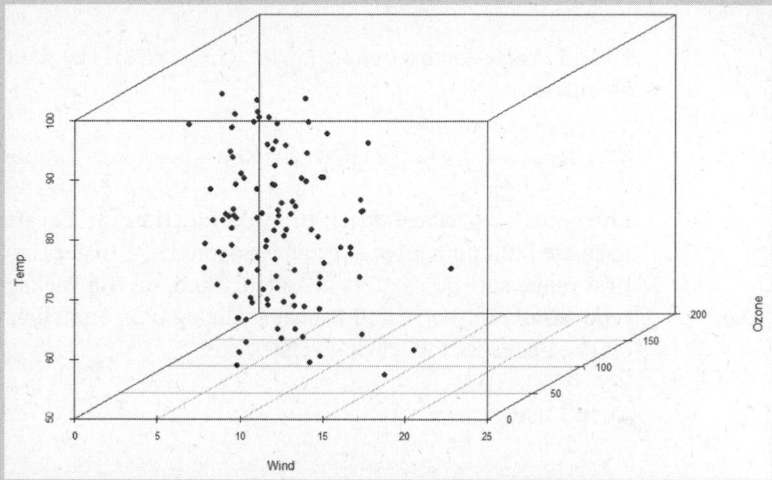

You can't do it in ggplot2. Instead, you have to install a package called scatter plot3d. (Other packages are also available for drawing 3-dimensional scatterplots.)

On the Packages tab, click Install. In the Install Packages dialog box, type **scatterplot3d** and then click Install. After the package downloads, find it in the Packages tab and click its check box, or type

```
>library(scatterplot3d)
```

The code for the 3d scatterplot is

```
with(aq.Ozone.Level,
(scatterplot3d(Wind ~ Temp + Ozone, pch = 19)))
```

The with statement keeps you from having to add the name of the data frame (along with a dollar sign, $) to each variable. (See Chapter 1.) The first argument to scatterplot3d( ) shows the relationship I mention earlier in this sidebar. The second argument specifies that the plot characters are black. You can add arguments to modify the appearance of the plot.

Scatterplot matrix

A matrix of scatterplots shows the pairwise relationships among more than two variables. Figure 3-10, earlier in this chapter, shows how the base R `pairs()` function renders this kind of matrix.

First, I create a subset of `aq.no.NA` (the `airquality` data frame after omitting all `NA` entries):

```
aq.subset <- subset(aq.no.NA,select = c(Ozone,Wind,Temp,Solar.R))
```

The `ggplot2` package doesn't have a function for a scatterplot matrix. `GGally`, a package built on `ggplot2`, provides `ggpairs()` to get the job done. To get `GGally`, first make sure `ggplot2` is installed. Then, on the Packages tab, select Install and type **GGally** in the Install Packages dialog box, and click Install. When it appears on the Packages tab, click its check box.

Then I use `ggpairs()`

```
> library(ggplot2)
> library(GGally)
> ggpairs(aq.subset)
```

to produce the scatterplot matrix in Figure 3-19.

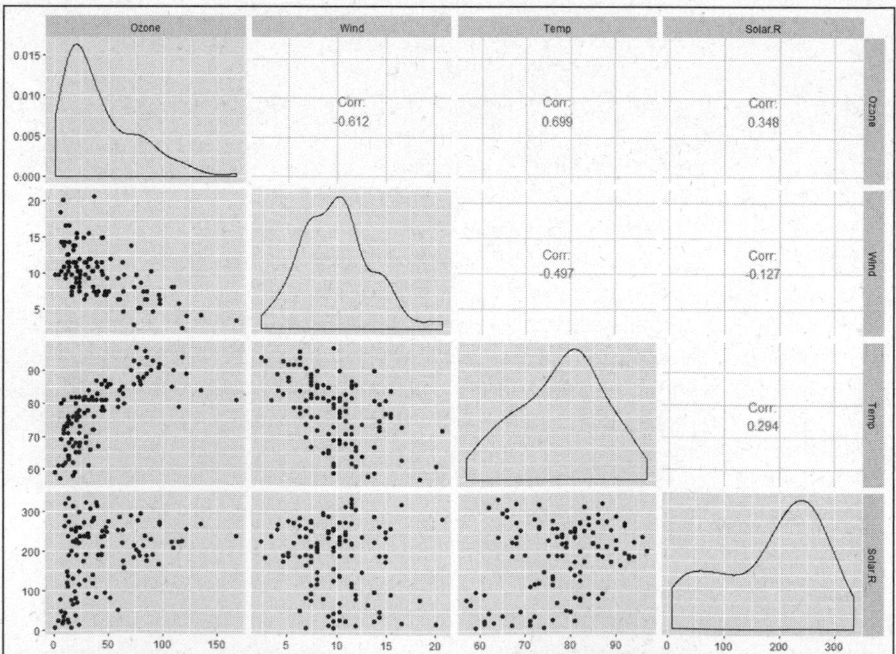

FIGURE 3-19: Scatterplot matrix rendered in `GGally`, which is built on `ggplot2`.

The main diagonal features density plots of the variables. (See the "Density plots" section, earlier in this chapter.) Below the main diagonal, each item is a scatter-plot that represents the relationship between the variable in its row and the variable in its column.

Above the main diagonal, each entry is a *correlation coefficient* — a statistic that summarizes the relationship between the variable in its row and the variable in its column. A correlation coefficient can range between −1.00 and 1.00. A positive coefficient (like .699 between `Temp` and `Ozone`) indicates a *direct* relationship: As one variable increases, the other increases. A negative coefficient (like −.612 between `Wind` and `Ozone`) indicates an *inverse* relationship: As one variable increases, the other decreases.

Box plots

Statisticians use box plots to quickly show how groups differ from one another. I fully explain this type of plot in the earlier "Box plots" section in this chapter. As in that section, I plot `Temp` against `Month` in the `airquality` data frame.

The `ggplot()` function is

```
ggplot(airquality, aes(x=as.factor(Month),y=Temp))
```

Whoa! What's that `as.factor()` in the first aesthetic mapping? In the `Month` variable in the data frame, the numbers 5–9 represent May–September. Thus, `ggplot()` interprets `Month` as a numerical variable. For the `ggplot2` box plot, this is a no-no: The x variable has to be a categorical variable, also known as a *factor.* (See the section about data frames in Chapter 1). This means that the values of `Month` have to be categories rather than numbers.

To get `ggplot()` to treat `Month` as a factor (and each month as a category), I use the `as.factor()` function.

REMEMBER

R honchos would say that I used `as.factor()` to "*coerce* `Month` into a factor."

What's the `geom` function? You can probably figure out that it's

```
geom_boxplot()
```

These two lines of code

```
ggplot(airquality, aes(x=as.factor(Month),y=Temp)) +
  geom_boxplot()
```

produce Figure 3-20.

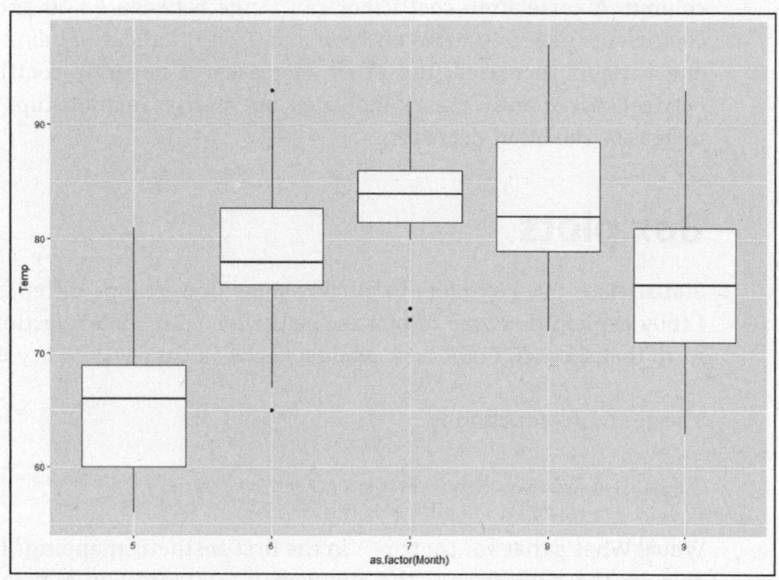

FIGURE 3-20: Box plot for Temp versus Month in ggplot2.

I can add some functions to spiff up the graph and produce Figure 3-21.

To visualize all the data points, I add

```
geom_point()
```

To change the axis names, it's

```
labs(y="Temperature",x="Month")
```

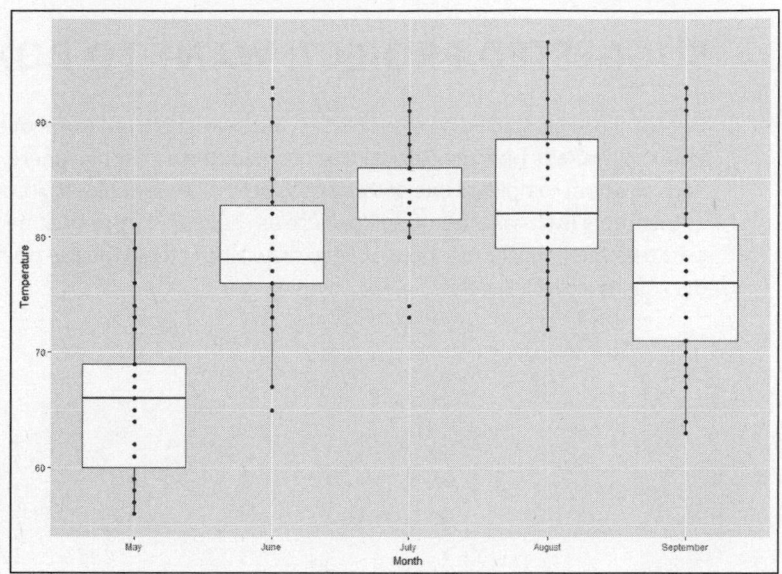

FIGURE 3-21: Embellished box plot for `Temp` versus `Month`.

To change the x-axis labels from 5–9 to May–September, I use a function called `scale_x_discrete()`:

```
scale_x_discrete(labels=c("May","June","July","August", "September"))
```

The whole megillah is

```
ggplot(airquality, aes(x=as.factor(Month),y=Temp)) +
  geom_boxplot()+
  geom_point()+
  labs(y="Temperature",x="Month")+
  scale_x_discrete(labels=c("May","June","July","August", "September"))
```

TIP

In contrast with the base R box plot, the lines perpendicular to the whiskers are missing from the `ggplot` version. You can add them, but it's a bit more trouble than it's worth.

SUGGESTED PROJECT: WANT TO BOX?

If you'd like to get started on a box plot of your own, check out the `anorexia` data frame in the `Mass` package. This data frame holds the data for 72 anorexia patients, each of whom completed one of three treatments. The variables (columns) are the type of treatment (which is a factor, so don't use `as.factor()`), pre-treatment weight, and post-treatment weight. Use `ggplot()` to draw a box plot of the pre-treatment weight data. It should look like this:

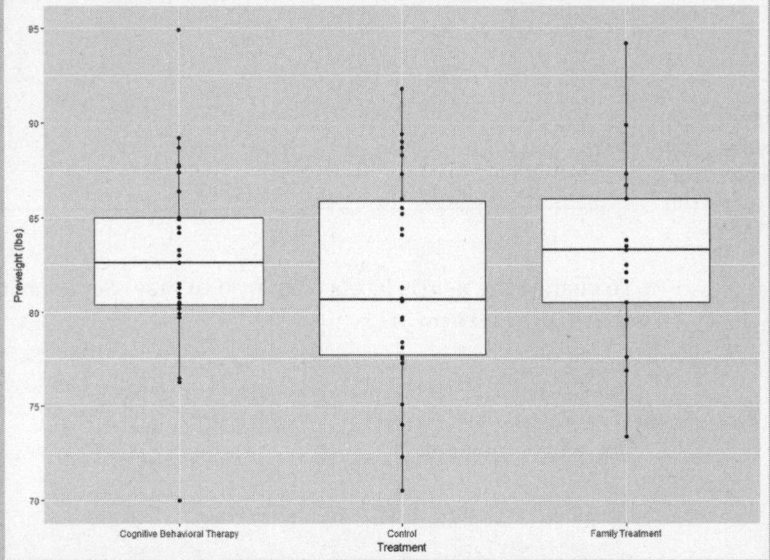

Then, if you're feeling ambitious, draw another box plot for the post-treatment weight data. Feeling even more ambitious? Plot post-treatment weight minus pre-treatment weight, and label the y-axis *Weight Change (lbs).* Which treatment appears to be the most effective? With the limited amount of analysis I've shown you (the `lm()` and `summary()` functions), are the differences among the three treatments "statistically significant?

2 Interacting with a User

IN THIS PART . . .

Create browser-based applications

Use the `shiny` package

Understand the anatomy of a `shiny` project

Visualize data in an interactive application

Use the `shinydashboard` package

Create a dashboard

IN THIS CHAPTER

» Introducing shiny

» Looking at a simple shiny project

» Developing your project

» Coming up with a more complex project

Chapter 4
Working with a Browser

As I emphasize in Chapter 3, R is rich with opportunities for visualizing data. In this chapter, I show how to create R applications whose visualizations depend on user input. I also show how to present these applications in a browser so that web users can interact with them. Putting an R application in a browser is a great way to share data and analyses. And you don't have to know HTML or JavaScript to get the job done!

Getting Your Shine On

A creation of RStudio honchos, `shiny` is the package that enables interactive, browser-based R applications. Use RStudio to install it in the usual way. On the Packages tab, click Install and then type **shiny** into the Install Packages dialog box. After the package finishes downloading, click the check box next to `shiny` on the Packages tab, or type

```
> library(shiny)
```

A couple of words about architecture before I move on and show how to create your first `shiny` project. Behind any web page with a `shiny` app is a computer that serves that page. The computer is running the R code (also known as a *script*) that creates the page. Though the computer can be a server that operates via the cloud, for the apps I show you in this chapter, the server is your laptop.

Creating Your First shiny Project

A `shiny` application is a directory that contains a file with R code. So, in your working directory (see Chapter 1), create a new directory called `shinydir1`.

RStudio gives you an easy way to do this: With the `shiny` package installed, select File ➪ New File ➪ Shiny Web App.

This menu command opens the New Shiny Web Application dialog box, shown in Figure 4-1.

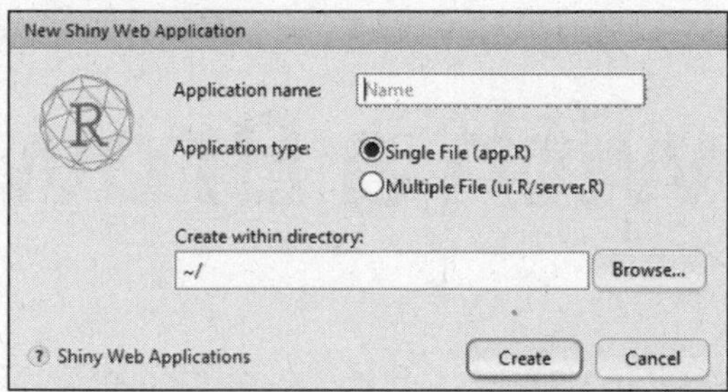

FIGURE 4-1: The New Shiny Web Application dialog box.

In the Application Name box, I enter a descriptive name for the app I'm about to create. I'm creating an interactive histogram that shows random sampling from a uniform distribution, so I type **UniformRandom** (no spaces!). For the Application Type option, I leave the Single File (app.R) radio button selected.

Finally, I create the directory. I click the Browse button to open the Choose Directory dialog box, which you see in Figure 4-2.

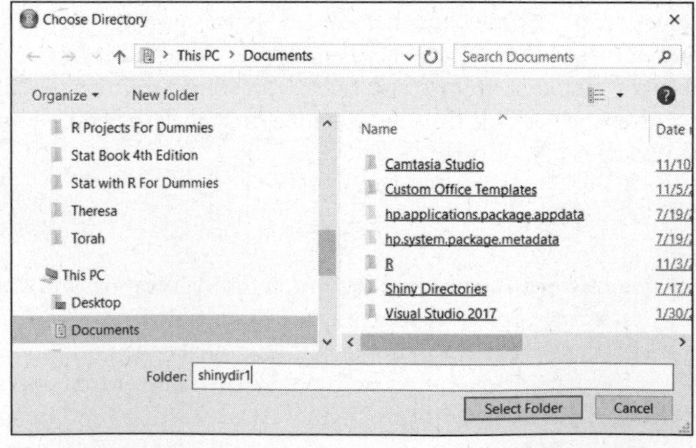

FIGURE 4-2: The Choose Directory dialog box.

In this dialog box, I create a new folder called `shinydir1` and click Select Folder. This closes the Choose Directory dialog box. Back in the New Shiny Web Application dialog box, I click Create.

After you complete these steps, you'll notice that the tab in the Scripts pane is now titled `app.R`. Every `shiny` app tab is labeled `app.R`. (Different `app.R` applications reside in different directories.) You'll also notice that an R script for a sample `shiny` app appears in the pane. Figure 4-3 shows you what I mean.

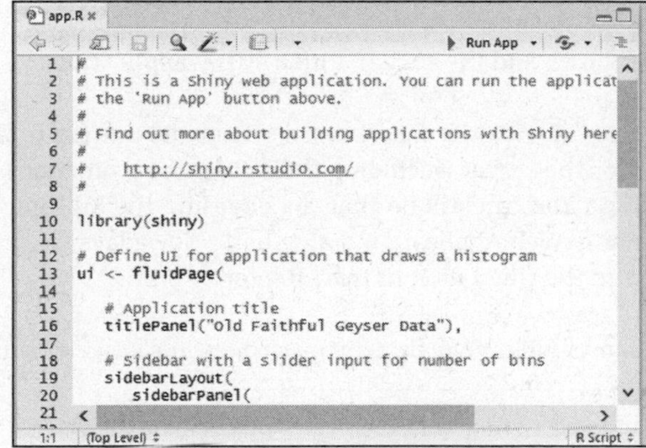

FIGURE 4-3: The Scripts pane after clicking Create in the New Shiny Web Application dialog box.

As the comment lines in the Scripts pane tell you, you can run this sample app by clicking the Run App button at the top of the pane. I'll leave it to you to run this application and see how the application reflects the code.

In this section, however, I delete the sample code and develop a similar (but somewhat more elaborate) application that teaches you some additional R skills as I explore `shiny`'s capabilities. With the Scripts pane active, I press Ctrl+A and press Delete. Now I have an empty Scripts pane.

The code for a `shiny` app has two main components: a *user interface* and a *server*.

The first order of business is to create a function that defines the *user interface* — the page that the user sees and interacts with. The fundamental structure of this script is

```
ui <- type_of_page()
```

Several types of pages are possible. Arguments in the parentheses determine the appearance and functionality of the page.

Then you create a set of instructions for the server to execute when the user interacts with the user interface. One way to begin is

```
server <- function(input,output){}
```

Inside the curly brackets, put the instructions you create.

Finally, the function

```
shinyApp(ui=ui, server=server)
```

ties together the `ui` and the `server` into a `shiny` application.

TECHNICAL STUFF

In the early days of `shiny`, it was necessary to create one file for the user interface and another for the server (including the `shinyApp()` function) and to store both in the directory. You can still do that (by choosing the Multiple File radio button in the New Shiny Web Application dialog box). Nowadays, only one file is necessary, and that's the way I do it in this chapter.

Figure 4-4 shows what your first `shiny` project looks like when all the pieces are in place.

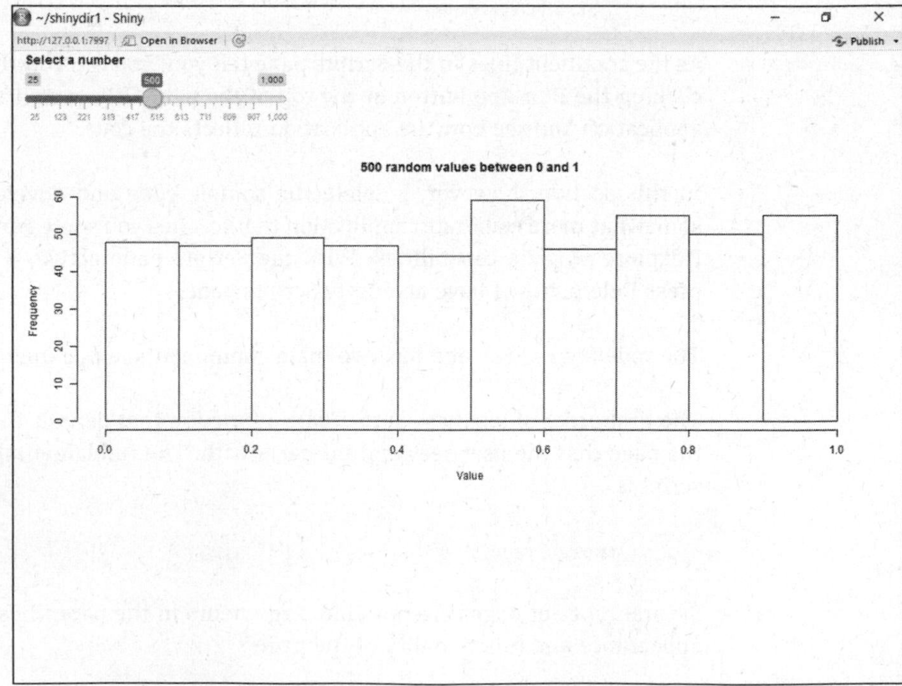

FIGURE 4-4: Your first `shiny` project.

It's a simple app, and it's typical of first projects with this package. The user manipulates a slider to determine the number of values to sample in a uniform distribution. The minimum value of the distribution is 0, and the maximum value is 1.

The histogram shows the results of the sampling. The minimum number of values is 25, the maximum number is 1,000, and the default is 500. Figure 4-4 shows the app in a window that RStudio opens.

To see the app in a browser, click Open in Browser in the upper left corner. (Spoiler alert: It looks pretty much the same.) As we proceed, I show you `shiny` apps in RStudio windows because they look better in the confines of the pages you're reading. Just bear in mind that it's easy enough to see the browser version by clicking Open in Browser.

The user interface

First things first. To define the user interface, I specify the type of page. For this application, I want a page that changes with the width of the browser: If I make the browser narrower, for example, I want the appearance of the page to change accordingly. This type of page is *fluid*, so the function that creates it is called `fluidPage()`:

```
ui <- fluidPage()
```

And that's the beginning of the user interface.

Next, I need a function that defines the slider and the input (the result of moving the slider) and another function that sets up the output. I put those two functions inside the parentheses.

For the slider, it's

```
sliderInput(inputId = "number",
            label = "Select a number",
            value = 500, min = 25, max = 1000)
```

The first argument establishes an identifier for the number the user selects by moving the slider. In the upcoming `server()` function, I refer to it as `input$number`.

The second argument adds the instruction above the slider. The remaining arguments set the default number, the minimum number, and the maximum number of values to sample from the uniform distribution.

Finally, I reserve an area for the output:

```
plotOutput("hist")
```

At this point, the app doesn't know what kind of output to plot. All it knows is that "hist" is the name of the output.

The user interface code is

```
ui <- fluidPage(
  sliderInput(inputId = "number",
              label = "Select a number",
              value = 500, min = 25, max = 1000),
  plotOutput("hist")
)
```

Think of sliderInput() as an input function and plotOutput() as an output function.

TECHNICAL STUFF

What does this code actually do? In the Scripts pane, highlight fluidPage() and all its arguments (don't include ui <- in your highlighting). Then press Ctrl+R to run the highlighted code. The result? A lot of HTML in the Console pane. This shows you that the user interface code generates a web page.

The server

As I point out earlier in this chapter, the starting point for the server is

```
server <- function(input,output){}
```

The first thing to put in the curly brackets is an R expression that represents the output. In the user interface, the name of the output is "hist". Here in the output, I refer to it as output$hist.

That expression receives the value of a function called renderPlot(), which, unsurprisingly, renders the plot.

A word about renderPlot(). The syntax of this function is

```
renderPlot({})
```

Inside renderPlot's curly brackets, you add as many lines of code as necessary to, well, render the plot. In this application, the base R graphics function hist() does the honors, as described in Chapter 3:

```
server <- function(input, output) {
  output$hist <- renderPlot({ hist(runif(input$number,min=0,max=1),xlab="Value",
main=paste(input$number,"random values between 0  and 1"))
   })
  }
```

That first argument to `hist()` is `runif()`. Do *not* pronounce it "run if"! It's not a *run* statement combined with an *if* statement or anything like that. Instead, think of the *r* as *random* and *unif* as *uniform*. This is R's way of saying, "Randomly sample from a uniform distribution." (The correct pronunciation is "r unif.") How would R say, "Randomly sample from a normal distribution"? If you guessed `rnorm()` you're absolutely right.

The first argument to `hist()` indicates that the data for the histogram comes from a random sample of values from a uniform distribution. How many values are in the sample? `input$number`, that's how many. The next two arguments to `runif()` set the distribution's minimum value to 0 and its maximum value to 1.

Now for the remaining arguments for `hist()`. If you've completed the examples in Chapter 3, you'll remember that `xlab` labels the x-axis, and `main` provides a title. Within `main`, I use the `paste()` function to add the value of `input$number` to the beginning of the title. The result is that the histogram title (as well as the histogram) changes each time the user moves the slider to a new number.

Final steps

To tie the user interface to the server, I add

```
shinyApp(ui = ui, server = server)
```

The entire script (including the `library()` function at the beginning) is

```
library(shiny)
ui <- fluidPage(
  sliderInput(inputId = "number",
              label = "Select a number",
              value = 500, min = 25, max = 1000),
  plotOutput("hist")
)
server <- function(input, output) {
  output$hist <- renderPlot({      hist(runif(input$number,min=0,max=1),
   xlab="Value",main=paste(input$number,"random values between 0 and 1"))
   })
  }
shinyApp(ui = ui, server = server)
```

Save the code (press Ctrl+S or choose File⇨Save) and then click the Run App button. That opens the display shown earlier, in Figure 4-4, and puts this in the Console pane:

```
> runApp('shinydir1/UniformRandom')

Listening on http://127.0.0.1:3328
```

The second line means that R is waiting for the user to do something. (Move the slider, in other words.) The URL on your machine will no doubt be different from the one on mine.

To end the session with the application, press Esc or close the RStudio window that shows the page. You can also click the little red stop sign in the upper right corner of the Console pane.

Getting reactive

I can write the server in a different way. Instead of this:

```
server <- function(input, output) {
  output$hist <- renderPlot({ hist(runif(input$number,min=0,max=1),xlab="Value",
main=paste(input$number,"random values between 0   and 1"))
  })
  }
```

I can write this:

```
server <- function(input, output) {
  histdata <- reactive({
    runif(input$number,min=0,max=1)
    })

  output$hist <- renderPlot({
    hist(histdata(),xlab="Value",
    main=paste(input$number,"random values between 0 and 1")
  )
  })
}
```

It accomplishes the same thing. Why bother setting a variable called `histdata` for the `runif()` function? And what's that `reactive({})` deal? And, finally, why do I have parentheses after `histdata` in the first argument to the `hist()` function?

Creating the `histdata` variable enables me to use the results of sampling from the uniform distribution for additional outputs — not just for the histogram. For example, I might want to add the data's mean, median, and standard deviation to the `shiny` app. I show you how to do that in just a moment.

What about `reactive({})`? To make the `shiny` app responsive to user input, I have to create `histdata` in a *reactive context* so that the variable can *react* to the input (when the user moves the slider to change the value of `input$number`, in other words). Accordingly, `reactive({})` provides that context.

"But wait a second," you might exclaim. "In the original version, I was able to explicitly use `runif()` in `renderPlot({})`. Why is that?" Because `renderPlot({})` is a reactive context. (The curly brackets are a giveaway.) For that reason, changes in `input$number` show up as changes in the histogram plot. If `renderPlot({})` is the only reactive context I use, it's not necessary to have another reactive context and create `histdata`.

TIP

In `shiny`, every `render` function is a reactive context.

Now for the parentheses next to `histdata` in `hist()`. When I create a reactive variable like `histdata`, I create an object I can *call* to see whether changes have occurred (in this case, to `input$number`), and it returns the changes. If it's callable and it returns something, it's a function, and to indicate that, I add the parentheses. So `histdata` is the reactive variable I define here, and when I use it again, it's `histdata()`. Got it?

TIP

I can't emphasize this enough: When you create a variable in a reactive context, *you must add the parentheses whenever you use it*. Forgetting to do that is the biggest roadblock when you're starting out with `shiny`.

Now my objective is to create a `shiny` app that shows not just the histogram of the sample from the uniform distribution but also the sample mean, median, and standard deviation. The app will look like Figure 4-5. The mean, median, and standard deviation are below the histogram, to the left.

In the user interface, I have to create space for those three items. Each one is a `textOutput`, so I add these three lines to the user interface:

```
textOutput("mean"),
textOutput("median"),
textOutput("sd")
```

Of course, I also have to make changes to the server. Remember, I add

```
histdata <- reactive({
    runif(input$number,min=0,max=1)
    })
```

at the beginning of the server code.

For the textOutputs, I add

```
output$mean <- renderText({paste("Mean =",round(mean(histdata()),3)
  )
  })
```

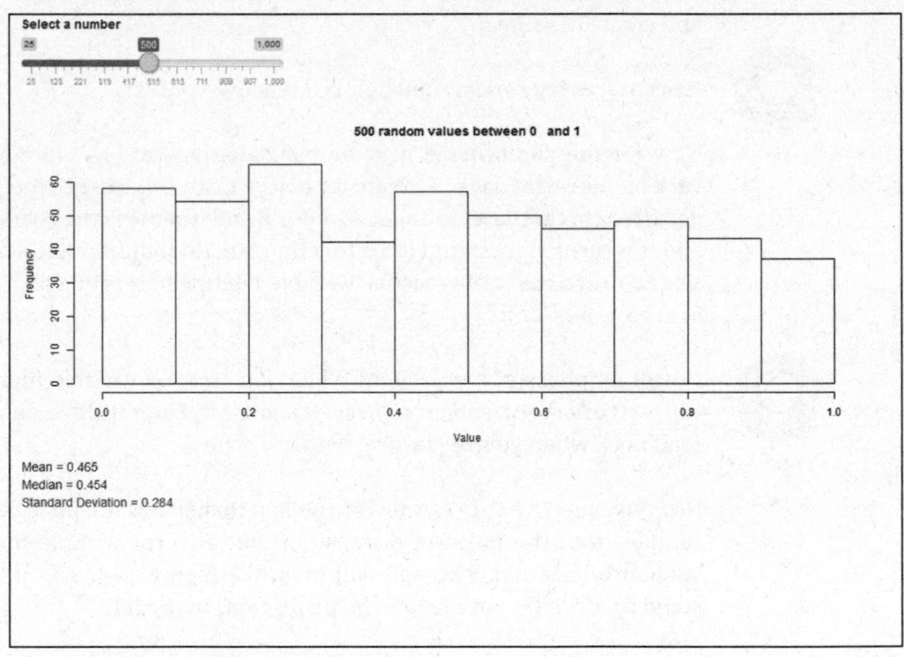

FIGURE 4-5: The shiny app with the mean, the median, and the standard deviation.

```
output$median <- renderText({paste("Median =",round(median(histdata()),3)
  )
  })

  output$sd <- renderText({paste("Standard Deviation =",round(sd(histdata()),3)
  )
  })
```

The whole thing is

```
library(shiny)
ui <- fluidPage(
  sliderInput(inputId = "number",
              label = "Select a number",
              value = 500, min = 25, max = 1000),
  plotOutput("hist"),
  textOutput("mean"),
  textOutput("sd")
)
server <- function(input, output) {

  histdata <- reactive({
    runif(input$number,min=0,max=1)
    })

  output$hist <- renderPlot({
    hist(histdata(),xlab="Value",
    main=paste(input$number,"random values between 0   and 1")
  )
  })

  output$mean <- renderText({paste("Mean =",round(mean(histdata()),3)
  )
  })

  output$median <- renderText({paste("Median =",round(median(histdata()),3)
  )
  })

  output$sd <- renderText({paste("Standard Deviation =",round(sd(histdata()),3)
  )
  })
}
shinyApp(ui = ui, server = server)
```

Working with ggplot

If you've read Chapter 3, you know that I'm a huge fan of the ggplot2 package. I hope you become one, too. In this section, I show you how to use ggplot functions to create the first version of the app from the preceding section. When it's done, it will look like Figure 4-6. (As in the preceding section, I show the app in an RStudio window. Click Open in Browser to see it in your browser.)

To get started, I follow the steps in the preceding section to create a new application called `UniformRandomggplot` in a new directory called `shinydir2`. Again, I delete the sample code and begin the coding with these two lines:

```
library(ggplot2)
library(shiny)
```

The user interface code remains the same as in the preceding section's first version:

```
ui <- fluidPage(
  sliderInput(inputId = "number",
              label = "Select a number",
              value = 500, min = 1, max = 1000),
  plotOutput("hist")
)
```

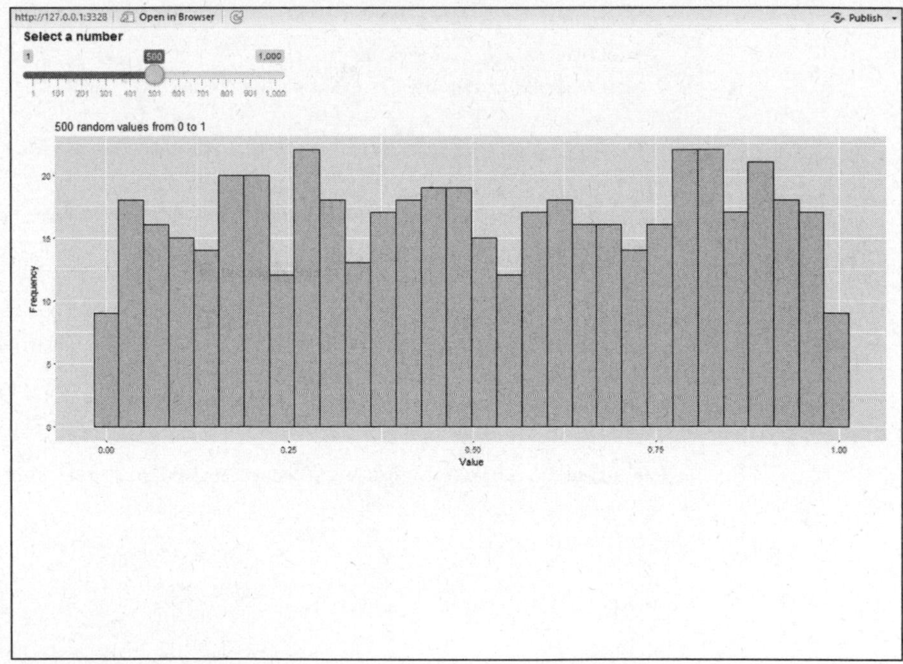

FIGURE 4-6: The first version of the `shiny` app from the preceding section, rendered in `ggplot2`.

Changing the server

The function that does the plotting has to change. Instead of a base R function, I'm going to put `ggplot()` into `renderPlot()`'s curly brackets. Recall from Chapter 3 that `ggplot()` has to have a data frame as its first argument. So I can't just pass `runif(input$number, min = 0, max=1)` as an argument to `ggplot()`.

Instead, I have to turn the sample of `input$number` values into a data frame, and here's how I do it:

```
df <- data.frame(runif(input$number, min=0,max=1))
```

That would be the first line of code I put into `renderPlot()`'s curly brackets.

The second argument to `ggplot()` is `aes()`, which maps the values in the data frame into the x-axis of the histogram. This means I have to have a name for the column of values in the `df` data frame:

```
colnames(df)<-c("Value")
```

Take another look at Chapter 1 if that looks strange to you. That's the second line of code in the curly brackets.

Now I can start on the plot:

```
ggplot(df,aes(x=Value))+
```

And I can add the histogram

```
geom_histogram(color = "black", fill = "grey80")+
```

and some landscaping:

```
labs(y="Frequency",title = paste(input$number,"random values from 0 to 1"))
```

Altogether, the code for the server looks like this:

```
server <- function(input, output) {
output$hist <- renderPlot({
    df <- data.frame(runif(input$number, min=0,max=1))
    colnames(df)<-c("Value")
    ggplot(df,aes(x=Value))+
             geom_histogram(color = "black",fill="grey80")+
             labs(y="Frequency",
title = paste(input$number,"random values from 0 to 1"))

    })
}
```

Remember to add

```
shinyApp(ui = ui, server = server)
```

With the code for the user interface (including the two `library()` functions) and the server (and `shinyApp()`) saved in `shinydir2`, click the Run App button to produce what you see in Figure 4-5.

A few more changes

In the Console pane, this line appears each time you move the slider:

```
`stat_bin()` using `bins = 30`. Pick better value with `binwidth`.
```

This indicates that R has taken a guess about how to render the appearance of the histogram. Specifically, R takes a shot at the binwidth — the width of each bar. (See Chapter 3.) Some modifications eliminate the guesswork.

I add a slider that enables the viewer to set the binwidth. To the user interface, I insert this code between the first `sliderInput()` and `plotOutput()`:

```
sliderInput(inputId = "binwidth",
            label = "Select a binwidth",
            value = .05, min = .01, max = .10),
```

The first argument sets the identifier for this particular input, the second puts a label above the slider. The third gives the starting binwidth, the fourth gives the minimum binwidth, and the fifth gives the maximum binwidth.

TIP

The (approximate) number of rendered bars is the range of values (1.00) divided by the selected binwidth. So the starting value (`.05`) produces 20 (ish) bars.

Changes to the `title` argument in the `labs()` function in the server add the binwidth information to the histogram title:

```
labs(y="Frequency",
title = paste(input$number,"random values from 0 to 1 with binwidth
   =",input$binwidth))
```

The whole megillah is shown here:

```
library(ggplot2)
library(shiny)
ui <- fluidPage(
  sliderInput(inputId = "number",
              label = "Select a number",
              value = 500, min = 1, max = 1000),
```

```
  sliderInput(inputId = "binwidth",
              label = "Select a binwidth",
              value = .05, min = .01, max = .10),
  plotOutput("hist")
)
server <- function(input, output) {

  output$hist <- renderPlot({
    df <- data.frame(runif(input$number, min=0,max=1))
    colnames(df)<-c("Value")
    ggplot(df,aes(x=Value))+
            geom_histogram(binwidth=input$binwidth,
                           color = "black",fill="grey80")+
            labs(y="Frequency",
title = paste(input$number,"random values from 0 to 1 with
   binwidth =",input$binwidth))

    })
}
shinyApp(ui = ui, server = server)
```

Press Ctrl+S to save it all in the `shinydir2` directory, and then run the app to produce the display in Figure 4-7.

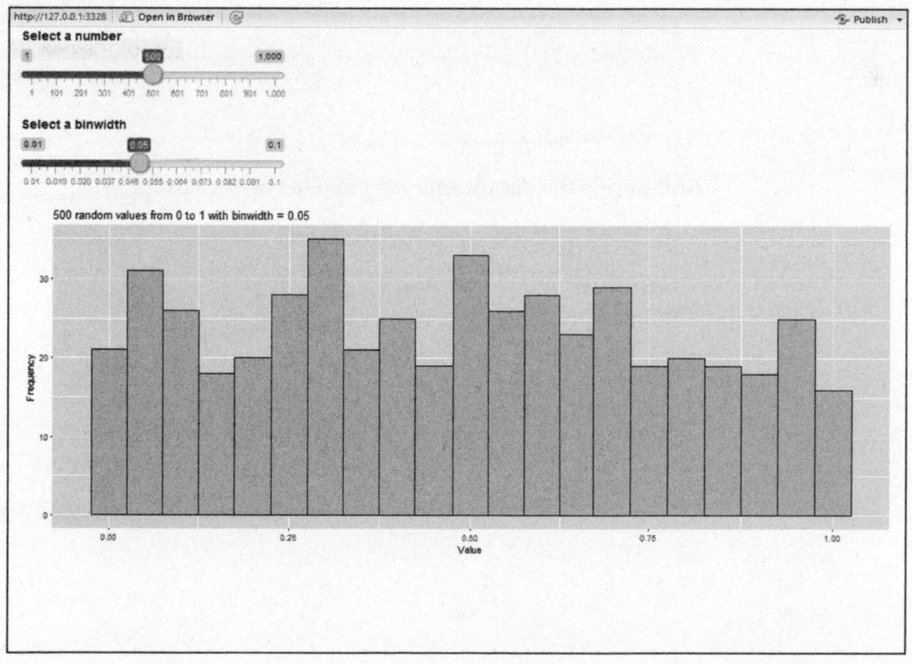

FIGURE 4-7: Adding a slider to enable the selection of binwidth.

Getting reactive with ggplot

To add the mean, median, and mode to the display you see in Figure 4-7 — the idea here is that it should match what you see in Figure 4-5 — I first add the textOutputs to the user interface, as before:

```
textOutput("mean"),
textOutput("median"),
textOutput("sd")
```

Things start to get a bit tricky in the server because I have to do two things: Use reactive({}) to create a variable for runif(), and create a data frame for ggplot(). Why is this tricky? Because in the simpler version with just the plot and not the statistics, I was able to accomplish both at once inside the reactive context of renderPlot():

```
df <- data.frame(runif(input$number, min=0,max=1))
```

In this version, however, I have to create the variable in a reactive context outside renderPlot({}) (so that I can use that variable to calculate the mean, median, and standard deviation), and the data frame inside renderPlot({}) so that ggplot() can use it.

Here's the variable (histdata) in reactive({}):

```
server <- function(input, output) {
  histdata <- reactive({(runif(input$number, min=0,max=1))

  })
```

And here's the data frame (df) inside renderPlot({}):

```

  output$hist <- renderPlot({
    df <-data.frame(histdata())
    colnames(df)<-c("Value")
    ggplot(df,aes(x=Value))+
      geom_histogram(binwidth=input$binwidth,
                     color = "black",fill="grey80")+
      labs(y="Frequency",
           title = paste(input$number,"random values from 0 to 1 with binwidth =",
              input$binwidth))
```

And finally, here are the output$s:

```
output$mean <- renderText({paste("Mean =",round(mean(histdata()),3)
  )
  })

  output$median <- renderText({paste("Median =",round(median(histdata()),3)
  )
  })

  output$sd <- renderText({paste("Standard Deviation =",round(sd(histdata()),3)
  )
  })
```

TIP

Yes, I'm going to harp on this: Notice that after I define histdata in reactive({}), it's histdata() whenever I use it again.

Make those changes and run the app. It should look like Figure 4-8:

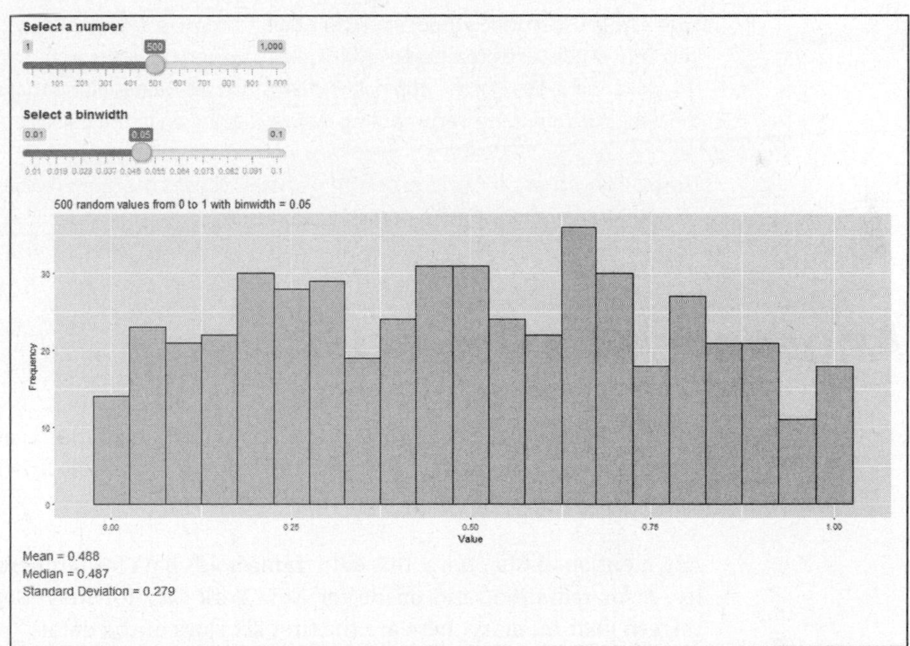

FIGURE 4-8: The ggplot2 version of the first shiny app, with statistics added.

HOW DOES ALL THIS WORK, REALLY?

When you drive, do you have to know the inner workings of your car's engine? Do you have to know exactly how your refrigerator keeps your food cold? If you answered yes to at least one of those questions, this sidebar is for you. Even if you didn't, you might still want to read it.

I hate to break this to you, boys and girls, but like computer animation, reactivity is an illusion. In computer animation, nothing moves across the screen: Instead, one pixel turns off, another turns on, and the illusion is that the pixel has moved from the first pixel's location to the second.

Likewise, in reactivity, it is *not* the case that the app only monitors the user and that when the user makes a change to the input (like moving the slider to change `input$number`), the output (like the plot in `output$hist`) changes accordingly. Instead, the server constantly recomputes everything in the app every few microseconds. So if the user moves the slider, for example (or changes the input in some other way), within microseconds the output updates.

Wait a (micro) second. Suppose the user doesn't make a change. Then what? Recomputation takes place anyway. It's just that everything recomputes its previous results, and it looks like the app hasn't changed at all. Bear in mind that whether or not the user does anything, recomputing is always going on in the background.

The illusion is that the user's action immediately causes the app's reaction. And, like computer animation, that's a pretty useful illusion!

Another shiny Project

In this section, I move from a `shiny` app based on random sampling to an app based on data. The data that forms the basis of this project is in the data frame `airquality`, which lives in the `datasets` package.

As I mention in Chapter 2, this data frame holds data for temperature, wind velocity, solar radiation, and ozone for New York City for May–September 1973. To refresh your memory, here are the first six rows of the data:

```
> head(airquality)
  Ozone Solar.R Wind Temp Month Day
1    41     190  7.4   67     5   1
2    36     118  8.0   72     5   2
```

```
3    12       149 12.6    74      5   3
4    18       313 11.5    62      5   4
5    NA        NA 14.3    56      5   5
6    28        NA 14.9    66      5   6
```

The objective is an app that shows a scatterplot of two user-selected variables (excluding Month and Day) along with statistical summaries (correlation and regression) of the relationship between the variables. I show you how to create two versions: one in base R graphics and the other in ggplot.

The base R version

Figure 4-9 shows the finished product. The user selects an x-variable from one drop-down menu, and a y-variable from the other. The application then produces a scatterplot, which contains the regression line that summarizes the relationship between the two variables. The first line of the scatterplot title includes the selected variables. The second line shows the correlation coefficient (r) between the two, along with the equation of the regression line in the plot.

I begin by using File⇨NewFile⇨Shiny Web App to create a new app called AirQuality in a new directory called shinydir3. I delete the sample code.

The first thing is to attach the library that contains the data frame:

```
library(datasets)
```

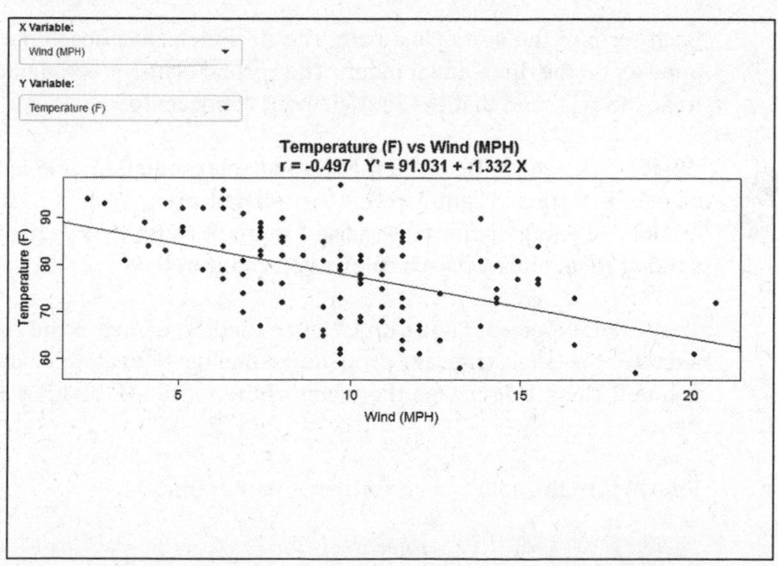

FIGURE 4-9: A shiny app for the airquality data frame.

I'll have to clean up the data by eliminating missing values. The function that does that, drop_na(), lives in the tidyr package, so I add

```
library(tidyr)
```

I describe drop_na() in Chapter 2.

One more package, tibble, supplies a useful function called rownames_to_column(), which I also describe in Chapter 2. I use it here in a moment, so I add its package:

```
library(tibble)
```

Next, I delete the missing values from airquality:

```
aq.no.missing <-drop_na(airquality)
```

The newly created data frame aq.no.missing is the one I use going forward.

The next task is to provide a set of options for the x-variable menu and for the y-variable menu. The options, of course, are the same for both variables. I create the vector:

```
options <- c("Ozone (parts per billion)" = "Ozone",
             "Solar (Langleys)" = "Solar.R",
             "Wind (MPH)" = "Wind",
             "Temperature (F)" = "Temp")
```

Each term of the vector is a pair. The first element of each pair is the label that appears on the drop-down menu. The second element is the name of the variable in aq.no.missing that the first element connects to.

TECHNICAL STUFF

What is a langley? Used as a measure of solar radiation, one langley is one small calorie per square centimeter of irradiated area. What's a small calorie? The amount of energy required to raise 1 gram of water by 1 degree Celsius. (A thousand of them make up each calorie you count in food.) Aren't you glad you asked?

Take another look at Figure 4-7. Notice that the names in the plot title and on the axes are the labels from the drop-down menus, not variable names from the data frame. I think this makes the whole thing more informative. How do I get this done?

First, I turn the options vector into a data frame:

```
df.options <-data.frame(options)
```

Here's what that data frame looks like:

```
> df.options
                          options
Ozone (parts per billion)   Ozone
Solar (Langleys)          Solar.R
Wind (MPH)                   Wind
Temperature (F)              Temp
```

For this data frame to be useful, the row names on the left have to constitute a data column, so

```
df.lv <-rownames_to_column(df.options)
```

makes that happen. I use `lv` in the new data frame name to denote `label` (the name that appears on the menu) and `value` (the corresponding variable name in the data frame). To complete this data frame, I name its columns:

```
colnames(df.lv) <- c("label","value")
```

This data frame now looks like this:

```
> df.lv
                      label   value
1 Ozone (parts per billion)   Ozone
2          Solar (Langleys) Solar.R
3                Wind (MPH)    Wind
4           Temperature (F)    Temp
```

On to the user interface:

```
ui <- fluidPage(
  selectInput("X", "X Variable:",
              options),

  selectInput("Y", "Y Variable:",
              options),

  plotOutput("scatter")


)
```

Once again, it's a fluid page. Each selectInput() is a drop-down menu. The first argument is its name, the second argument is its onscreen label, and the third is the options vector that presents the choices. And plotOutput() sets aside the space for the plot.

Now for the server. The overall structure of the server, remember, is

```
server <- function(input,output) { }
```

The first item between the brackets assigns the user selections input$X and input$Y to a data frame I call selections. I do this in a reactive context (see the earlier section "Getting reactive"):

```
selections <- reactive({
    aq.no.missing[, c(input$X, input$Y)]

  })
```

REMEMBER

Here I go again: I've created selections in a reactive context (within reactive({}), in other words), and the next time I use it, I have to refer to it as selections().

The comma within the square brackets means "all rows in the aq.no.missing data frame." The second expression c(input$X, input$Y) limits those rows to just the variables the user has selected. The result is that I can now refer to all rows in the first selected variable as

```
selections()[,1]
```

and to all the rows in the second as

```
selections()[,2]
```

which I will do almost immediately. Stay tuned.

The next item in the server is the output function, whose overall structure is

```
output$scatter <- renderPlot({})
```

The code for rendering the output goes between the curly brackets.

And now, as promised, I use those references to the two selected variables. I assign the first user selection to a variable called x_column:

```
x_column <- selections()[,1]
```

and the second to y_column:

```
y_column <- selections()[,2]
```

The correlation coefficient is

```
correlation <-cor(x_column,y_column)
```

and the regression is

```
regression <- lm(y_column ~ x_column)
```

To put the equation of the regression line into the title, I have to know its intercept (where the line meets the y-axis) and its slope (how slanted it is). In base R graphics, I also have to have those pieces of information to plot the regression line.

The result of a regression analysis is a list. For a regression analysis of Temp dependent on Wind, for example, part of that list looks like this:

```
Coefficients:
            Estimate Std. Error t value Pr(>|t|)
(Intercept) 91.0305      2.3489  38.754  < 2e-16 ***
Wind        -1.3318      0.2226  -5.983 2.84e-08 ***
---
```

To retrieve the intercept from the list, the expression is

```
intercept <- regression$coefficients[1]
```

And to retrieve the slope, it's

```
slope <- regression$coefficients[2]
```

(For the full skinny on correlation and regression, see the book I shamelessly plugged earlier.)

Two more pieces of information and I'm ready to plot. So far, the R code has worked with the variable names that correspond to the user selections, like Wind and Temp. In the plot, remember, I want to use the names on the menus — Wind (MPH) and Temperature (F) — for the title and for the axis labels.

So I'm looking for the label names that correspond to the selected variable names. Here's where that df.lv data frame comes into play. For the label for the x-variable, I'm looking for

```
X_Label <- df.lv$label[whose corresponding df.lv$value     matches input$X]
```

Fortunately, R provides a neat little trick that fills the bill. It's a function called which(), and here's how to use it:

```
X_Label <- df.lv$label[which(df.lv$value == input$X)]
```

And for the label for the y-variable, it's

```
Y_Label <- df.lv$label[which(df.lv$value == input$Y)]
```

And now, here's the plot() function:

```
plot(x=x_column,y=y_column,xlab = X_Label,ylab = Y_Label,
         cex.axis = 1.5,cex.lab = 1.5, pch = 20, cex = 2,
         main = paste(Y_Label,"vs",X_Label,
                    "\n r =",round(correlation,3),"
             Y' =",round(intercept,3),"+",round(slope,3),"X"),
         cex.main=1.8)
```

The first two arguments, x and y, are the variables to plot. The next two, xlab and ylab, are the titles for the axes. The cex.axis argument specifies the size of the numbers on the axes, and cex.lab is the size of the axes labels. The value 1.5 means "1.5 times the normal size of a character." The next argument, pch, means that the plot character is a filled circle, and its size, cex, is 2.

The argument main is the title. I use paste() to put Y_Label and X_Label into the title. \n means to continue on the next line, where I paste the rounded correlation (rounded to three places) as well as the rounded intercept and the rounded slope into the regression equation. The size of the title, cex.main, is 1.8.

One more function draws the regression line:

```
abline(intercept,slope)
```

Here's the whole thing, including the shinyApp() function at the end:

```
library(datasets)
library(tidyr)
library(tibble)
```

```
aq.no.missing <-drop_na(airquality)

options <- c("Ozone (parts per billion)" = "Ozone",
             "Solar (Langleys)" = "Solar.R",
             "Wind (MPH)" = "Wind",
             "Temperature (F)" = "Temp")
df.options <-data.frame(options)
df.lv <-rownames_to_column(df.options)
colnames(df.lv) <- c("label","value")

ui <- fluidPage(
  selectInput("X", "X Variable:",
              options),

  selectInput("Y", "Y Variable:",
              options),

  plotOutput("scatter")


)
server <- function(input, output) {
  selections <- reactive({
    aq.no.missing[, c(input$X, input$Y)]

  })


  output$scatter <- renderPlot({

    x_column <- selections()[,1]
    y_column <- selections()[,2]

    correlation <-cor(x_column,y_column)
    regression <- lm(y_column ~ x_column)
    intercept <- regression$coefficients[1]
    slope <- regression$coefficients[2]

    X_Label <- df.lv$label[which(df.lv$value == input$X)]
    Y_Label <- df.lv$label[which(df.lv$value == input$Y)]

    plot(x=x_column,y=y_column,xlab = X_Label,ylab = Y_Label,
         cex.axis = 1.5,cex.lab = 1.5, pch = 20, cex = 2,
         main = paste(Y_Label,"vs",X_Label,
```

```
                    "\n r =",round(correlation,3),"
              Y' =",round(intercept,3),"+",round(slope,3),"X"),
            cex.main=1.8)
      abline(intercept,slope)
    })


  }


shinyApp(ui = ui, server = server)
```

Save the file, and run the app!

The ggplot version

Rendered in `ggplot()`, this app looks like Figure 4-10.

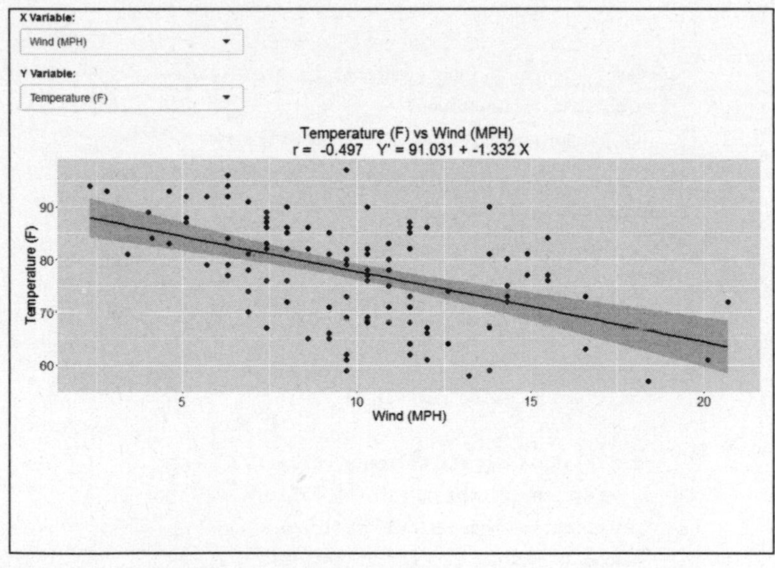

FIGURE 4-10: The app from the preceding section, rendered in ggplot.

The code is the same as in the base R version, except that I have to add

```
library(ggplot2)
```

to the beginning, and of course I have to change the plotting function in `output$scatter`.

Instead of plot(), I begin with ggplot():

```
ggplot(selections(),aes(x=x_column,y=y_column))+
```

The first argument is the data frame that supplies the data, and aes() then maps the first selected variable to x, and the second selected variable to y.

Next, I add geom_point() to specify that I want points to appear in the plot:

```
geom_point(size=3) +
```

and the argument shows how big the points should be.

Adding a labs() function renders the x-axis, y-axis, and title:

```
labs(x = X_Label,y = Y_Label,
        title = paste(Y_Label,"vs",X_Label,
        "\n r = ",round(correlation,3),"                         Y' =",round(in
            tercept,3),"+",round(slope,3),"X"))+
```

To set the sizes of the fonts, I use a theme() function:

```
theme(axis.title.x = element_text(size=18),
         axis.text.x = element_text(size=17),
         axis.title.y = element_text(size=18),
         axis.text.y = element_text(size=17),
         plot.title = element_text(hjust = 0.5,size=20))+
```

In plot.title, hjust =0.5 centers the title.

Finally, geom_smooth() plots the regression line:

```
geom_smooth(method="lm",col="black")
```

The first argument specifies a linear model (linear regression, in this example), and the second makes the line black. Notice that, unlike in base R, it's not necessary to specify the slope or the intercept.

The shadow around the regression line in Figure 4-10 represents the *standard error of estimate* — a measure of variability around the line. The tighter the shadow, the better the fit of the line to the data. (Note what happens when the x-variable and the y-variable are the same.). To eliminate the shadow, add se=FALSE as an argument to geom_smooth().

Here's the entire set of functions for the ggplot version:

```
ggplot(selections(),aes(x = x_column,y = y_column))+
      geom_point(size=3) +
      labs(x = X_Label,y = Y_Label,
           title = paste(Y_Label,"vs",X_Label,
           "\n r = ",round(correlation,3),"
           Y' =",round(intercept,3),"+",round(slope,3),"X"))+
      theme(axis.title.x = element_text(size=18),
            axis.text.x = element_text(size=17),
            axis.title.y = element_text(size=18),
            axis.text.y = element_text(size=17),
            plot.title = element_text(hjust = 0.5,size=20))+
      geom_smooth(method="lm",col="black")
```

Substitute this set of functions for the plot() function and abline() in the base R version, save, and run the application.

Suggested Project

Feeling adventurous? Take what you learned in this last project and try it out on a different data frame. It's a great way to build up your skill set.

I suggest Cars93, which lives in the MASS package. I use it in some examples in Chapter 3. Just to refresh your memory, this data frame provides information on a number of variables (way more than four!) for 93 models of cars from 1993.

Good luck!

IN THIS CHAPTER

» Introducing `shinydashboard`

» Exploring dashboard layouts

» Creating a dashboard

Chapter 5
Dashboards — How Dashing!

A *dashboard* is a collection of graphics that make it easy for a user to access and understand information. Think about the dashboard in a car: It shows how fast the car is moving, how much gas is in the tank, the temperature, and a number of other pieces of information that help a driver understand the state of a car at any moment.

In this chapter, I show you how to use R to create dashboards that show multiple pieces of information about data.

The shinydashboard Package

In Chapter 4, I introduce you to `shiny`, a package for creating interactive applications in R. Like `shiny`, the `shinydashboard` package is a creation of the same folks who brought us RStudio. As its name indicates, it has all the elements of shiny (like user interface, server, and reactivity), and you use it to create dashboards. If, as you work with this package, you get the idea that a dashboard is a `shiny` app on steroids, you've pretty much got it.

Here's what I mean. Figure 5-1 shows a dashboard I created in `shinydashboard`. It shows a random sample from a uniform distribution with values between 0 and 1, and it shows the mean, median, and standard deviation of the sample. The user moves a slider to set the sample size. It's the same example I use to introduce shiny in Chapter 4. Compare this figure with Figure 4-5 and you'll see that this app presents the same information, but in a snazzier way.

How do you create something like this? Read on.

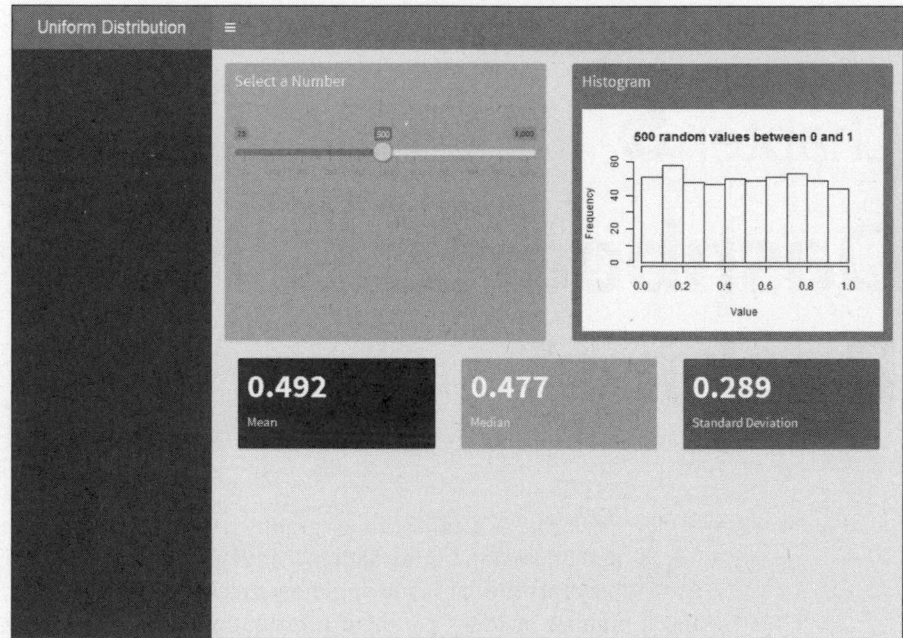

FIGURE 5-1: First shiny app from Chapter 4 rendered in shinydashboard.

Exploring Dashboard Layouts

The first step in creating a dashboard is to install the shinydashboard package. On the Packages tab in RStudio, click Install. In the Install Packages dialog box, type **shinydashboard** and then click Install.

After the package installation is finished, check its box on the Packages tab. Make sure the box next to shiny on the Packages tab is also checked.

Select File ➪ New File ➪ Shiny Web App from the main menu.

Doing this opens the New Shiny Web Application dialog box. Type **Dashboard-Development** (or another descriptive title) in the Application Name box. Use the Browse button to open the Choose Directory dialog box and create a new directory for the app. In the new file, clear out all the sample code.

Getting started with the user interface

A dashboard user interface consists of a header, a sidebar, and a body. In shinydashboard code, that looks like this:

```
library(shinydashboard)

ui <- dashboardPage(
  dashboardHeader(title = "This is the Header"),
  dashboardSidebar(),
  dashboardBody()
)
```

I add a server

```
server <- function(input, output) {}
```

and the shinyapp() function:

```
shinyApp(ui, server)
```

With all this code typed into the new DashboardDevelopment file, clicking the Run App button creates the screen you see in Figure 5-2.

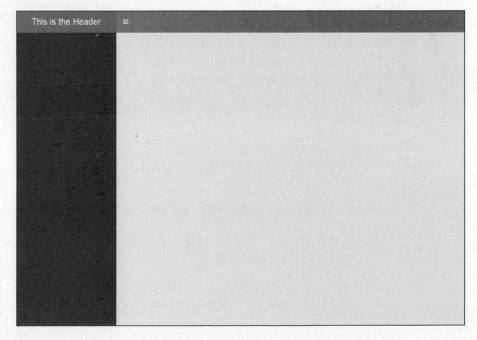

FIGURE 5-2: The beginning of a shiny dashboard dashboard.

Building the user interface: Boxes, boxes, boxes . . .

The user interface so far, of course, doesn't allow a user to do anything. In shinydashboard, you use *boxes* to build the user interface. I add them inside a fluidRow (something like fluidPage in a shiny app; see Chapter 4) in dashboardBody() — one box for the slider and one box for the plot:

```
  dashboardBody(

    fluidRow(

      box(
        title = "Select a Number",
        sliderInput(inputId = "number",
                    label = "",
                    value = 500, min = 25, max = 1000)),

      box(
      title = "Histogram",
         plotOutput("hist", height = 250))
      )
  )
```

TIP

Notice the label argument to sliderInput(). I don't want a label in the slider, but omitting the argument results in an error message.

TIP

The height argument in plotOutput() sets a height for the graph inside the box, not for the entire box.

I also have to add code to the server to render the plot:

```
server <- function(input, output) {
    output$hist <- renderPlot({})
}
```

Running this app produces the elements for the screen shown in Figure 5-3.

The app still doesn't do anything. If you've read Chapter 4, you know what's coming next in the way of code.

I use reactive({}) to set a variable (histdata) for the results of random sampling from a uniform distribution whose values are between 0 and 1:

```
histdata <- reactive({runif(input$number,min=0,max=1)})
```

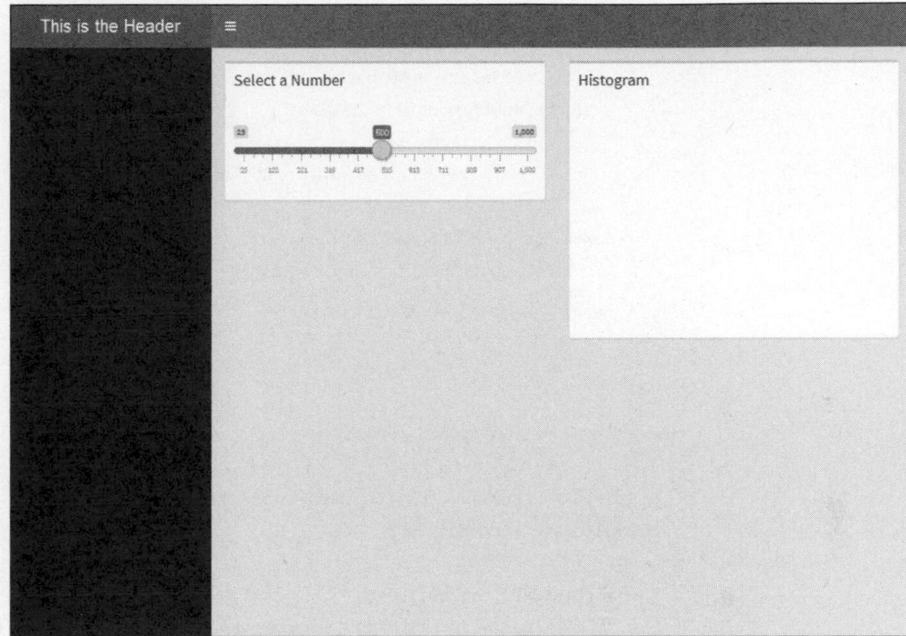

FIGURE 5-3: Adding a slider and a plot.

And, in order to draw the graph of the sample, I add `hist()` and appropriate arguments to `renderPlot({})`:

```
output$hist <- renderPlot({

    hist(histdata(),xlab="Value",
main=paste(input$number,"random values between 0 and 1"))
  })
```

The first argument in `hist` is the variable I just set within `reactive({})` (along with parentheses!), and the next two add the x-axis title and the main title.

Here's all the code at this point:

```
library(shinydashboard)

ui <- dashboardPage(
  dashboardHeader(
    title = "Uniform Distribution"
    ),
  dashboardSidebar(),
  dashboardBody(

    fluidRow(
```

```
    box(
        title = "Select a Number",
        sliderInput(inputId = "number",
                    label = "",
                    value = 500, min = 25, max = 1000)),

      box(title = "Histogram",
          plotOutput("hist", height = 250))
      )
    )
)

server <- function(input, output) {

  histdata <- reactive({runif(input$number,min=0,max=1)})
  output$hist <- renderPlot({

    hist(histdata(),xlab="Value",
         main=paste(input$number,"random values between 0 and 1"))
  })

  }

shinyApp(ui, server)
```

Notice that in `dashboardHeader()` I changed the `title` to `"Uniform Distribution"`. This code produces the functionality in Figure 5-4. Moving the slider now changes the histogram and the heading just above it.

Each box can have a `status`. Although it's not strictly necessary, I assign a `warning` status to the slider, and a `primary` status to the plot:

```
     box(title = "Select a Number",
            status="warning",
            sliderInput(inputId = "number",
                    label = "",
                    value = 500, min = 25, max = 1000)),
      box(title = "Histogram",
             status="primary",
             plotOutput("hist", height = 250))
      )
```

Each status is associated with a color, so this change adds a little color to the box edges: yellow for the slider (although it looks more like gold) and light blue for the plot.

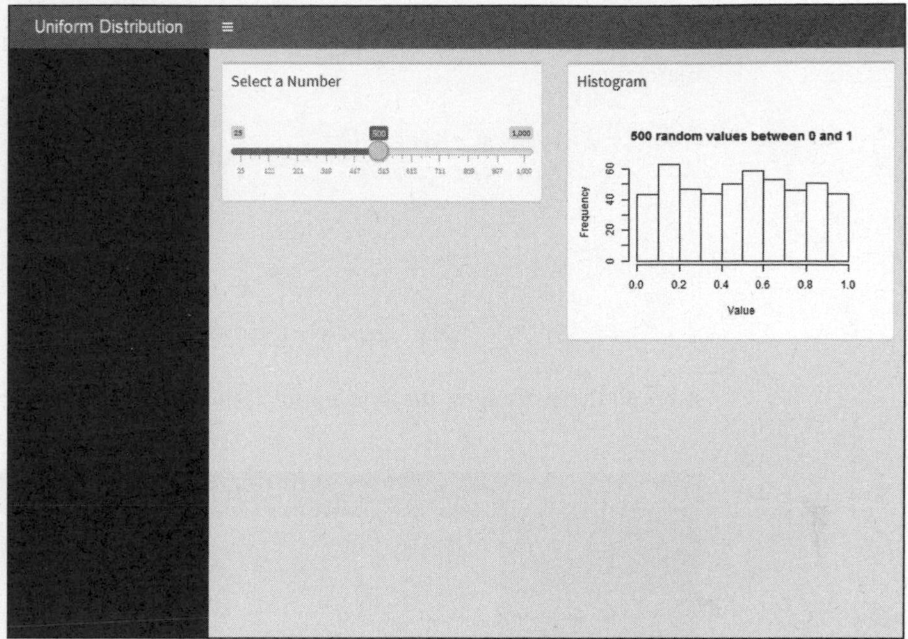

FIGURE 5-4: Adding functionality.

TIP

The other possible statuses and their associated colors are success (green), info (aqua), and danger (red). (No shades of gray here. Sorry.)

I add more color to those boxes by setting the background argument for each box:

```
box(title = "Select a Number",
     background ="yellow",
     status="warning",
     sliderInput(inputId = "number",
              label = "",
              value = 500, min = 25, max = 1000)),
box(title = "Histogram",
                    background ="light-blue",
      status="primary",
      plotOutput("hist", height = 250))
)
```

I'd like the two boxes to be the same height (it's good user interface design). I've already set the height of the plot to 250 (pixels). Do I set the height of the slider to 250? Nope. The value of height in plotOutput() is the height of the plot, not the height of the box that contains it. The box adds an extra 62 pixels (discovered via trial-and-error), so if I set the height of the slider to 312, the two boxes match up:

```
box(title = "Select a Number",
         background ="yellow",
         status="warning",
                    height = 312,
         sliderInput(inputId = "number",
               label = "",
               value = 500, min = 25, max = 1000)),
```

After all these changes, the developing dashboard looks like Figure 5-5.

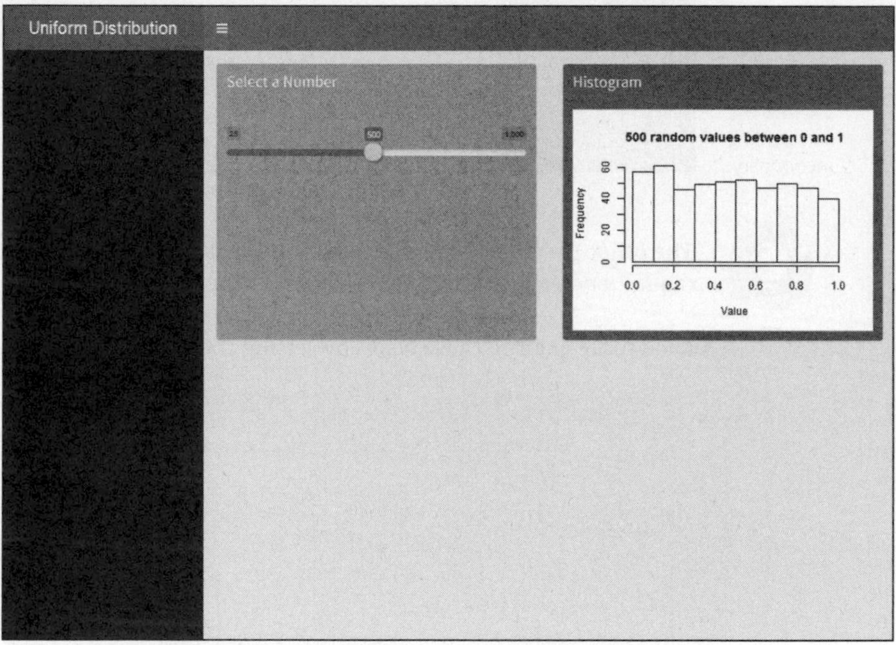

FIGURE 5-5: The dashboard, after adding status and background and changing the height of the slider.

All that's left is to add the boxes for the mean, median, and standard deviation. In `shinydashboard`, boxes that show values are called, appropriately enough, `valueBoxes`. So in the user interface, I add

```
valueBoxOutput("meanBox"),
valueBoxOutput("medianBox"),
valueBoxOutput("sdBox")
```

And in the server, I add functions that render the `valueBoxes`. Just as `renderPlot()` provides the reactive context for rendering the plot, you can probably guess that `renderValueBox()` provides the reactive context for rendering the `valueBox`, and `valueBox()` does the rendering:

```
output$meanBox <- renderValueBox({
  valueBox(
    round(mean(histdata()),3),"Mean",
    color = "navy"
  )
})

output$medianBox <- renderValueBox({
  valueBox(
    round(median(histdata()),3),"Median",
    color = "aqua"
  )
})

output$sdBox <- renderValueBox({
  valueBox(
    round(sd(histdata()),3), "Standard Deviation",
    color = "blue"
  )
})
```

For each `valueBox()`, the first argument is the value in the box (the statistic rounded to three decimal places), which appears as a kind of title, the second is the subtitle, and the third, of course, is the color.

The whole code is shown here:

```
library(shinydashboard)

ui <- dashboardPage(
  dashboardHeader(
    title = "Uniform Distribution"
    ),
  dashboardSidebar(),
  dashboardBody(

    fluidRow(
      box(
          title = "Select a Number",
```

```
          background = "yellow",
          status="warning",
          height = 312,
        sliderInput(inputId = "number",
                    label = "",
                    value = 500, min = 25, max = 1000)),

      box(title = "Histogram",
           background = "light-blue",
           status="primary",
           plotOutput("hist", height = 250))
      ),
      valueBoxOutput("meanBox"),

      valueBoxOutput("medianBox"),

      valueBoxOutput("sdBox")

  )
)

server <- function(input, output) {

  histdata <- reactive({runif(input$number,min=0,max=1)})

  output$hist <- renderPlot({    hist(histdata(),xlab="Value",main=paste
   (input$number,"random values between 0 and 1"))
  })

  output$meanBox <- renderValueBox({
    valueBox(
      round(mean(histdata()),3),"Mean",
      color = "navy"
    )
  })

  output$medianBox <- renderValueBox({
    valueBox(
      round(median(histdata()),3),"Median",
      color = "aqua"
    )
  })
```

```
    output$sdBox <- renderValueBox({
      valueBox(
        round(sd(histdata()),3), "Standard Deviation",
        color = "blue"
      )
    })
    }

  shinyApp(ui, server)
```

Click Run App and you'll see a dashboard that looks just like Figure 5-1.

Lining up in columns

So the dashboard in Figure 5-1 shows two rows of boxes. How about arranging the boxes in columns? I can put the slider and the plot in one column and the statistics boxes in another. Figure 5-6 shows what I mean.

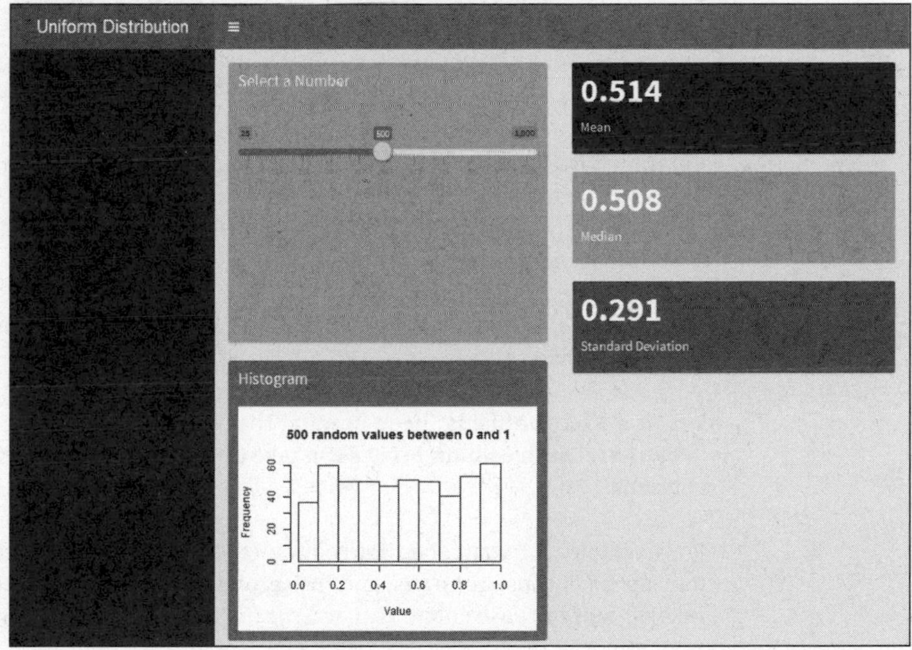

FIGURE 5-6: The dashboard, with the boxes in columns.

To get this done, I keep everything in a `fluidRow()`, and within the row I add a `column()` that encompasses the boxes for that column. Here's the overall structure, with some lines of code omitted for clarity:

```
fluidRow(
      column(

        box( ... This is the slider ... ),

        box( ... This is the plot ... )

       ),

      column(

        valueBoxOutput("meanBox"),

        valueBoxOutput("medianBox"),

        valueBoxOutput("sdBox")
       )

     )
```

Column-based layouts require specifications for `width`. I have to specify the width of each column and the width of each box in that column. Remember when I specified `height` (of the slider and the plot) in pixels? When I specify `width`, it's measured in columns.

Wait. What? I'm dealing with columns and the measurement unit of their width is . . . columns?

Yes, it's a bit confusing. Keep in mind that the `dashboardBody` is divided into 12 "columns." Each column I *create* can take up a number of those 12 `dashboardBody` columns.

For example, if I want the first column (the one with the slider and the plot) to take up six of those columns, and the second column (with the statistics boxes) to take up four of those columns, I add the `width` argument to each one:

```
fluidRow(
      column(width = 6

        box( ... This is the slider ... ),

        box( ... This is the plot ... )

        ),

      column(width = 4

        valueBoxOutput("meanBox"),

        valueBoxOutput("medianBox"),

        valueBoxOutput("sdBox")
        )

      )
```

But wait — there's more: I also have to specify the width of each box. For each box, I add `width=NULL`:

```
fluidRow(
      column(width = 6

        box( ... This is the slider ... width = NULL),

        box( ... This is the plot ... width = NULL )

        ),

      column(width = 4

        valueBoxOutput("meanBox", width = NULL),

        valueBoxOutput("medianBox", width = NULL),

        valueBoxOutput("sdBox", width = NULL)
        )

      )
```

TIP

Why didn't I specify `width` in the first (row-based) layout? I could have, but default values kicked in very nicely. In the first row, each of the two boxes takes up half the 12 columns (so each `width` is 6). In the second row, each of the three boxes takes up one third of the 12 columns (so each `width` is 4). If I add another box to the second row . . . it goes into the next row.

So the code for the `dashboardBody()` is

```
dashboardBody(

    fluidRow(
      column(width=6,
        box(
          title = "Select a Number",
          solidHeader = TRUE,
          background = "yellow",
          status="warning",
          width = NULL,
          height = 312,
          sliderInput(inputId = "number",
                      label = "",
                      value = 500, min = 25, max = 1000)),

        box(title = "Histogram",
          solidHeader=TRUE,
          background = "light-blue",
          status="primary",
          width = NULL,
          plotOutput("hist", height = 250))
        ),

      column(width = 4,

        valueBoxOutput("meanBox",width = NULL),

        valueBoxOutput("medianBox",width = NULL),

        valueBoxOutput("sdBox",width = NULL)
        )

      )
  )
```

This code, along with the rest of the user interface and everything else, produces the screen you see in Figure 5-6.

A nice trick: Keeping tabs

Another type of dashboard box acts like a box full of tabbed documents. It's called `tabBox` and I show how to use it in Figure 5-7. I've put the mean and the median `valueBoxOutputs` in separate tabs in a `tabBox` called `Central Tendency`. In this context, a tabbed document is called a `tabPanel`. I've put the standard deviation `valueBoxOutput` and a new variance `valueBoxOutput` in separate `tabPanels` in a `tabBox` called `Variability`. Clicking a `tabPanel` reveals its associated statistical value.

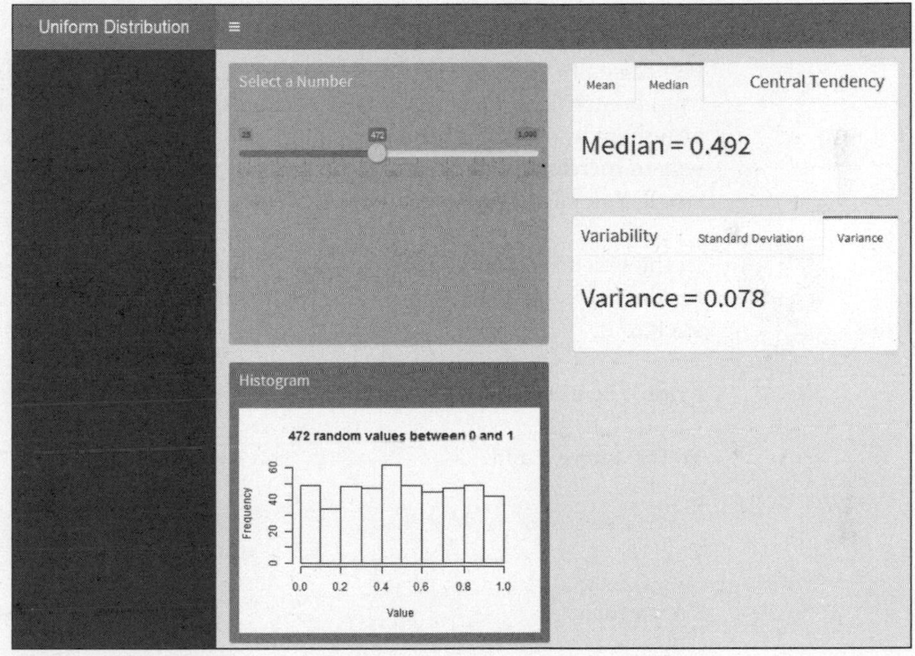

FIGURE 5-7: The dashboard, with `tabBoxes` labeled Central Tendency and Variability.

As you can see in the figure, the statistical values are in text rather than in `value Boxes`. So I work with `textOutput()` in the user interface and `renderText()` in the server.

To construct this version, I add this code to the user interface:

```
tabBox(
        title = "Central Tendency",
        id = "tabs1", height = 150, width = NULL,
        tabPanel("Mean",
h2(textOutput("meantext")),width = NULL),
        tabPanel("Median", h2(textOutput("mediantext")),width = NULL)
      ),
```

```
        tabBox(
          title = "Variability",
          id = "tabs2", height = 150, width = NULL,
          side = "right",
          tabPanel("Variance",
h2(textOutput("vartext")),width = NULL),
          tabPanel("Standard Deviation", h2(textOutput("sdtext")),width = NULL)
```

Each tabBox has a title, an id, a height, and a width. The important action is in the tabPanels. Each one has a textOutput and each textOutput has an id (like "meantext") so that the server can track it.

Pay close attention to a particular aspect of each tabPanel — the h2() that surrounds each textOutput(). The h2() comes from HTML. It sets the font size of its argument by declaring the argument to be a "level 2 heading." So it's a nice, quick way to increase the font size of the textOutput. If I don't do this, the font is very small. You might try experimenting with h1() and h3().

TIP

In the second tabBox, I added side = "right" to show you an alternative layout for the title and the tabPanels. I recommend that you pick one tabBox layout and stick to it.

I won't be using the valueBoxOutputs, so I delete them.

To the server, I add

```
output$meantext <-renderText({
paste("Mean =",round(mean(histdata()),3))})

output$mediantext <-renderText({
paste("Median =",round(median(histdata()),3))})

   output$vartext <-renderText({
paste("Variance =",round(var(histdata()),3))})

   output$sdtext <-renderText({
paste("Standard Deviation =",
round(sd(histdata()),3))})
```

And I delete all the renderValueBox({}) functions.

Do I also need `render({})` functions for the `tabBoxes`? Not in this case. If each `tabPanel` in the first `tabBox`, for example, just contains some unique text that I want to show, I'd add that text as an argument in each `tabPanel` and add

```
output$tabs1Selected <- renderText({
     input$tabs1
   })
```

to the server. But that's not necessary here.

Just to clarify, the whole set of code is shown here:

```
library(shinydashboard)

ui <- dashboardPage(
  dashboardHeader(
    title = "Uniform Distribution"
    ),
  dashboardSidebar(),
  dashboardBody(

    fluidRow(
      column(width=6,
        box(
          title = "Select a Number",
          solidHeader = TRUE,
          background = "yellow",
          status="warning",
          width = NULL,
          height = 312,
          sliderInput(inputId = "number",
                    label = "",
                    value = 500, min = 25, max = 1000)),

        box(title = "Histogram",
          solidHeader=TRUE,
          background = "light-blue",
          status="primary",
          width = NULL,
          plotOutput("hist", height = 250))
       ),
```

```
        column(width = 6,

          tabBox(
            title = "Central Tendency",
            id = "tabs1", height = 120, width = NULL,
            tabPanel("Mean",
h2(textOutput("meantext")),width = NULL),
            tabPanel("Median",
h2(textOutput("mediantext")),width = NULL)
          ),

          tabBox(
            title = "Variability",
            id = "tabs2", height = 120, width = NULL,
            side = "right",
            tabPanel("Variance",
h2(textOutput("vartext")),width = NULL),
            tabPanel("Standard Deviation", h2(textOutput("sdtext")),width = NULL)
          )

           )
          )
        )
  )


server <- function(input, output) {

  histdata <- reactive({runif(input$number,min=0,max=1)})

  output$hist <- renderPlot({

  hist(histdata(),xlab="Value",
main=paste(input$number,"random values between 0 and 1"))
  })

  output$meantext <-renderText({
paste("Mean =",round(mean(histdata()),3))})

  output$mediantext <-renderText({
paste("Median =",round(median(histdata()),3))})

  output$vartext <-renderText({
paste("Variance =",round(var(histdata()),3))})
```

```
  output$sdtext <-renderText({
paste("Standard Deviation =",
round(sd(histdata()),3))})


  }


shinyApp(ui, server)
```

Click Run App for a dashboard that looks (and acts) like the dashboard shown in Figure 5-7.

Suggested project: Add statistics

One way to sharpen your `shinydashboard` skills is to extend this tabbed version. Add a `tabBox` that provides statistics for the appearance of the histogram. The statistics are called *skewness* (how weighted the histogram is to the left or the right), and *kurtosis* (how peaked or how flat the histogram is). Functions for these statistics live in a package called `moments`.

When you're done, your dashboard should look similar to Figure 5-8.

FIGURE 5-8: The dashboard, with a `tabBox` for statistics that describe the histogram's appearance.

TIP

Move the slider and check the resulting values for skewness and kurtosis against the appearance of the histogram. You might just get a feel for what those two statistics are all about!

Suggested project: Place valueBoxes in tabPanels

It's possible to render the statistics in the `tabPanels` in a different way. Instead of `textOutput` you can use `valueBoxes`, as in the original, nontabbed version. The idea is to move each `valueBox` inside a `tabPanel`. Your finished product should look like Figure 5-9. If you're feeling ambitious, add the Appearance `tabBox` from the previous suggested project!

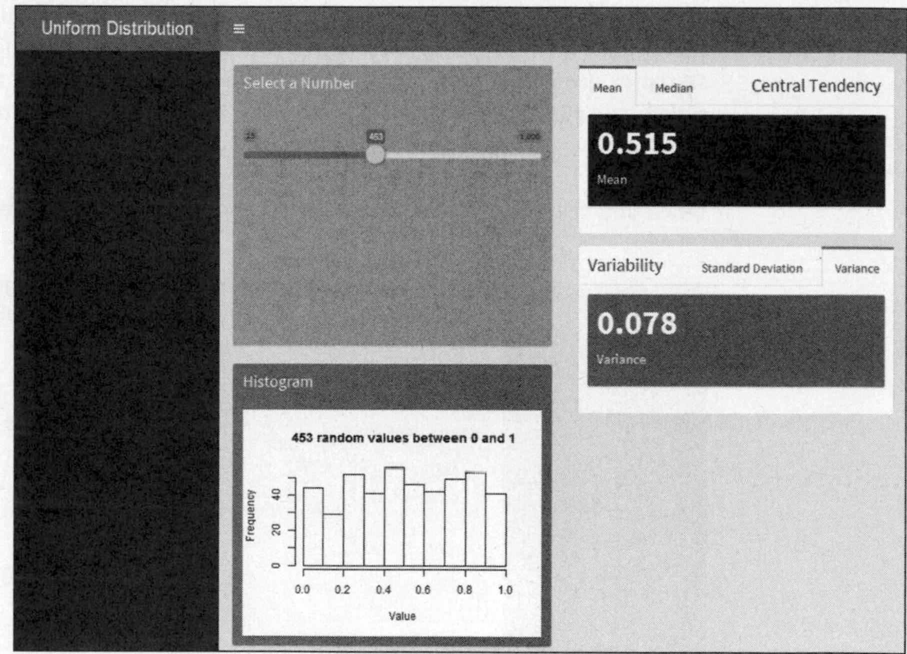

FIGURE 5-9: The dashboard, with statistics presented in `valueBoxes` in the `tabPanels`.

Working with the Sidebar

In this section, I show you some more `shinydashboard` features, beginning with the sidebar. Similar to the tabbed boxes I show you earlier, the sidebar is a way of navigating through content. Click a sidebar menu item and its corresponding content appears.

I create a dashboard with two content-screens. The first is a repeat of the first version of sampling from a uniform distribution, with statistics presented in `valueBoxes`. The second involves sampling from a standard normal distribution (mean = 0, standard deviation = 1). In this one, the statistics appear in another kind of box: the `infoBox`. Clicking icons on the sidebar navigates between the sections.

The first screen, shown in Figure 5-10, looks very much like Figure 5-1. The only difference is in the sidebar. The sidebar has a Square icon that represents the uniform distribution, and a Bell icon that represents the standard normal distribution. (See what I did there?). Also, I changed the title of the whole thing to Sampling.

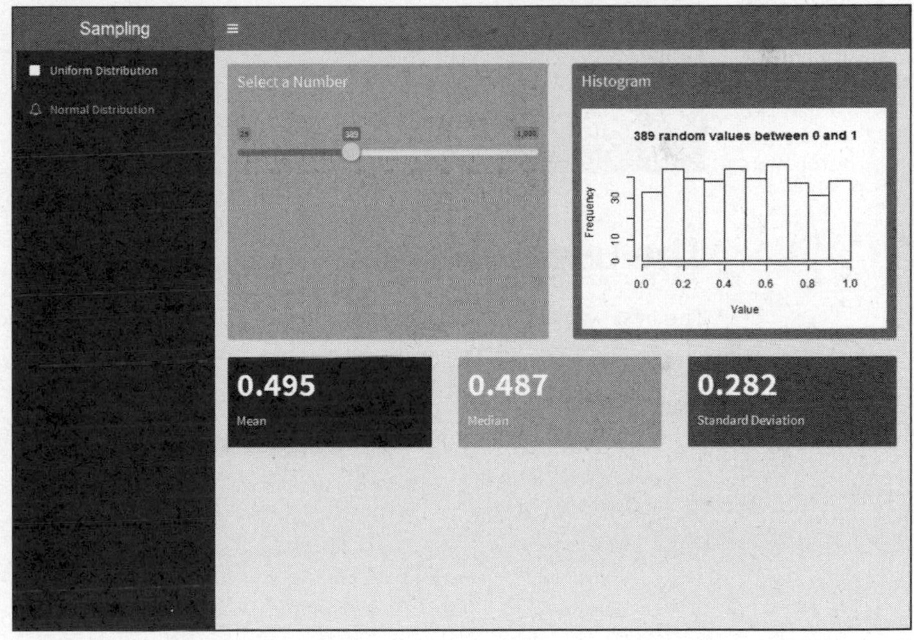

FIGURE 5-10: The first screen of the dashboard, showing sampling from a uniform distribution.

Figure 5-11 shows the second screen. The slider is a bit different, and the graph is a density plot rather than a histogram. (See Chapter 3.) The statistics, as I mention earlier, are in `infoBoxes`.

I begin the project by selecting File ➪ New File ➪ Shiny Web App from the main menu in order to create a new file called `sidebarDevelopment` in a new directory.

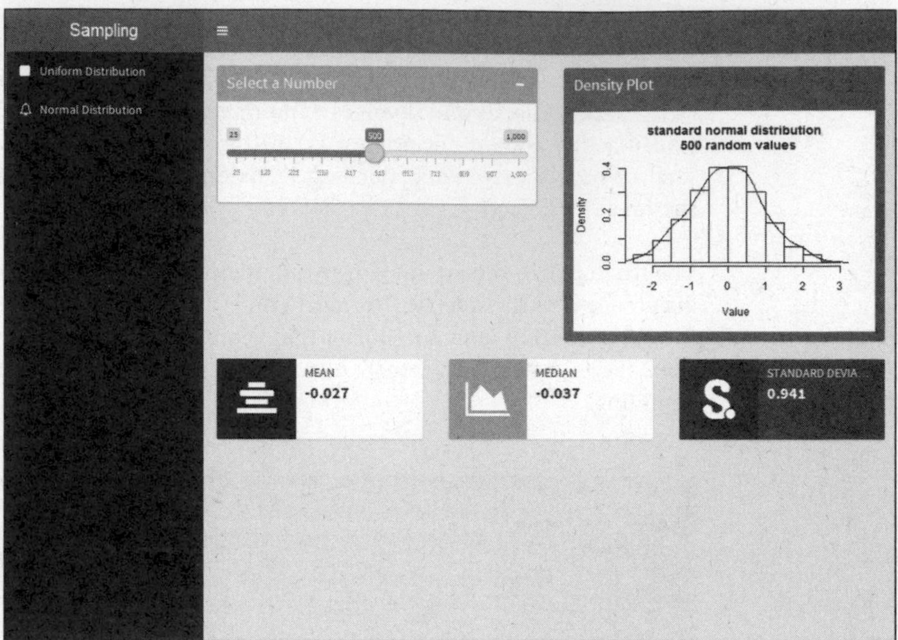

FIGURE 5-11: The second screen of the dashboard, showing sampling from a standard normal distribution.

The user interface

The best way to start off the user interface is to show you its overall structure:

```
ui <- dashboardPage(
 dashboardHeader(
   title = "Sampling"
 ), # dashboardHeader
 dashboardSidebar(
   sidebarMenu(
     menuItem( ... Uniform distribution stuff ... ),
     menuItem( ... Standard Normal Distribution stuff ... )

   ) # sidebarMenu

  ), # dashboardSidebar

 dashboardBody(
   tabItems(

     tabItem( ... Uniform distribution stuff ... ),

     tabItem( ... Standard Normal Distribution stuff ... )
```

```
        ) # tabItems

      ) # dashboardBody

    ) # dashboardPage
```

The close parentheses can get a bit confusing (trust me!), so I added comments where I thought they'd help.

The first difference from the earlier projects in this chapter, of course, is the `sidebarMenu()` in `dashboardSidebar()`. The `sidebarMenu` consists of `menuItems`.

The second difference is the `tabItems()` in `dashboardBody()`. As you can see, `tabItems()` consists of, well, `tabItems`. Each `tabItem` corresponds to a `menuItem`, which is why clicking a `menuItem` causes `tabItem` content to appear.

Here's the `sidebarMenu()`:

```
sidebarMenu(
      menuItem("Uniform Distribution", tabName = "uniform", icon = icon("square")),
      menuItem("Normal Distribution", tabName = "normal",
icon = icon("bell-o"))
    )
```

For each `menuItem`, the first argument is the text that appears on the menu, the second is the name that will also appear in the corresponding `tabItem`, and the third is the `icon()` function that renders the icon in the menu. These icons (like "square" and "bell-o") are special characters that you can find at `http://fontawesome.io/icons`.

Here is `tabItems()`, along with its component `tabItems`:

```
tabItems(


      tabItem(
tabName = "uniform",


              fluidRow(


                box(
                  title = "Select a Number",
                  solidHeader = TRUE,
                  background = "yellow",
```

```
              status="warning",
              height = 312,
              sliderInput(inputId = "number",
                          label = "",
                          value = 500, min = 25,
max = 1000)),

            box(title = "Histogram",
              solidHeader=TRUE,
              background = "light-blue",
              status="primary",
              plotOutput("hist", height = 250)),

            valueBoxOutput("meanBox"),

            valueBoxOutput("medianBox"),

            valueBoxOutput("sdBox")

          )

        ),

      tabItem(tabName = "normal",

            fluidRow(
              box(title = "Select a Number",
                solidHeader = TRUE,
                collapsible = TRUE,
                status="warning",
                sliderInput(inputId = "normnumber",
                            label = "",
                            value = 500, min = 25,
                            max = 1000)),

              box(title = "Density Plot",
                solidHeader=TRUE,
                background = "light-blue",
                status="primary",
                plotOutput("density", height = 250)),

              infoBoxOutput("meanInfoBox"),
```

```
            infoBoxOutput("medianInfoBox"),

            infoBoxOutput("sdInfoBox")

          )

    )
```

The first `tabItem` (`tabName = "uniform"`) is just a rehash of the first project: the slider, histogram, and statistics in `valueBox`es.

The second `tabItem` (`tabName="normal"`) shows some new features. First, notice `collapsible = TRUE` in the box that creates the slider. This creates the little minus sign in the upper right corner of the slider. (Refer to Figure 5-11.) Clicking it collapses the slider and turns the minus sign into a plus sign. And this `tabItem` features `infoBox`es rather than `valueBox`es.

The server

The server code begins with `reactive({})` functions for the uniform distribution and for the standard normal distribution:

```
histdata <- reactive({runif(input$number,min=0,max=1)})
densitydata <- reactive({rnorm(input$normnumber)})
```

Next are the functions for rendering the histogram:

```
output$hist <- renderPlot({
 hist(histdata(),xlab="Value",
    main=paste(input$number,
    "random values between 0 and 1"))
  })
```

and for rendering the density plot:

```
  output$density <- renderPlot({
    hist(densitydata(),xlab="Value",
      main=paste("standard normal distribution \n",
       input$normnumber,"random values"),
      probability=TRUE)
    lines(density(densitydata()))
```

If the `hist()` function for the density plot looks strange to you, go back and reread the first section of Chapter 3. The `probability=TRUE` argument puts density on the y-axis, and the `lines()` function adds the line for the density plot.

Next, I add the `render({})` functions for the `valueBoxes`:

```
output$meanBox <- renderValueBox({
    valueBox(
      round(mean(histdata()),3),"Mean",
      color = "navy"
    )
  })

  output$medianBox <- renderValueBox({
   valueBox(
      round(median(histdata()),3),"Median",
      color = "aqua"
    )
  })

  output$sdBox <- renderValueBox({
    valueBox(
     round(sd(histdata()),3), "Standard Deviation",
      color = "blue"
    )
  })
```

and add the `render({})` functions for the `infoBoxes`:

```
output$meanInfoBox <- renderInfoBox({
    infoBox("Mean",
      round( mean(densitydata()),3),
   icon=icon("align-center"),
      color = "navy")
  })

  output$medianInfoBox <- renderInfoBox({
    infoBox(icon=icon("area-chart"), "Median",
      round(median(densitydata()),3),
      color = "aqua")
  })

  output$sdInfoBox <- renderInfoBox({
    infoBox("Standard Deviation",
      round(sd(densitydata()),3),icon=icon("scribd"),
      fill = TRUE,
      color = "blue")
  })
```

In the third infoBox, I show what happens if fill=TRUE.

TIP

I'm not sure that the icons I used are the most appropriate. Perhaps you can find some better ones.

REMEMBER

It's okay to use icons in the valueBoxes. I just chose not to.

Putting all this code between the curly brackets in

```
server <- function(input, output) {}
```

and adding

```
shinyApp(ui, server)
```

at the end, and adding

```
library(shinydashboard)
```

at the beginning produces the framework for Figures 5-10 and 5-11 when I click Run App.

Suggested project: Relocate the slider

The sidebar can have more than just menuItems. For example, you can put a slider or other kinds of input in the sidebar, and that's what this suggested project is all about.

Suppose the objective is to see what a specific sample size looks like from a uniform distribution and compare with a standard normal distribution. The user selects a number from a slider in the sidebar and then uses the sidebar menu to see the uniform distribution results or the standard normal distribution results. The dashboard looks like Figure 5-12 with Uniform Distribution selected.

Figure 5-13 shows the dashboard with Normal Distribution selected.

Give it a try. You'll have to come up with values for width and height for the sidebar and its slider, and for each plot, to make your dashboard look like Figures 5-12 and 5-13. You'll also have to adjust some aspects of the slider's appearance.

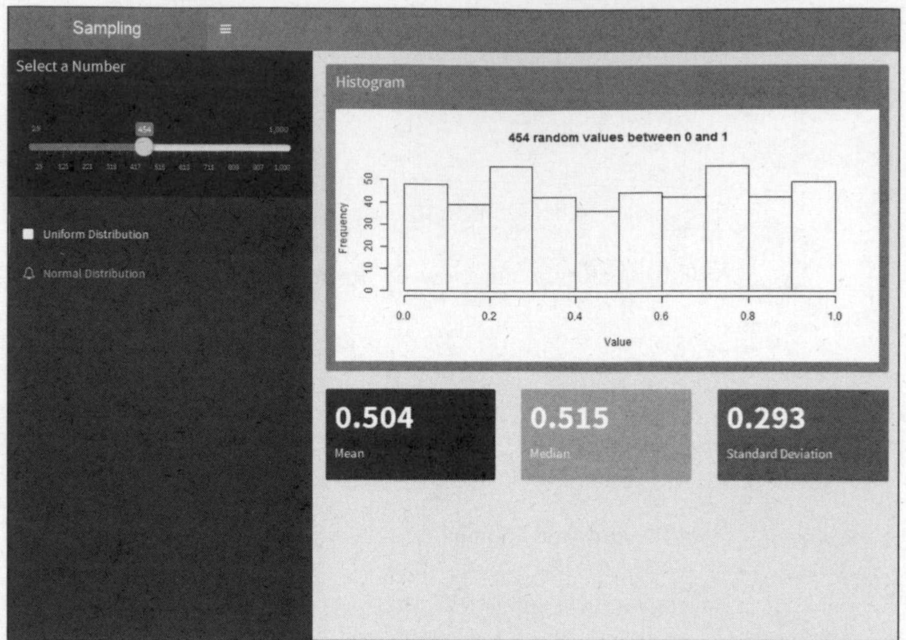

FIGURE 5-12: The dashboard, with the slider in the sidebar and Uniform Distribution selected.

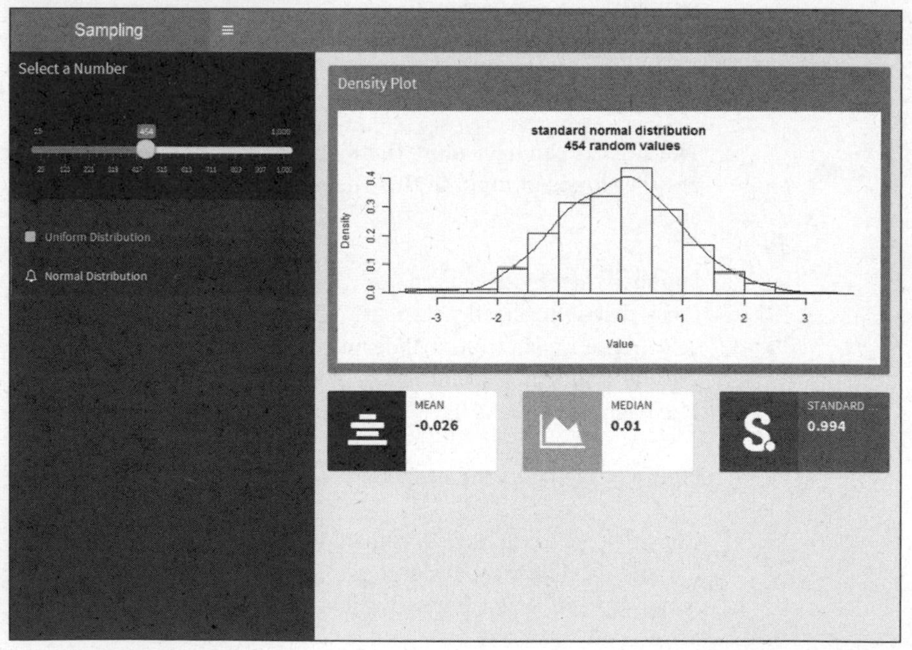

FIGURE 5-13: The dashboard, with Normal Distribution selected.

Interacting with Graphics

In the projects I've shown you so far in this chapter, plot changes follow user interactions with components like sliders or drop-down menus. In this section, I reverse the process: When the dashboard opens, a plot appears, the user interacts with the plot, and other user interface components change.

As you learn how to make this happen, you'll see some additional dashboard and graphics capabilities along the way.

Clicks, double-clicks, and brushes — oh, my!

To this point, all I've done with `plotOutput()` is set the `height` and `width` of the plot. The `plotOutput()` function offers more possibilities: It takes arguments called `click`, `dblclick`, `hover`, and `brush`.

TIP

Brush? What's that? If you've ever dragged the mouse while you pressed and then released the left mouse button (and I know you have!), you've brushed. A joke about doing this after every meal suggests itself, but I won't pursue it.

I can set the `click` argument to a value like `"single_click"`. When I click the plot, the plot sends the xy-coordinates of the click to the server. The values of those coordinates are stored in `input$single_click`. The `dblclick` argument works the same way: If I set `dblclick` to `"double_click"` and click a point twice in rapid succession, the plot sends the coordinates to the server, and the values are stored in `input$double_click`. You can probably figure out how `hover` works.

The `brush` argument works a bit differently. When you brush across the plot, you create, in effect, a box. Four pairs of xy-coordinates define the box: `xmin, ymin` (the lower left corner), `xmax, ymax` (the upper right corner), `xmin, ymax` (the upper left corner), and `xmax, ymin` (the lower right corner). Setting `brush` to `"brushed"` and dragging the mouse and then releasing the mouse button sends `xmin`, `xmax`, `ymin`, and `ymax` to the server. I get to those values via `input$brushed`.

To show you all this in action, I work with a data frame called `UScereal` in the `MASS` package. This data frame holds nutritional information (and some other stuff) for about 65 brands of cereal sold in the United States. The initial of each cereal manufacturer (Kellogg's, Post, General Mills, Quaker Oats, Ralston Purina, and Nabisco) represents the manufacturer's name.

Figure 5-14 shows a dashboard with a plot that presents Calories versus Proteins (gm) of each cereal. The measurements are per portion, and a portion is 1 cup (240 ml). I thought it would add pizzazz to the graph if each data point identifies the manufacturer — hence, all the letters inside the plot.

Below the plot is a box that shows the coordinates for the different types of mouse interactions. Here's how to do it:

As usual, I begin the project by selecting File ⇨ New File ⇨ Shiny Web App to create a new file called `mouseActions` in a new directory.

I start with the libraries:

```
library(shinydashboard)
library(MASS)
```

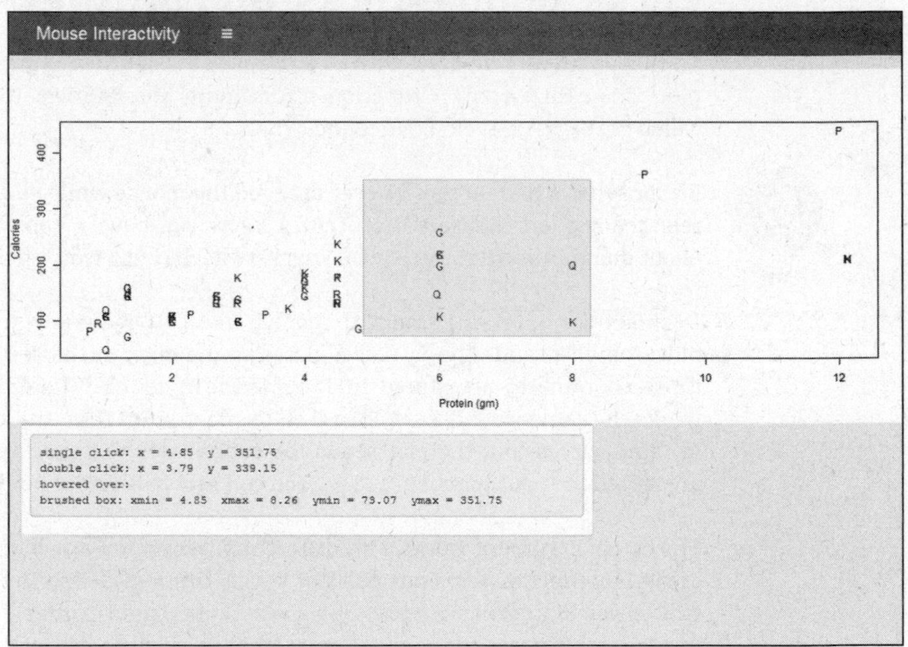

FIGURE 5-14: Data on US cereals, showing interaction with the plot.

Next comes the user interface:

```
ui <- dashboardPage(
  dashboardHeader(title="Mouse Interactivity"),
  dashboardSidebar(collapsed=TRUE),
  dashboardBody(
    fluidRow(
                  plotOutput("CerealPlot",
                 click = "single_click",
                 dblclick = "double_click",
```

```
                    hover = "hovering",
                    brush = "brushing"
  ),

                    box((verbatimTextOutput("coords")),width =8)
  )
 )
)
```

The box toward the end of the code holds the coordinates for the mouse actions. Its output method — verbatimTextOutput — is a quick way of presenting the values. This saves me from putting the values in valueBoxes or in infoBoxes.

And finally, the server, which begins with the function for rendering the plot:

```
server <- function(input, output) {
  output$CerealPlot <- renderPlot({
    plot(x=UScereal$protein, y=UScereal$calories,
         xlab="Protein (gm)",
         ylab="Calories",
         pch=as.character(UScereal$mfr))
  })
```

The last argument, pch, puts those manufacturer initials in the plot.

The next reactive context renders the coordinate values:

```
output$coords <- renderText({})
```

The renderText({}) function is for rendering character strings, like the coordinate values.

Three functions are placed between the curly brackets of renderText({}). The first is for the coordinates that click, dblclick, and hover return:

```
xy_points <- function(datapoints) {
      if(is.null(datapoints)) return("\n")
      paste("x =", round(datapoints$x, 2), " y =", round(datapoints$y, 2), "\n")
    }
```

If the user hasn't performed a particular action, the function returns a newline character. Ultimately, the function outputs rounded values of the x-coordinate and the y-coordinate.

The second function is for the four coordinates that a brush produces:

```
xy_points_range <- function(datapoints) {
      if(is.null(datapoints)) return("\n")
      paste("xmin =", round(datapoints$xmin, 2),
" xmax =", round(datapoints$xmax, 2),
            " ymin =", round(datapoints$ymin, 2),
" ymax =", round(datapoints$ymax, 2))
    }
```

The third function puts the coordinate values on the screen:

```
paste0(
      "single click: ", xy_points(input$single_click),
      "double click: ", xy_points(input$double_click),
      "hovered over: ", xy_points(input$hovering),
      "brushed box: ", xy_points_range(input$brushing)
    )
```

TIP

For the third function, `paste0()` works a little better than `paste()`.

With those three functions inside the curly brackets of `renderText({})`, and with the close curly bracket for `server({})`and with`shinyApp(ui = ui, server = server)` at the end, clicking Run App produces the dashboard shown in Figure 5-15. You can click, double-click, hover, and brush to watch the effects on the coordinate values. One helpful feature is that the coordinates are in terms of the units on the axes, not in terms of pixels.

Why bother with all this?

Interacting with the data points on a plot is a great way to select data points and then render the rows of selected data in a table. Figure 5-15 shows a dashboard that presents data resulting from a single click on the plot. The click was on the cluster of data points above the 4 on the x-axis.

The coding for this is, believe it or not, easier than for the immediately preceding section. What makes the data row rendering possible is a neat little function called `nearPoints()`. This function takes the coordinates of the click and finds the rows in the associated data frame.

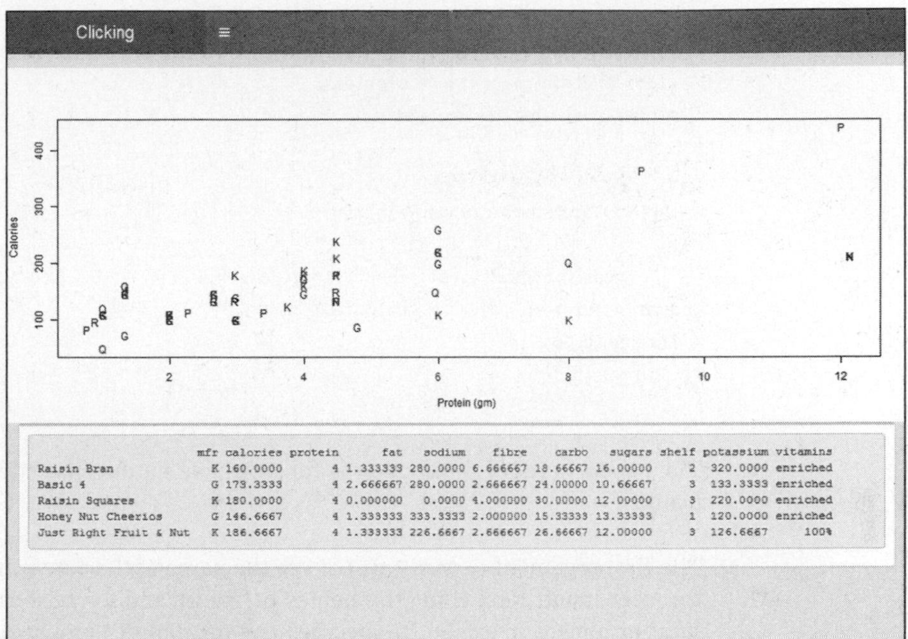

	mfr	calories	protein	fat	sodium	fibre	carbo	sugars	shelf	potassium	vitamins
Raisin Bran	K	160.0000	4	1.333333	280.0000	6.666667	18.66667	16.00000	2	320.0000	enriched
Basic 4	G	173.3333	4	2.666667	280.0000	2.666667	24.00000	10.66667	3	133.3333	enriched
Raisin Squares	K	180.0000	4	0.000000	0.0000	4.000000	30.00000	12.00000	3	220.0000	enriched
Honey Nut Cheerios	G	146.6667	4	1.333333	333.3333	2.000000	15.33333	13.33333	1	120.0000	enriched
Just Right Fruit & Nut	K	186.6667	4	1.333333	226.6667	2.666667	26.66667	12.00000	3	126.6667	100%

FIGURE 5-15: Clicking the plot causes the rows of selected data to appear.

I'll tell you all about it, but first here's the beginning of the code for the dashboard in Figure 5-15:

```
library(shinydashboard)
library(MASS)
ui <- dashboardPage(
  dashboardHeader(title="Clicking"),
  dashboardSidebar(collapsed=TRUE),
  dashboardBody(
    fluidRow(
                  plotOutput("CerealPlot",
             click = "single_click"
                   ),


                  box((verbatimTextOutput("coords")),width =12)
  )
 )
)
```

The server code is

```
server <- function(input, output) {
  output$CerealPlot <- renderPlot({
```

```
  plot(x=UScereal$protein, y=UScereal$calories,
xlab="Protein(gm)",ylab="Calories",
pch=as.character(UScereal$mfr))
  })

  output$coords <- renderPrint({

     nearPoints(UScereal, input$single_click,
xvar = "protein", yvar = "calories",
threshold=20)
  })
}
```

The `renderPrint({})` function is for printable output, like the rows of the data frame.

The first argument to `nearPoints()` is the name of the data frame. The second is the user input. Next come the names of the x- and y-variables in the plot. The final argument, `threshold`, specifies the maximum number of pixels from the click to include:

Add

```
shinyApp(ui = ui, server = server)
```

and that's all there is to it.

TIP

The `nearPoints()` function also works with `dblclick` and `hover`.

Brushing proceeds in a similar way. The only difference is that brushing requires `brushedPoints()`, which works very much like `nearPoints()`.

For a dashboard like the one shown in Figure 5-16, the only changes I make to the code are

```
dashboardHeader(title="Brushing"),
```

and

```
plotOutput("CerealPlot",
             brush = "brushing"
  ),
```

in the user interface, and

```
brushedPoints(UScereal, input$brushing, xvar = "protein", yvar = "calories")
```

in the `renderPrint({})` function in the server.

Figure 5-16 shows the result, including a brush box and the selected data.

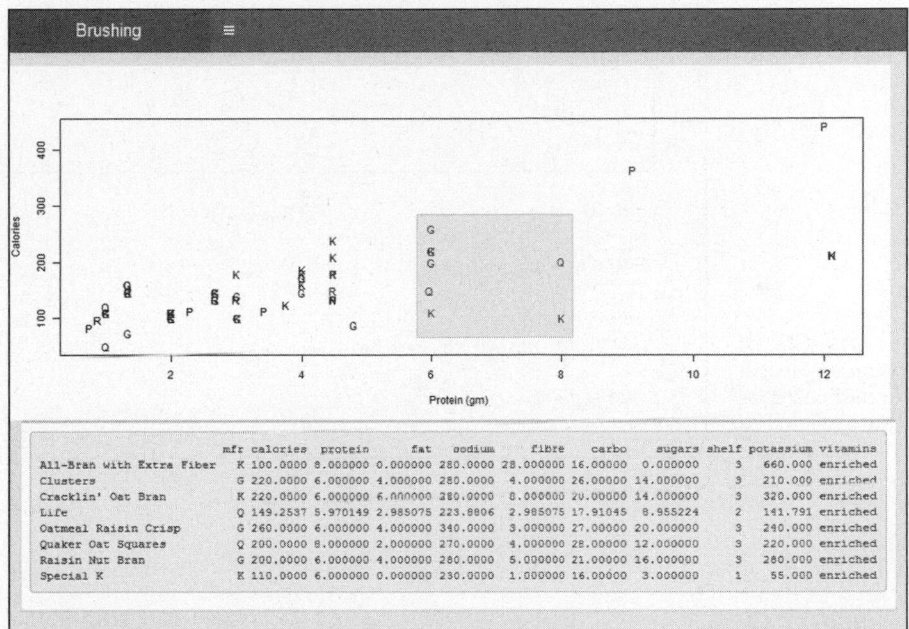

	mfr	calories	protein	fat	sodium	fibre	carbo	sugars	shelf	potassium	vitamins
All-Bran with Extra Fiber	K	100.0000	8.000000	0.000000	280.0000	28.000000	16.00000	0.000000	3	660.000	enriched
Clusters	G	220.0000	6.000000	4.000000	280.0000	4.000000	26.00000	14.000000	3	210.000	enriched
Cracklin' Oat Bran	K	220.0000	6.000000	6.000000	280.0000	8.000000	20.00000	14.000000	3	320.000	enriched
Life	Q	149.2537	5.970149	2.985075	223.8806	2.985075	17.91045	8.955224	2	141.791	enriched
Oatmeal Raisin Crisp	G	260.0000	6.000000	4.000000	340.0000	3.000000	27.00000	20.000000	3	240.000	enriched
Quaker Oat Squares	Q	200.0000	8.000000	2.000000	270.0000	4.000000	28.00000	12.000000	3	220.000	enriched
Raisin Nut Bran	G	200.0000	6.000000	4.000000	280.0000	5.000000	21.00000	16.000000	3	280.000	enriched
Special K	K	110.0000	6.000000	0.000000	230.0000	1.000000	16.00000	3.000000	1	55.000	enriched

FIGURE 5-16: Using a brush (mouse-drag and release) to select data.

Suggested project: Experiment with airquality

The `airquality` data frame, which you find in the `datasets` package, provides a nice data set to experiment with. I've used it before. Just to refresh your memory, here are the first six rows:

```
> head(airquality)
  Ozone Solar.R Wind Temp Month Day
1    41     190  7.4   67     5   1
2    36     118  8.0   72     5   2
3    12     149 12.6   74     5   3
4    18     313 11.5   62     5   4
5    NA      NA 14.3   56     5   5
6    28      NA 14.9   66     5   6
```

For a dashboard with brushing capability, your project should look like Figure 5-17.

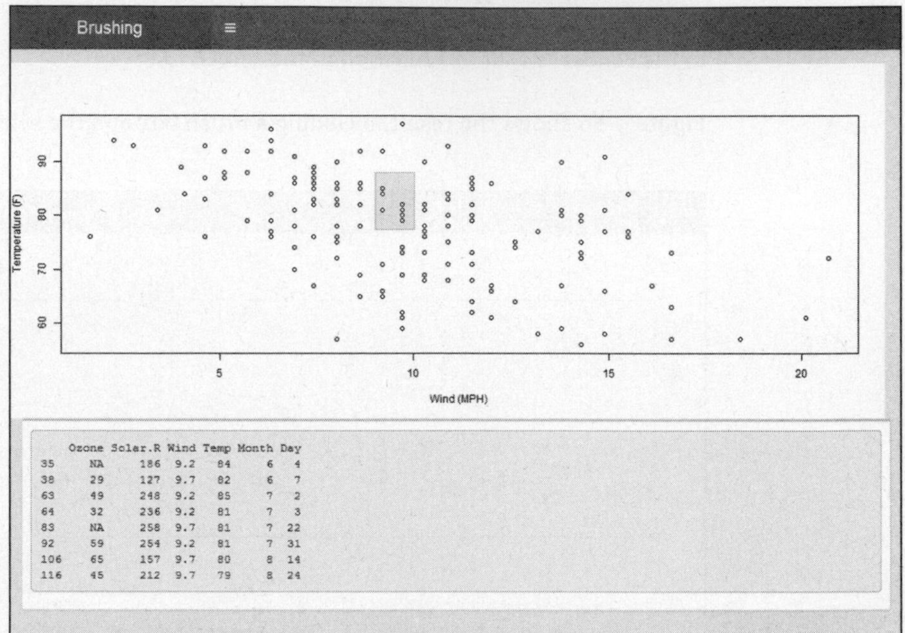

FIGURE 5-17: A brush-capable dashboard for the `airquality` data frame.

3 Machine Learning

IN THIS PART . . .

Create machine learning analyses with the `rattle` package

Build decision trees and random forests

Put support vector machines to work

Use *k*-means clustering

Build neural networks

IN THIS CHAPTER

» Types of machine learning

» Working with the UCI Machine Learning repository

» Understanding the `iris` dataset

» Introducing the `rattle` package

» Using `rattle` with the `iris` dataset

Chapter 6

Tools and Data for Machine Learning Projects

Machine learning (ML) is the application of artificial intelligence (AI) to statistics and statistical analysis. ML techniques automate the search for patterns in data. Sometimes, the objective is to figure out a rule for classifying individuals based on their characteristics: For example, does a particular X-ray mean the X-rayed person is sick or well? Is a particular flower a member of one species or another?

In other efforts, the objective is prediction: Given a sequence of stock market data, will the market go up or down? Given the last three days of weather data, will it rain tomorrow or not?

Think of the characteristics of the X-rays or flowers (or the stock market or weather) as *inputs*. Think of the targets (sick or well, rain or shine) as *outputs*. The learner sees the inputs and their associated outputs and has to come up with some function or rule that characterizes the linkage. Then, when faced with a new input, the learner can apply what it has learned and classify the input (or make a prediction) accordingly.

Learning a function or rule that links inputs with outputs is called *supervised learning.*

TECHNICAL STUFF

If the outputs are categories (sick or well, rain or shine), this is a *classification* problem. If the set of outputs is continuous, it's *regression*.

In another type of learning, the learner receives a set of inputs and the goal is to use the inputs' characteristics to find a structure for the set — to partition the set into subsets, in other words. No specific target outputs are involved.

Early zoologists faced this type of problem. They learned enough about the characteristics of animals to partition "vertebrates" (animals with backbones) into "mammals," "reptiles," "amphibians," "birds," and "fish." Then when they encountered a new animal, they could observe its characteristics and assign it to the appropriate subset. (I'm guessing that assigning whales, bats, dolphins, and duck-billed platypuses to "mammals" might have been a bit dicey at first.)

Discovering the structure in a set of inputs is called *unsupervised learning.*

In any event, an ML technique does its work without being explicitly programmed. It changes its behavior on the basis of experience, with the goal of becoming increasingly accurate.

The UCI (University of California-Irvine) ML Repository

For this book's machine learning projects, I work with datasets that reside in the Machine Learning Repository at the University of California-Irvine (home of the Anteaters!). You'll find this repository at

```
http://archive.ics.uci.edu/ml/index.php
```

Downloading a UCI dataset

Many (but not all) of the UCI datasets are in comma-separated value (CSV) format: The data are in text files with a comma between successive values. A typical line in this kind of file looks like this:

```
5.1,3.5,1.4,0.2,Iris-setosa
```

This is the first line from a well-known dataset called `iris`. The rows are measurements of 150 iris flowers — 50 each of three species of iris. The species are called *setosa*, *versicolor*, and *virginica*. The data are sepal length, sepal width, petal length, petal width, and species. One typical ML project is to develop a mechanism that can learn to use an individual flower's measurements to identify that flower's species.

What's a sepal? On a plant that's in bloom, a sepal supports a petal. On an iris, sepals look something like larger petals underneath the actual petals. In that first line of the dataset, notice that the first two values (sepal length and width) are larger than the second two (petal length and width).

You can find `iris` in numerous places, including the `datasets` package in base R. The point of this exercise, however, is to show you how to get and use a dataset from UCI.

So, to get the data from the UCI ML repository, point your browser to

```
http://archive.ics.uci.edu/ml/datasets/Iris
```

Click on the Data Set Description link. This opens a page of valuable information about the data set, including source material, publications that use the data, column names, and more. In this case, this page is particularly valuable because it tells you about some errors in the data (which I show you how to fix).

Returning to the previous page, click on the Data Folder link. On the page that opens, click the `iris.data` link. This opens the page that holds the dataset in CSV format.

To download the dataset, I use the `read.csv()` function. I can do this in several ways. To accomplish everything at once — to use just one function to read the file into R as a dataframe complete with column names — use this code:

```
iris.uci <- read.csv(url("http://archive.ics.uci.edu/ml/machine-learning-
   databases/iris/iris.data"),
                        header=FALSE, col.names = ("sepal.length","sepal.
                           width","petal.length","petal.width",
                        "species"))
```

The first argument is the web address of the dataset. The second indicates that the first row of the dataset is a row of data and does *not* provide the names of the columns. The third argument is a vector that assigns the column names. The column names come from the Data Set Description web page. That page gives `class` as the name for the last column, but I decided that `species` is correct. (And that's the name in the `iris` dataset in the `datasets` package.)

If you think that's a little too much to put in one function, here's another way:

```
iris.uci <- read.csv(url("http://archive.ics.uci.edu/ml/machine-learning-
  databases/iris/iris.data"), header=FALSE)

colnames(iris.uci)<-c("sepal.length","sepal.width","petal.length","petal.
  width","species")
```

I prefer still another way. With the dataset web page open, I press Ctrl+A to select everything on the page, and I press Ctrl+C to put all the data on the clipboard. Then

```
iris.uci <- read.csv("clipboard", header=FALSE,
    col.names=
    c("sepal.length","sepal.width","petal.length","petal.width","species"))
```

gets the job done. This way, I don't have to deal with the web address.

Cleaning up the data

Here are the first six rows of the dataframe:

```
> head(iris.uci)
  sepal.length sepal.width petal.length petal.width     species
1          5.1         3.5          1.4         0.2 Iris-setosa
2          4.9         3.0          1.4         0.2 Iris-setosa
3          4.7         3.2          1.3         0.2 Iris-setosa
4          4.6         3.1          1.5         0.2 Iris-setosa
5          5.0         3.6          1.4         0.2 Iris-setosa
6          5.4         3.9          1.7         0.4 Iris-setosa
```

Correcting errors

On the Data Set Description web page under Relevant Information, this message appears (after some other stuff):

> The 35th sample should be: 4.9,3.1,1.5,0.2,"Iris-setosa" where the error is in the fourth feature.
>
> The 38th sample: 4.9,3.6,1.4,0.1,"Iris-setosa" where the errors are in the second and third features.

Here is the 35th sample:

```
> iris.uci[35,]
   sepal.length sepal.width petal.length petal.width     species
35          4.9         3.1          1.5         0.1 Iris-setosa
```

To change the fourth feature to `0.2`, type this code into RStudio and run it:

```
> iris.uci[35,4]=0.2
```

And now it's correct:

```
> iris.uci[35,]
   sepal.length sepal.width petal.length petal.width     species
35          4.9         3.1          1.5         0.2 Iris-setosa
```

The 38th sample is

```
> iris.uci[38,]
   sepal.length sepal.width petal.length petal.width     species
38          4.9         3.1          1.5         0.1 Iris-setosa
```

This code changes the second and third features to 3.6 and 1.4:

```
> iris.uci[38,2:3]= c(3.6,1.4)
```

So the 38th sample is now

```
> iris.uci[38,]
   sepal.length sepal.width petal.length petal.width     species
38          4.9         3.6          1.4         0.1 Iris-setosa
```

Eliminating the unnecessary

In the `species` column, every entry begins with `Iris-`. I'd like to eliminate it from every entry. I do that with a function called `mapvalues()` that lives in the `plyr` package. Its usage is pretty straightforward:

```
library(plyr)
iris.uci$species <- mapvalues(iris.uci$species, from =
             c("Iris-setosa","Iris-versicolor", "Iris-virginica"), to =
                c("setosa", "versicolor", "virginica"))
```

After running this code, the head of `iris.uci` is

```
> head(iris.uci)
  sepal.length sepal.width petal.length petal.width species
1          5.1         3.5          1.4         0.2  setosa
2          4.9           3          1.4         0.2  setosa
3          4.7         3.2          1.3         0.2  setosa
4          4.6         3.1          1.5         0.2  setosa
5            5         3.6          1.4         0.2  setosa
6          5.4         3.9          1.7         0.4  setosa
```

Exploring the data

It's a good idea to explore the data and develop a sense of familiarity with it. One quick way to explore the data is to use the `summary()` function:

```
> summary(iris.uci)
  sepal.length    sepal.width     petal.length    petal.width          species
 Min.   :4.300   Min.   :2.000   Min.   :1.000   Min.   :0.100   setosa    :50
 1st Qu.:5.100   1st Qu.:2.800   1st Qu.:1.600   1st Qu.:0.300   versicolor:50
 Median :5.800   Median :3.000   Median :4.350   Median :1.300   virginica :50
 Mean   :5.843   Mean   :3.054   Mean   :3.759   Mean   :1.199
 3rd Qu.:6.400   3rd Qu.:3.300   3rd Qu.:5.100   3rd Qu.:1.800
 Max.   :7.900   Max.   :4.400   Max.   :6.900   Max.   :2.500
```

This gives you an idea of each variable's range (`Max` – `Min`), and central tendency (`Median` and `Mean`). You can quickly see that sepals are both longer and wider than petals, as I mention earlier.

The Summary statistics provide information about the distributions. To visualize and compare the distributions of the variables, one strategy is to plot a few histograms together to come up with what you see in Figure 6-1.

Here's how to plot those distributions:

```
par(mfrow=c(2,2))
for(i in 1:4){hist(iris.uci[,i],xlab=colnames(iris.uci[i]), cex.lab=1.2,
   main="")}
```

The `par()` function is a pretty hot item in base R graphics. It allows me to *set* (find out the values of) the parameters of a plot. It's so rich in possibilities that I could write a chapter or so just on how this function works. Instead, I'll spare you all the details and show you how I apply this function as needed. Here, the `mfrow` argument divides the screen into two rows and two columns so that the sepal variables are in one row and the petal variables are in the other. (Think of `mfrow` as "multiple figures by row.")

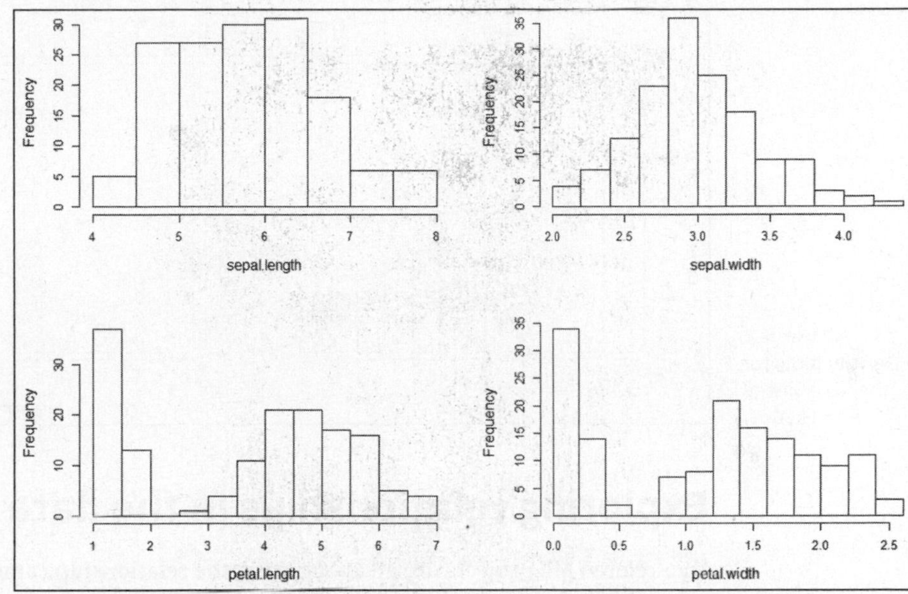

FIGURE 6-1: The distributions of the variables in `iris.uci`.

The `for` loop goes through the first four columns of the dataframe and draws a histogram for each one, labelling the x-axis with the column name. The `cex.lab` argument enlarges the axis labels slightly and the `main=""` argument eliminates the default title from each histogram.

The histograms show that the petal variables are skewed and the sepal variables are more symmetrical.

TIP

To put the two sepal variables into one column and the two petal variables into another, the `par()` function is

```
par(mfcol=c(2,2))
```

Quick suggested project: Density plots

Here's a neat little exercise to strengthen your graphics skillset (and your `for` loop skills): Turn these histograms into density plots. (See Chapter 3 to find out how.) Your finished product should look like Figure 6-2.

The density plots are another way of showing the symmetry and the skewness in the variables.

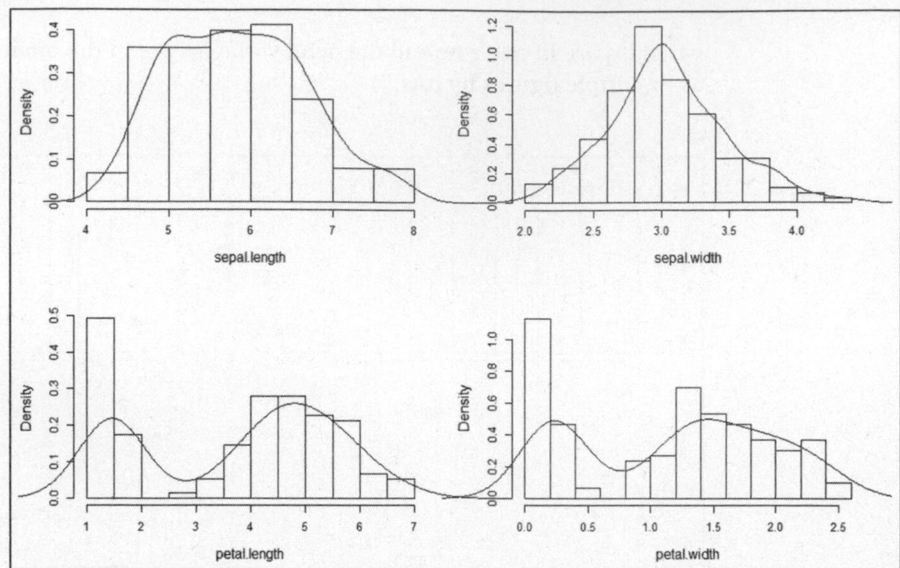

FIGURE 6-2: Density plots for the variables of `iris.uci`.

Exploring relationships in the data

Iris-related ML projects are all about using the relationships among the variables to correctly classify individual flowers. So in addition to summaries and graphics of each variable, I want to look at the relationships among the variables and how those relationships change across the species.

Base R graphics

A scatterplot matrix visualizes those intervariable relationships. (See Chapter 3.) Figure 6-3 shows the base R version of that matrix for `iris.uci`.

I eliminated the lower panel of the matrix because it shows the same data as the upper half but with x and y variables interchanged. I put a legend in that area. The legend indicates that black represents *setosa*, gray represents *versicolor*, and white represents *virginica*. Before I tell you how I did all this, let's take a look at the graph and try to understand what it's saying.

The main diagonal cells, of course, have the names of the variables. Each non-main-diagonal cell represents the relationship between the variable in the cell's row and the variable in the cell's column. So the cell in row 1, column 2 plots the relationship between `sepal.length` and `sepal.width`. The cells in column 5 show the relationships between each of the four measured variables and `species`. In effect, they show the distributions of the measurements within each species.

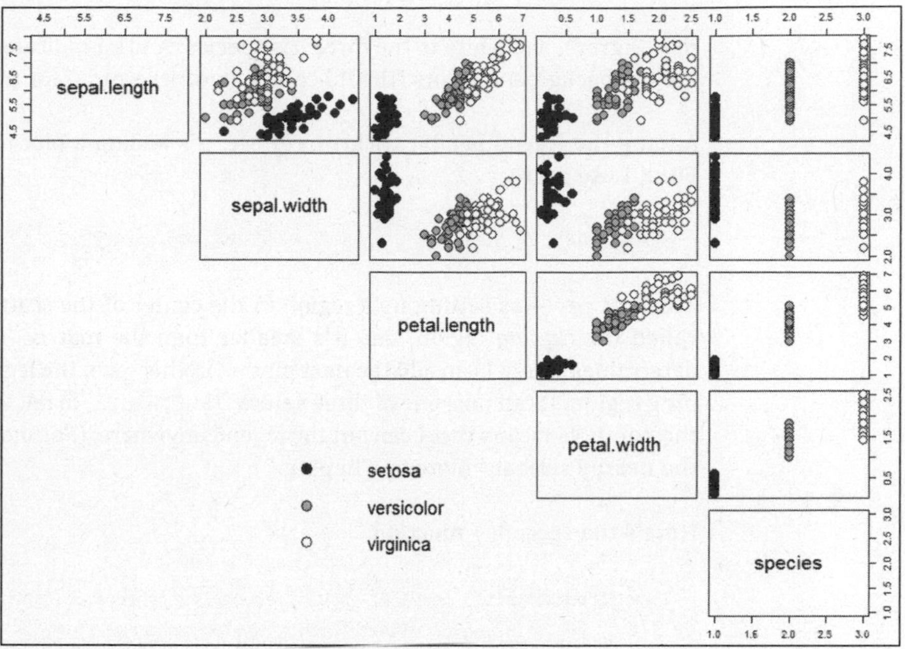

FIGURE 6-3: Scatterplot matrix for the `iris.uci` dataframe rendered in base R.

The cells that plot pairwise relationships among the four numeric variables seem to show that the setosas (the black-filled points) are separate and distributed somewhat differently than the other two species. The least amount of overlap in *versicolor* and *virginica* appears (to me, anyway) to be in `petal.length` versus `petal.width`. As for the cells in column 5, `petal.length` and `petal.width` seem to have the least amount of overlap across the species. By that, I mean that the range of one species has less extension into the range of another. All this suggests that `petal.length` and/or `petal.width` might provide a strong basis for a process that has to learn how to assign irises to their proper species.

To create the scatterplot matrix, I use the `pairs()` function:

```
pairs(iris.uci,lower.panel=NULL,cex=2,pch=21,cex.labels = 2,
    bg = c("black","grey","white")[iris.uci$species])
```

The first argument is the dataframe; the second eliminates the lower panel. The third expands the plot character to twice its size, and the fourth specifies a filled circle as the plot character. The fifth argument doubles the size of the labels in the main diagonal so that you can read them more easily. The final argument is the business end of the whole thing: This one assigns the colors black, gray (excuse me — grey), and white to the three iris species. And bg indicates that those colors are the background colors (the fill colors, in other words) for the plot characters.

Adding the legend is a bit tricky. In effect, it's adding a plot to an existing plot. First, I use par():

```
par(xpd=NA)
```

Think of par() as setting up a region in the center of the scatterplot matrix. It's called the *clipping* region, and it's smaller than the matrix. The xpd argument determines where I can add the next plot — in this case, the legend — to the clipping region. It can take one of three values: TRUE, FALSE, or NA. Without belaboring the point, NA means that I can put the legend anywhere. (For more on clipping, see the nearby sidebar "More on Clipping.")

Here's the legend() function:

```
legend("bottomleft", inset=c(-.5,0), legend=levels(iris.uci$species),
        pch=21,pt.bg=c("black","grey","white"),pt.cex=2,
        y.intersp=.2,cex=1.5,bty="n")
```

The first argument is the location of the legend. The second, inset, is its location relative to the clip region. The negative number for the first argument means that it's to the left of the clipping region, and the 0 means that it's at the bottom. The third argument specifies the terms that appear in the legend. (It's unusual for an argument to have the same name as its function, but there you have it.) I could have used a vector of the species names, but this way is much cooler.

The next three arguments pertain to the symbol in the legend: pch = 21 specifies a filled circle; the pt.bg argument gives the fill colors; pt.cex = 2 doubles the size of the filled circle.

The value of the next argument, y.intersp, shrinks the space between lines of the legend. Without this argument, the legend spreads all over the page. Then cex increases the font size of the text in the legend, and bty="n" means no border around the legend.

Running those three functions produces the plot shown in Figure 6-3. I supplied the values for the arguments based on resolution and screen size, so your plot might look a little different from mine. Feel free to change the values as needed.

MORE ON CLIPPING

Here's an exercise to help you understand clipping, `par()`, and `xpd` a little better, but first you have to complete the project in the earlier section "Quick suggested project: Density plots." In that one, I ask you to turn four histograms into four density plots. (See Figure 6-2.) Without totally letting the cat out of the bag, you have to use the `lines()` function to visualize each density plot after you create each histogram. Inside the `for` loop, just before you call `lines()`, insert `par(xpd=NA)` and note what happens to the ends of the density-plot lines when you run the code. Then change `NA` to `FALSE` and note the effects on the line-ends, and, finally, change to `TRUE` and see what happens.

The ggplot version

As a fan of `ggplot`, I have to show you how to do all this the `ggplot` way. Figure 6-4 shows you a ggplot-rendered scatterplot matrix.

Gorgeous, isn't it? Again, before I show you how to create this, I tell you what it all means. The species correspond to black for *setosa*, gray for *versicolor*, and lighter gray for *virginica.* The first four main diagonal cells show density plots for the three species for each variable. The fifth is a histogram of the species. The bottom row presents histograms that correspond to the density plots.

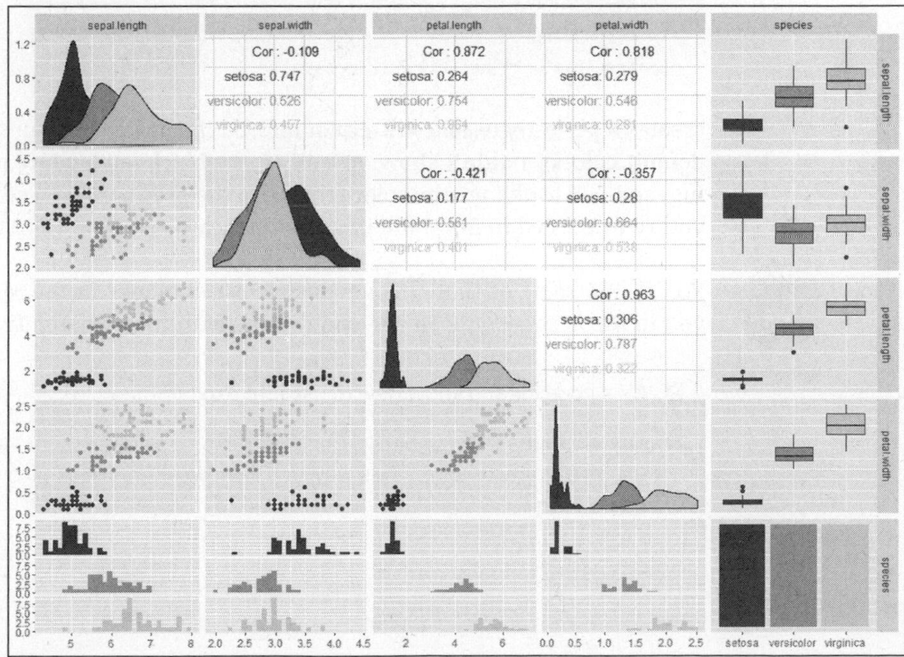

FIGURE 6-4: Scatterplot matrix for `iris.uci` rendered in `ggplot`.

The main diagonal cells and the bottom-row cells clearly show how setosa differs from the other two species with respect to the two petal variables. The scatterplots in each cell visualize the relationship between the cell's row variable and the cell's column variable. These relationships also show the difference between setosa and the other two species.

Above the main diagonal, each cell in columns 2–4 shows the correlation between its row variable and its column variable. Each cell also shows the correlation for each species. It's instructive to note that the individual correlations can vary greatly from the overall correlation.

The fifth column's first four cells are box plots for the three species with respect to each variable. The box plots show the species overlap for the two sepal variables, and little overlap for the petal variables. As is the case with the base R version, the emerging picture is that the petal variables are the stronger indicators of species membership.

On to plot creation. It would be great if `ggplot2` had a function called `ggpairs()` that aesthetically maps `color` to `species` and, like `pairs()` in base R, renders the matrix for you. It doesn't, but a package called `GGally` does, and this package is based on `ggplot2`. To load it, select the Packages tab and click Install. In the Install Packages dialog box, type **GGally**. After it downloads, find `GGally` on the Packages tab and click its check box. Then this code

```
library(ggplot2)
library(GGally)
ggpairs(iris.uci, aes(color = species))
```

creates a perfectly usable scatterplot matrix. It's usable on your *screen*, that is. The default colors wouldn't show up well on the black-and-white page you're reading, so I had to change the color scheme to the grey scale you see in Figure 6-4. If you're interested in how I did this, see the nearby sidebar "Three shades of grey."

REMEMBER

You'll find some of these data exploration techniques in the ML package I show you in the next section. So why did I show them to you here? Two reasons:

- It's a good idea to know how to use R to explore data.
- The package I show you uses these R functions to implement some of its exploration techniques. This way, you'll know where these techniques come from.

THREE SHADES OF GREY

To create Figure 6-4 with black, gray, and lighter gray as the species colors, I first have to create the plot matrix:

```
library(ggplot2)
library(GGally)
plot.matrix <-ggpairs(iris.uci,aes(color= species))
```

Why do I assign the plot matrix to the variable on the left? Because I have to go through the matrix, cell by cell, and change the default colors to grey scale. Using the variable name makes it easy to do that.

To go through the matrix. I use a `for` loop embedded in another `for` loop. The first loop deals with the rows, the second with the columns. Thus, the code goes through each cell in the first row, then each cell in the second, and so on:

```
for(i in 1:5) {
  for(j in 1:5){
      plot.matrix[i,j] <- plot.matrix[i,j] +
       scale_color_grey()  +
       scale_fill_grey()
    }
  }
```

The code inside the embedded `for`-loop makes the changes. In the cells above the main diagonal, `scale_color_grey()` changes the colors of the correlation coefficients and their associated species names. In the cells below the main diagonal, `scale_color_grey()` changes the colors of the points in each scatterplot. The `scale_fill_grey()` function changes the fill colors of the density plots in the main diagonal, the histograms in the bottom row, and the boxplots in the fifth column.

Finally,

```
plot.matrix
```

puts the plot on the screen.

Introducing the `Rattle` package

R has numerous functions and packages that deal with ML. Data science honcho Graham Williams has created `Rattle`, a graphical user interface (GUI) to many of these functions. I use `Rattle` for this book's ML projects.

Much of what `Rattle` does depends on a package called `RGtk2`, which uses R functions to access the Gnu Image Manipulation Program (GIMP) toolkit. (GIMP is a widely used open source image editor.) So the first thing to do is download and install this package. On the Packages tab, click Install. In the Install Packages dialog box, type **RGtk2** and click Install. After the download finishes, find `RGtk2` on the Packages tab and click its check box.

Now do the same for `Rattle`: On the Packages tab, click Install. In the Install Packages dialog box, type **rattle** and click Install. When the download finishes, find `Rattle` on the Packages tab and click its check box.

In R Studio's Script panel, type

```
rattle()
```

and then press Ctrl+R to run. Figure 6-5 shows the window that opens. The window might not be visible at first — it might have opened behind other windows, for example — so you might have to hunt around for it, but you'll find it. Expand it to make it look like Figure 6-5.

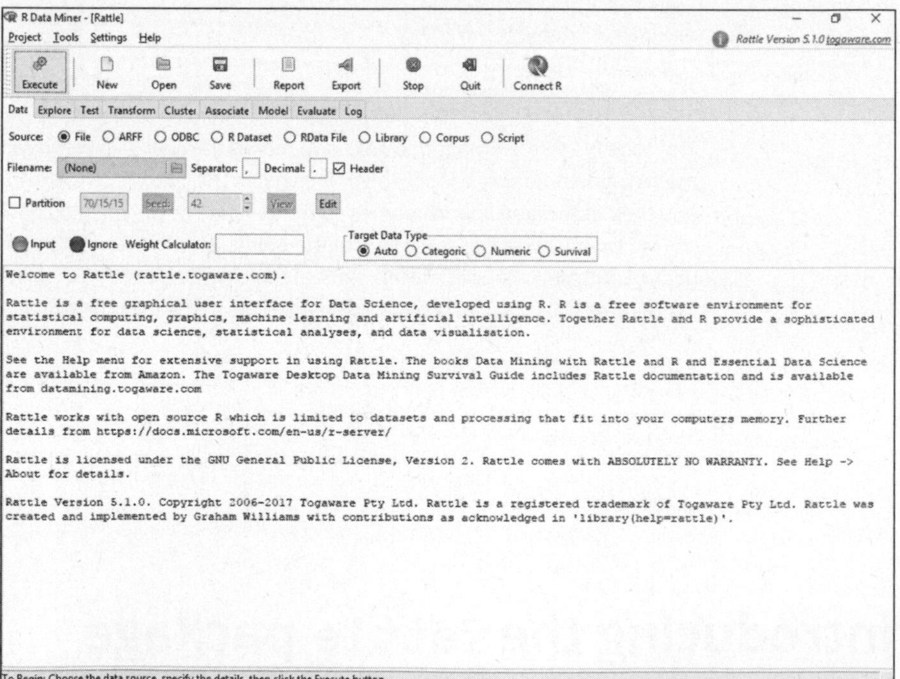

FIGURE 6-5: The `Rattle` window.

The main panel presents a welcome message and some info about `Rattle`. The menu bar at the top features Project (for starting, opening, and saving `Rattle` projects), Tools (a menu of choices that correspond to buttons and tabs), Settings (that deal with graphics), and Help.

The row below the menu bar holds icons, the most important of which is Execute. The idea is to look at each tab and make selections, and then click Execute to carry out those selections. (If you're a Trekkie, think of clicking the Execute icon as Captain Picard saying "Make it so!")

The next row holds the tabs. The first tab (on the left) is for Data. This tab presents the welcome message and, more importantly, allows you to choose the data source. The Explore tab is for — you guessed it — exploring data. The Test tab supplies two-sample statistical tests. If you have to transform data, the Transform tab is for you. The Cluster tab enables several kinds of cluster analysis, a type of unsupervised learning. The Associate tab sets you up with association analysis, which identifies relationships between variables. The Model tab provides several kinds of ML, including decision trees, support vector machines, and neural networks. The next tab allows you to Evaluate your ML creation. The Log tab tracks your interactions with Rattle as R script, which can be quite instructive if you're trying to learn R.

TIP

Remember that `Rattle` is a GUI to R functions for some complex analyses, and you can't always know in advance what those functions are or which packages they live in. Accordingly, a frequent part of the interaction with `Rattle` is a dialog box that opens and says that you have to install a particular package, and asks whether you want to install it. Always click Yes.

Using `Rattle` with `iris`

So I downloaded the `iris` data set from the UCI ML Repository, cleaned it up a bit, and explored it. Then I installed `Rattle`. Now I put `Rattle` to work.

Getting and (further) exploring the data

The first thing to do is bring the dataset into `Rattle`. On the Data tab, I select the source by clicking the radio button next to R Dataset. This causes a Data Name box to open just below the radio buttons.

Clicking the down arrow on the Data Name box opens a drop-down menu, as shown in Figure 6-6.

On the menu, I click `iris.uci`. Next, I click the Execute icon. This causes the Data tab to look like Figure 6-7.

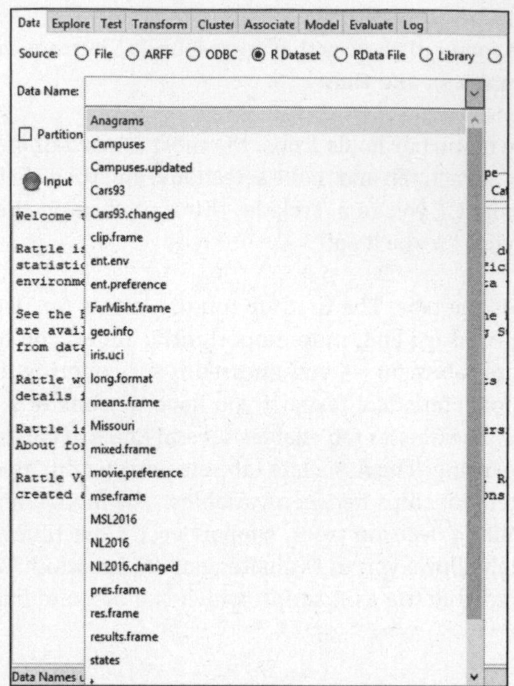

FIGURE 6-6: The dropdown menu in the Data Name box on the Rattle data tab.

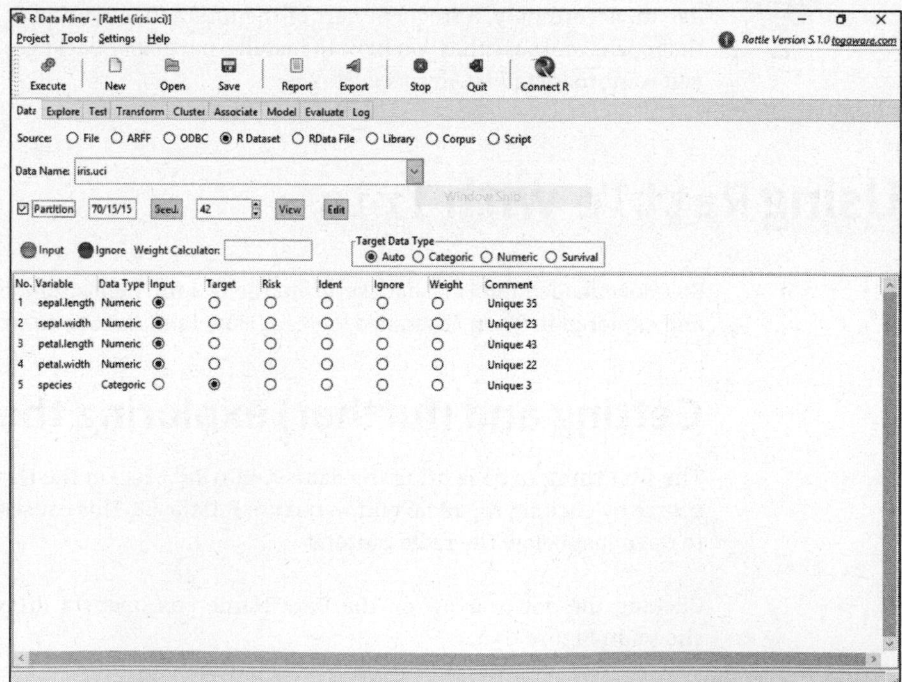

FIGURE 6-7: The Rattle Data tab, after loading the iris.uci dataframe.

Notice the check box next to Partition. This partitions the data into a training set, a validation set, and a test set, which are required for many types of ML. For what I'm about to do, though, that's not necessary. I'm just going to quickly show you some of `Rattle`'s capabilities by doing a hierarchical clustering analysis to look at the structure of the data set. So I uncheck that check box.

Notice also the variable names and the selected radio buttons in the main panel. As you can see, `Rattle` has a pretty good idea about the types of data in this data set.

Now for some exploration. Clicking the Explore tab shows the page you see in Figure 6-8.

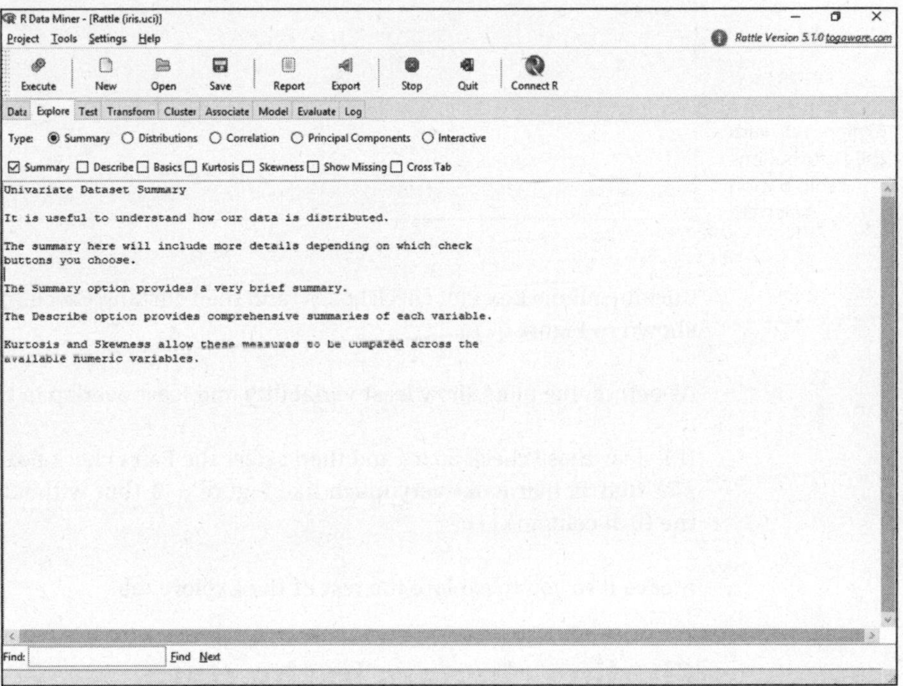

FIGURE 6-8: The `Rattle` Explore tab.

To explore the distributions of the variables, I click the Distributions radio button, and the tab looks like Figure 6-9.

TIP

A `Rattle` plot shows up on the RStudio Plots tab. For an expanded version, click on Zoom.

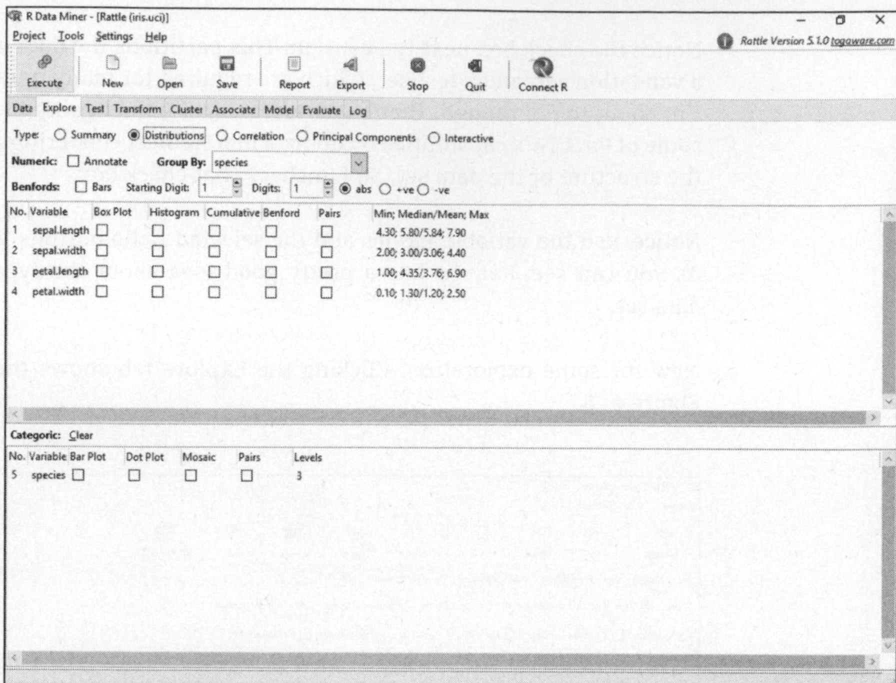

FIGURE 6-9: The `Rattle` Explore tab, with the Distributions radio button selected.

Clicking all the Box Plot check boxes (and then clicking Execute) results in the plot shown in Figure 6-10.

As before, the plots show least variability and least overlap in the petal variables.

If I clear those check boxes and then select the Pairs check boxes, I get a scatter-plot matrix that looks very much like Figure 6-4 (but without the fifth row and the fifth column).

I leave it to you to explore the rest of the Explore tab.

Finding clusters in the data

Now for some ML. In subsequent chapters, I provide detailed explanations of ML techniques, but here I show you just the superficial aspects of a hierarchical cluster analysis, a type of unsupervised learning that, as I mention earlier, finds the underlying structure in the data set. The analysis reveals the structure as a set of clusters organized in a hierarchy. I'm cheating a bit here because I know the structure: It's three species and, as data exploration suggests, *setosa* somehow is different from *versicolor* and *virginica*.

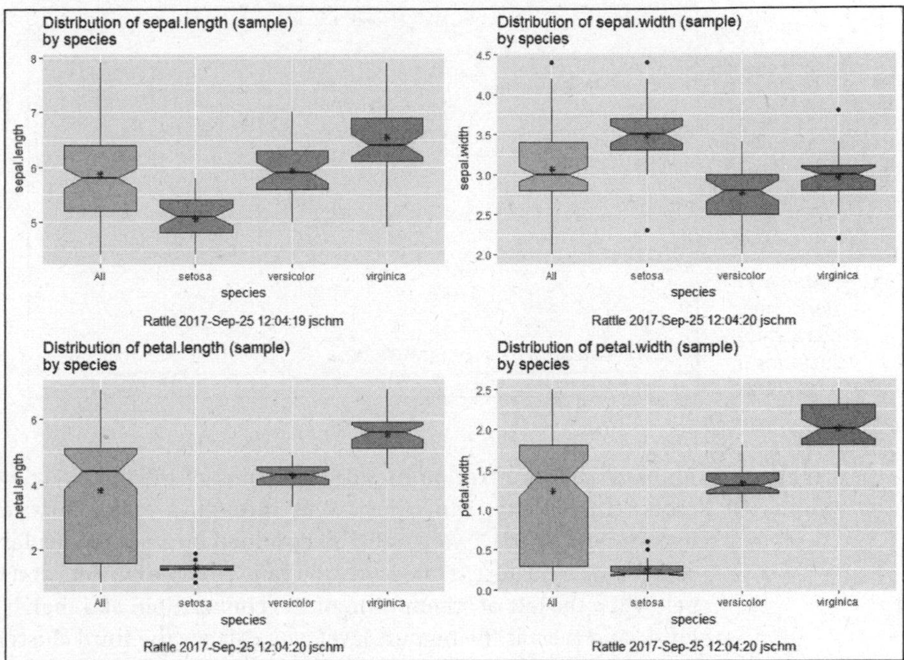

FIGURE 6-10: `Rattle`-rendered box plots for the four numeric variables in `iris.uci`.

We might guess, then, that the observations form "clusters" on the basis of their species. So that's three clusters.

What's the "hierarchy"? The overlap between *versicolor* and *virginica* in the scatterplots (and their separation from *setosa*) suggests that they form a "higher-order" cluster, leaving out *setosa*. Then, at a higher level, *setosa* forms a cluster with the other two, resulting in one big cluster that represents the whole data set. That's the hierarchy.

Or, looking at it another way, the data set partitions into two clusters: one consisting of *versicolor* and *virginica* and the other consisting of just *setosa*. The first cluster then breaks down into two clusters, one for each species perhaps.

It's simple for the `iris` data set because everything is pretty much cut-and-dried. With a larger data set that has more variables and more categories, things can get pretty complicated and this type of analysis can reveal unanticipated structures.

To do the hierarchical clustering, I select the Cluster tab and click the Hierarchical radio button. Clicking Execute makes the Cluster tab look like Figure 6-11.

In the Clusters box, I change the number to 3 and click Execute. (I said I was cheating, remember?) I'd like a picture of the hierarchical clustering I describe earlier, and that appears in a picture called a *dendrogram*. (In Greek, *dendro* means "tree.") So I click Dendrogram and the result is shown in Figure 6-12.

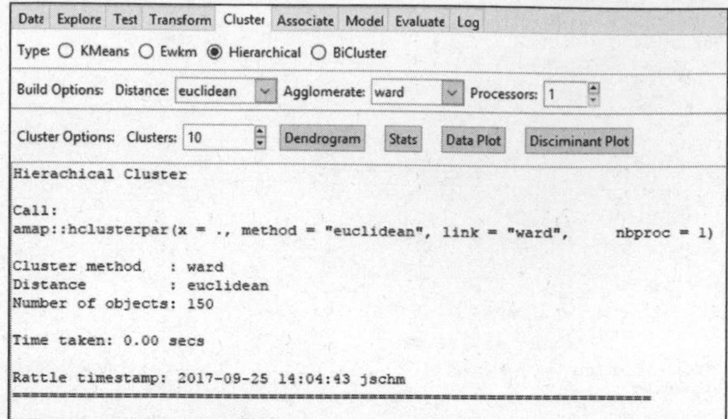

FIGURE 6-11: Performing hierarchical clustering in `Rattle`.

Think of this as a tree on its side, and think of the individual observations as the roots. (In my city, which just went through a major hurricane, that's not an uncommon sight!) Two parallel lines joined by a perpendicular line at their ends represents a cluster. At one level, you can see three clusters and numerous clusters below (to the left of) them. Two of the clusters join at a higher (more rightward) level. And then at the highest level, you can see the third cluster joining them.

TIP

With the Cluster box default value of 10, the dendrogram looks similar to Figure 6-12.

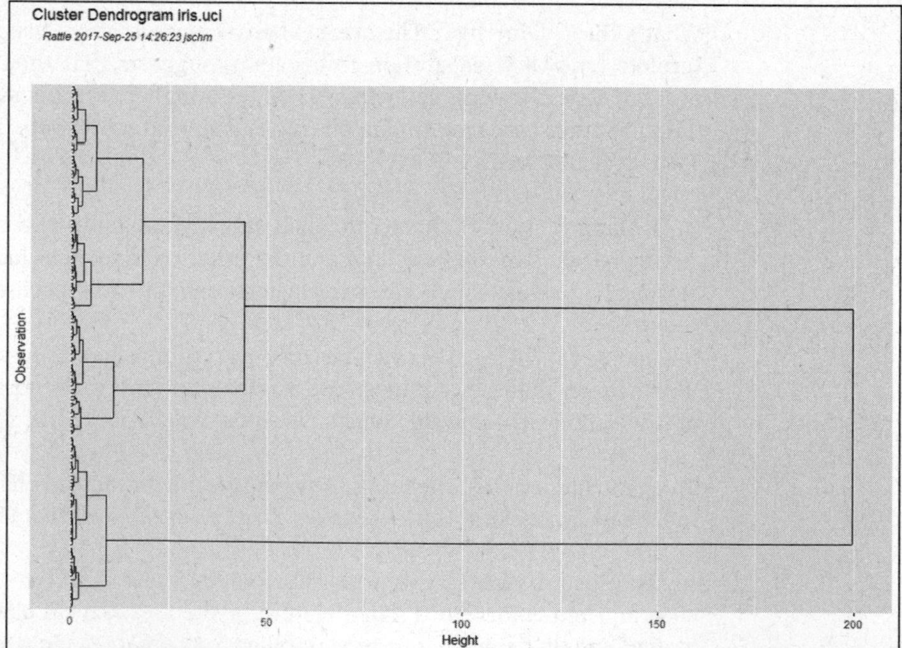

FIGURE 6-12: Dendrogram for the `iris.uci` data set.

LOOKING AT THE RATTLE LOG

As I mention earlier in this chapter, the Log tab shows your interactions with Rattle as R code. Here's a good example of working with the Rattle log.

In the hierarchical clustering analysis, click on Data Plot. You see a plot that looks very much like Figure 6-3. To find the code that produced this plot, select the Log tab and scroll down until you find this:

```
plot(crs$dataset[, c(1:4)], col=cutree(crs$hclust,3))
```

Copy and paste that line into the RStudio Script panel and then press Ctrl+R to run it.

On the Plots tab, you see the same scatterplot matrix, but without the title. The plotting characters aren't filled, and their border colors (black, red, and green) are the colors of the clusters to which Rattle has assigned them. (I don't show you this, because the red and green border colors would be hard to distinguish on a black-and-white page.)

To make the matrix look more like Figure 6-3, change `cr$dataset[, c(1:4)]` to `cr$dataset[, c(1:5)]`. This change adds the fifth row and the fifth column.

Add the argument `lower.panel=NULL` to eliminate everything below the main diagonal. Then add plot character arguments so that the code is

```
plot(crs$dataset[, c(1:5)], col=cutree(crs$hclust, 3), lower.panel=NULL,
    pch=21,cex=2,
          bg = c("black","grey","white")[iris.uci$species])
```

Now the border color of each character corresponds to its assigned cluster, and its fill color corresponds to its species. If you run this code, you see that in the scatterplots, some of the plot characters have red borders and are filled with gray and some red-border characters are filled with white. In the fifth column, all points in the rightmost group should have green borders, but some have red borders. What does all this tell us? That the clustering isn't perfect! That is, the three clusters do not correspond exactly with the three species.

Poking around in the Rattle log was a pretty good idea!

The Rattle Evaluation tab has procedures for evaluating your ML creations, and I discuss them in subsequent chapters.

It's tempting to say that the three clusters correspond to the three species. But do they really? A quick glance at the dendrogram shows that the three possibly-corresponding-to-the-species clusters don't appear to have equal numbers of observations at their lowest levels. So maybe the cluster-species correspondence isn't exact. Also, see the nearby sidebar "Looking at the `Rattle` log."

Where do the numbers on the Height axis come from? What's the rule for admitting an observation to a cluster? Or for joining one cluster to another? Important questions all, but my objective here is just to acquaint you with `Rattle`.

As was the case with Explore, feel free to look at the remaining options on this tab.

IN THIS CHAPTER

» Finding out about decision trees

» Creating a decision tree for the `iris` dataset

» Working with a decision tree for the `Acute inflammations` dataset from UCI

Chapter 7 Decisions, Decisions, Decisions

A *decision tree* is a graphical way of representing knowledge. As its name implies, it's a tree-like structure that shows decisions about something, and it's useful in many fields, from management to medicine.

Think of a decision tree as a way to structure a sequence of questions and possible answers. One prominent use of a decision tree is to show the flow of decision-making to a nontechnical audience.

Decision Tree Components

Figure 7-1 shows a decision tree for classifying irises along with decision tree terminology. You might recall from Chapter 6 that the `iris` dataset (downloaded from the UCI Machine Learning (ML) Repository and designated as `iris.uci`) consists of 150 rows and 5 columns. The 150 rows represent individual flowers, with 50 each of the *setosa, versicolor,* and *virginica* species. The five columns are `sepal.length`, `sepal.width`, `petal.length`, `petal.width`, and `species`.

The decision tree is really an upside down tree, and it consists of *nodes* and *branches*. Each node presents a question (like petal.length < 2.6, and the question mark is implicit), and branches emanating from the node represent possible answers (yes/no, for example).

(Alternative branches remind me of something the late, great Yogi Berra reputedly said: "When you come to a fork in the road, take it." Not entirely relevant, but I can't write a book without quoting Yogi Berra.)

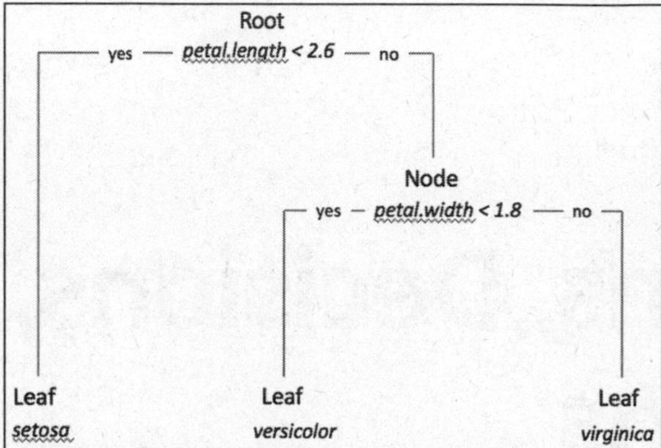

FIGURE 7-1: A decision tree for classifying irises.

Roots and leaves

The tree starts from a top-level node called the *root* and ends in bottom-level nodes called *leaves*. (I told you it was upside down.) Each leaf contains a category — in this case, a particular species of iris.

A node that branches to a node below it is the *parent* of the one below. The lower node on a branch is the *child* of the one above it. So a root has no parents and a leaf has no children. An *internal node* has at least one child.

Think of a sequence of branches from the root to a leaf as a *classification rule*. In Figure 7-1, one rule is, "If an iris's petal length is greater than or equal to 2.6 and its petal width is less than 1.8, then the iris is a *versicolor*."

REMEMBER

A decision tree with categories in the leaves is called a *classification tree*. A decision tree with numerical values (like "predicted miles per gallon" or "predicted length of hospital stay") in the leaves is called a *regression tree*.

Tree construction

If you had to build a decision tree based on the `iris.uci` data frame, how would you do it? In effect, the job is to create a series of yes/no questions that split the data into smaller and smaller subsets until you can't split the subsets any more.

So you'd examine the variables and find for one of them a value that splits the data into two subsets, perhaps one that has all the *setosa* and the other that has all the rest. Let's call them A and B.

How about splitting them further? If you were careful, you'd find a value such that A had two subsets (A1 and A2), one of which (A1) contained all the *setosa* and the other (A2) containing nothing. Because A2 has no members, you can't split it any more. So A is a leaf.

Now look at B. This one holds all the non-*setosa* irises. The same variable (or perhaps another one) might hold the key to a productive split into B1 and B2. That split value (whatever the variable and whatever the value) probably won't put all *versicolor* into B1 and all *virginica* into B2.

Why? You might remember from Chapter 6 that data exploration revealed some overlap between these two species regardless of the variable. So the split won't be perfect, but it might put the vast majority of one species in B1 (along with a tiny group of miscategorized cases) and the vast majority of the other in B2 (again, with a tiny group of miscategorized cases). Ideally, the miscategorizations are so few that you can't split any further. So B1 and B2 are leaves.

This is called *recursive partitioning*, and you could go through the data and do all this manually.

Or you could use R.

Decision Trees in R

R has a package that uses recursive partitioning to construct decision trees. It's called `rpart`, and its function for constructing trees is called `rpart()`. To install the `rpart` package, click Install on the Packages tab and type **rpart** in the Install Packages dialog box. Then, in the dialog box, click the Install button. After the package downloads, find `rpart` in the Packages tab and click to select its check box.

Growing the tree in R

To create a decision tree for the `iris.uci` data frame, use the following code:

```
library(rpart)
iris.tree <- rpart(species ~ sepal.length + sepal.width + petal.length + petal.
   width, iris.uci, method="class")
```

The first argument to rpart() is a formula indicating that species depends on the other four variables. [The tilde (~) means "depends on." See the section "R Formulas" in Chapter 2.] The second argument is the data frame you're using. The method = "class" argument (it's the third one) tells rpart() that this is a classification tree. (For a regression tree, it's method = "anova".)

TIP

You can abbreviate the whole right side of the formula with a period. So the shorthand version is

```
species ~ .
```

The left side of the code, iris.tree, is called an *rpart object*. So rpart() creates an rpart object.

At this point, you can type the rpart object

```
iris.tree
```

and see text output that describes the tree:

```
n= 150

node), split, n, loss, yval, (yprob)
      * denotes terminal node

1) root 150 100 setosa (0.33333333 0.33333333 0.33333333)
  2) petal.length< 2.45 50   0 setosa (1.00000000 0.00000000 0.00000000) *
  3) petal.length>=2.45 100  50 versicolor (0.00000000 0.50000000 0.50000000)
    6) petal.width< 1.75 54   5 versicolor (0.00000000 0.90740741 0.09259259) *
    7) petal.width>=1.75 46   1 virginica (0.00000000 0.02173913 0.97826087) *
```

The first line indicates that this tree is based on 150 cases. The second line provides a key for understanding the output. The third line tells you that an asterisk denotes that a node is a leaf.

Each row corresponds to a node on the tree. The first entry in the row is the node number followed by a right parenthesis. The second is the variable and the value that make up the split. The third is the number of classified cases at that node. The fourth, loss, is the number of misclassified cases at the node. Misclassified? Compared to what? Compared to the next entry, yval, which is the tree's best guess of the species at that node. The final entry is a parenthesized set of proportions that correspond to the proportion of each species at the node.

You can see the perfect classification in node 2, where loss (misclassification) is 0. By contrast, in nodes 6 and 7 loss is not 0. Also, unlike node 2, the parenthesized proportions for nodes 6 and 7 do not show 1.00 in the slots that represent the correct species. So the classification rules for *versicolor* and *virginica* result in small amounts of error.

Drawing the tree in R

Now you plot the decision tree, and you can see how it corresponds to the rpart() output. You do this with a function called prp(), which lives in the rpart.plot package.

WARNING

The rpart package has a function called plot.rpart(), which is supposed to plot a decision tree. My version of R can't find it. It can find the function's documentation via ?plot.rpart but it can't find the function. Weird. It's enough to make me *plotz* (which in another language means something like "implode and explode simultaneously").

With rpart.plot installed, here's the code that plots the tree shown in Figure 7-2:

```
library(rpart.plot)
prp(iris.tree,type=2,extra="auto",nn = TRUE,branch=1,varlen=0,yesno=2)
```

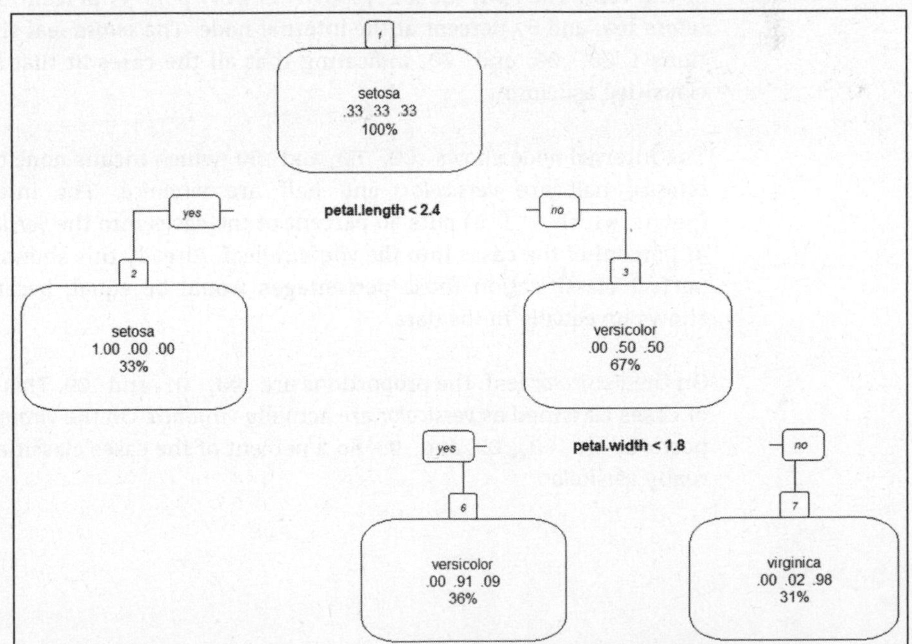

FIGURE 7-2: Decision tree for iris.uci, created by rpart() and rendered by prp().

The first argument to `prp()` is the rpart object. That's the only argument that's necessary. Think of the rpart object as a set of specifications for plotting the tree. I've added the other arguments to make the plot prettier:

- **`type = 2`** means "label all the nodes"
- **`extra = "auto"`** tells `prp()` to include the information you see in each rounded rectangle that's in addition to the species name
- **`nn = TRUE`** puts the node-number on each node
- **`branch = 1`** indicates the lines-with-corners style of branching shown in Figure 7-2. These are called "square-shouldered branches", believe it or not. For slump-shouldered branches (I made that up) try a value between 0 and 1
- **`varlen=0`** produces the full variable names on all the nodes (instead of names truncated to 8 characters)
- **`yesno=2`** puts yes or no on all the appropriate branches (instead of just the ones descending from the root, which is the default). Note that each left branch is yes and each right branch is no

At the root node and the internal node, you see the split. The rounded rectangle at each node shows a species name, three proportions, and the percentage of the data encompassed at that node.

At the root, the proportions are .33 for each species, and 100 percent of the data is at the root. The split (`petal.length < 2.4`) puts 33 percent of the data at the *setosa* leaf and 67 percent at the internal node. The *setosa* leaf shows the proportions `1.00`, `.00`, and `.00`, indicating that all the cases at that leaf are perfectly classified as *setosas*.

The internal node shows `.00`, `.50`, and `.50`, which means none of these cases are *setosas*, half are *versicolor*, and half are *virginica*. The internal node split (`petal.width < 1.8`) puts 36 percent of the cases into the *versicolor* leaf and the 31 percent of the cases into the *virginica* leaf. Already this shows a problem: With perfect classification those percentages would be equal, because each species shows up equally in the data.

On the *versicolor* leaf, the proportions are `.00`, `.91`, and `.09`. This means 9 percent of cases classified as *versicolor* are actually *virginica*. On the *virginica* leaf, the proportions are `.00`, `.02`, and `.98`. So 2 percent of the cases classified as *virginica* are really *versicolor*.

Bottom line: For the great majority of the 150 cases in the data, the classification rules in the decision tree get the job done. But the rules aren't perfect, which is typically the case with a decision tree.

Decision Trees in `Rattle`

`Rattle` provides a GUI to R's tree-construction and tree-plotting functions. To use this GUI to create a decision tree for `iris.uci`, begin by opening `Rattle`:

```
library(rattle)
rattle()
```

I'm assuming that you've downloaded and cleaned up the `iris` dataset from the UCI ML Repository and called it `iris.uci`. I mention that at the beginning of this chapter, and I walk you through all the download and cleanup steps in Chapter 6.

On `Rattle`'s Data tab, in the Source row, click the radio button next to R Dataset. Click the down arrow next to the Data Name box and select `iris.uci` from the drop-down menu. Then click the Execute icon in the upper left corner. Your screen should look like Figure 6-7, in Chapter 6.

TIP

If you haven't downloaded the UCI iris dataset and you just want to use the `iris` dataset that comes with base R, click the Library radio button. Then click the down arrow next to the Data Name box and select

```
iris:datasets:Edgar Anderson's iris data
```

from the drop-down menu. Then click Execute.

I recommend downloading from UCI, though, to get the hang of it. Downloading from the UCI ML Repository is something you'll be doing a lot.

Still on the Data tab, select the Partition check box. This breaks down the dataset into a training set, a validation set, and a test set. The default proportions are 70 percent training, 15 percent validation, and 15 percent test. The idea is to use the training set to construct the tree and then use the test set to test its classification rules. The validation set provides a set of cases to experiment with different variables or parameters. Because I don't do that in this example, I set the percentages to 70 percent training, 0 percent validation, and 30 percent test.

The Seed box contains a default value, 42, as a seed for randomly assigning the dataset rows to training, validation, or testing. Changing the seed changes the randomization.

Creating the tree

Decision tree modeling resides on the Model tab. It opens with Tree selected. Figure 7-3 shows this tab.

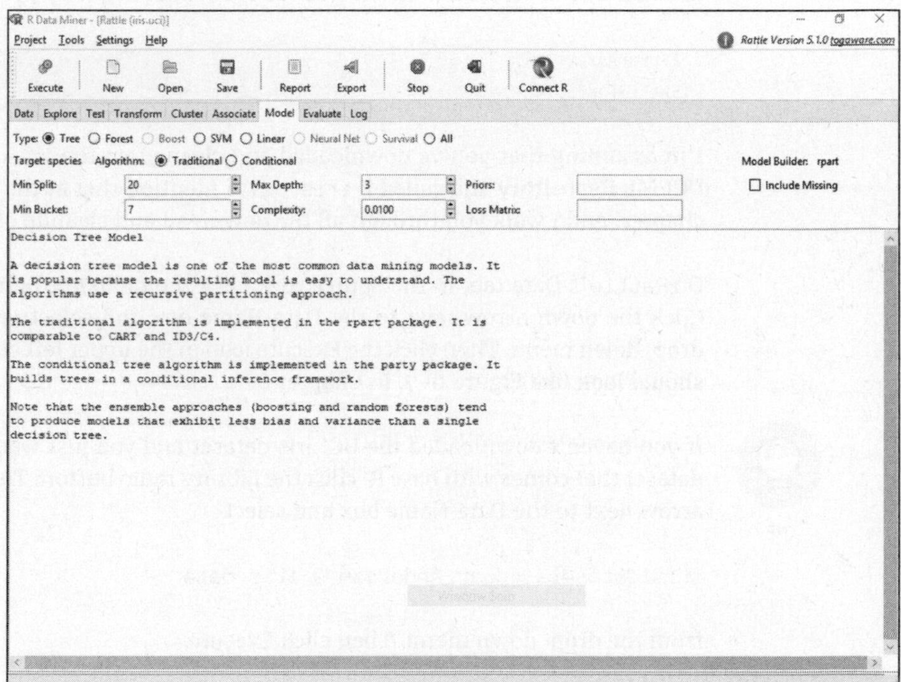

FIGURE 7-3: The Rattle Model tab.

A number of onscreen boxes provide access to `rpart()`'s arguments. (These are called *tuning parameters*.) Moving the cursor over a box opens helpful messages about what goes in the box.

For now, just click Execute to create the decision tree. Figure 7-4 shows what then happens on the Model tab.

The text in the main panel is output from `rpart()`, with a few more arguments than I use earlier in this chapter. It looks a lot like the output I show you earlier, with some extra info. Note that the tree is based on the 105 cases (70 percent of 150) that constitute the training set. Unlike the tree created earlier, this one just uses `petal.length` in its splits.

The rest of the output is from a function called `printcp()`. The abbreviation `cp` stands for *c*omplexity *p*arameter, which controls the number of splits that make up the tree. Without delving too deeply into it, I'll just tell you that if a split adds less than the given value of `cp` (on the Model tab, the default value is .01), `rpart()` doesn't add the split to the tree. For the most complex tree possible (with the largest number of possible splits, in other words), set `cp` to `.00`. (See the section "Quick Suggested Project: Understanding the complexity parameter," toward the end of this chapter.)

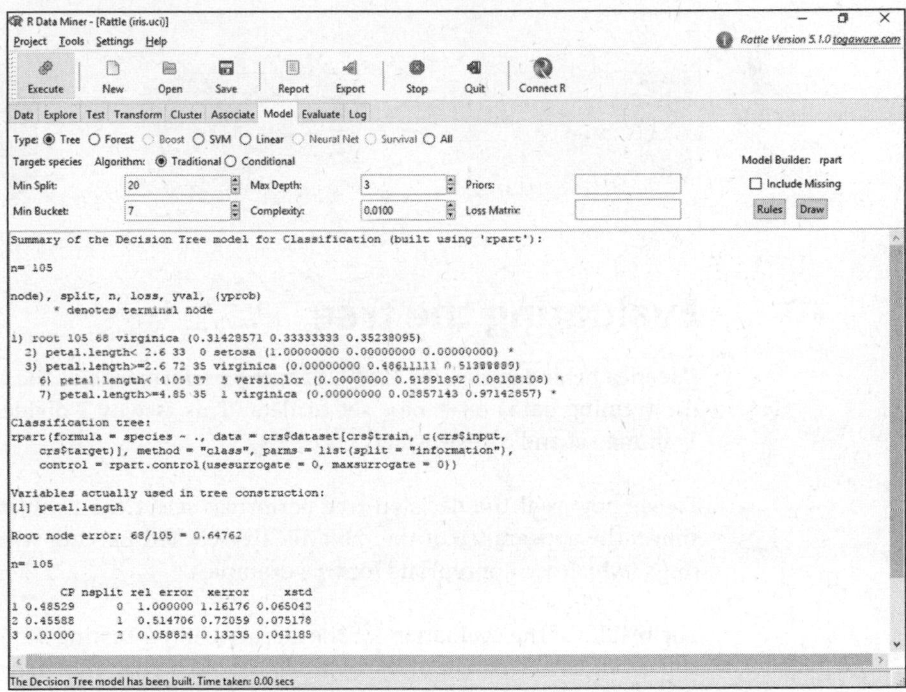

FIGURE 7-4: The `Rattle` Model tab, after creating a decision tree for `iris.uci`.

Drawing the tree

Clicking the Draw button produces the decision tree shown in Figure 7-5, rendered by `prp()`. The overall format of the tree is similar to the tree shown earlier, in Figure 7-2, although the details are different and the boxes at the nodes have fill color.

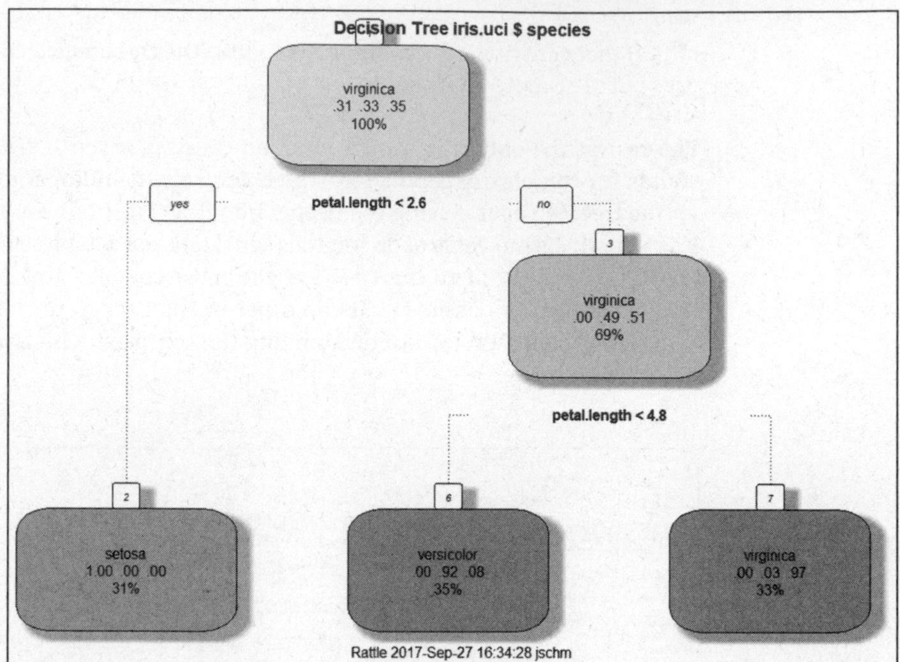

FIGURE 7-5: A decision tree for `iris.uci`, based on a training set of 105 cases.

Evaluating the tree

The idea behind *evaluation* is to assess the performance of the tree (derived from the training data) on a new set of data. This is why I divided the data into a Training set and a Testing set.

To see how well the decision tree performs, select the Evaluate tab. Figure 7-6 shows the appearance of the tab after I've clicked Execute with the default settings (which are appropriate for this example).

The results of the evaluation for the 45 cases in the Testing set (30 percent of 150) appear in two versions of an *error matrix*. Each row of a matrix represents the actual species of the flower. Each column shows the decision tree's predicted species of the flower. The first version of the matrix shows the results by counts; the second, by proportions.

Correct identifications are in the main diagonal. So in the first matrix, the cell in row 1, column 1 represents the number of times the decision tree correctly classified a *setosa* as a *setosa* (17). The zeros in the other two cells in row 1 indicate no misclassified *setosas*.

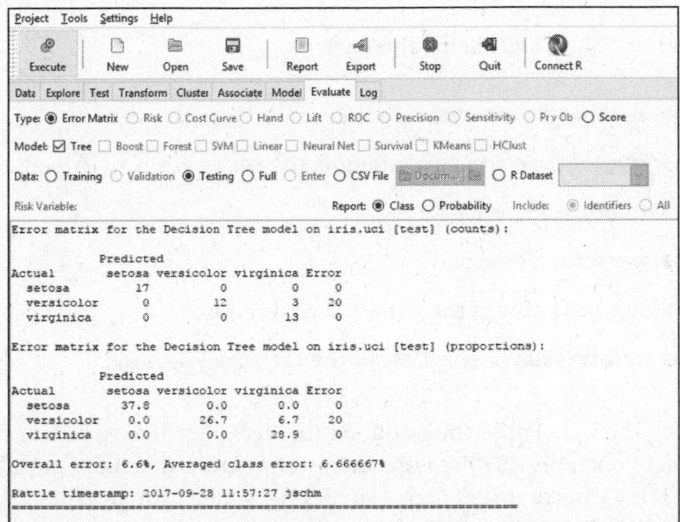

FIGURE 7-6: The Rattle Evaluate tab, after evaluating the decision tree for `iris.uci`.

The cell in row 2, column 3 shows that the tree incorrectly classified three *virginicas* as *versicolors*. The fourth column shows that the error rate is 20 percent (3/(12 + 3)).

Row 3 shows no misclassifications, so dividing the 20 percent by 3 (the number of categories) gives the averaged class error you see at the bottom of the figure. The overall error is the number of misclassifications divided by the total number of observations.

Project: A More Complex Decision Tree

The decision tree for the `iris` dataset is pretty straightforward and yields a relatively low error rate. The following sections lay out a project that results in a more complex tree.

The data: Car evaluation

In the UCI ML Repository, you'll find the `Car Evaluation` dataset. It lives at `http://archive.ics.uci.edu/ml/datasets/Car+Evaluation`.

As the dataset's description tells you, the designers created the dataset to demonstrate expert system technology, so it's a bit on the "artificial" side. I use it here to give you some practice creating decision trees. The idea is that, given a set of cars' attributes and their values, the decision is whether a specific car is unacceptable, acceptable, good, or very good.

The attributes and their values are

- **buying (the purchase price):** `v-high`, `high`, `med`, `low`
- **maint (the cost of maintaining the car):** `v-high`, `high`, `med`, `low`
- **doors:** `2`, `3`, `4`, `more`
- **persons:** `2`, `4`, `more`
- **lug_boot (size of the trunk):** `small`, `med`, `big`
- **safety (estimated safety of the car):** `low`, `med`, `high`

Click the Data Folder link and, on the new page that appears, click the `car.data` link to open the CSV data file. Using my preferred method of putting the data into an R data frame, press Ctrl+A to highlight the entire page and then Ctrl+C to copy it to the clipboard.

Then the line

```
car.uci <- read.csv("clipboard",header=FALSE)
```

creates the data frame for this project. Now it's time to name the columns:

```
colnames(car.uci) = c("buying","maintenance","doors","persons","lug_boot",
   "safety", "evaluation")
```

The Data Set Description refers to the target as `class`, but I think `evaluation` is more to the point. Just as a check on what the data looks like, type:

```
head(car.uci)
```

Running that command produces:

```
  buying maintenance doors persons lug_boot safety evaluation
1  vhigh       vhigh     2       2    small    low      unacc
2  vhigh       vhigh     2       2    small    med      unacc
3  vhigh       vhigh     2       2    small   high      unacc
4  vhigh       vhigh     2       2      med    low      unacc
5  vhigh       vhigh     2       2      med    med      unacc
6  vhigh       vhigh     2       2      med   high      unacc
```

With `Rattle` installed,

```
library(rattle)
rattle()
```

opens the Rattle screen. On the Data tab, select the R Dataset radio button. Click the down arrow next to the Data Name box, and select car.uci from the drop-down menu. Check the Partition check box to partition the data into a training set, a validation set, and a test set. After you click the Execute icon, the Data tab looks like the one shown in Figure 7-7.

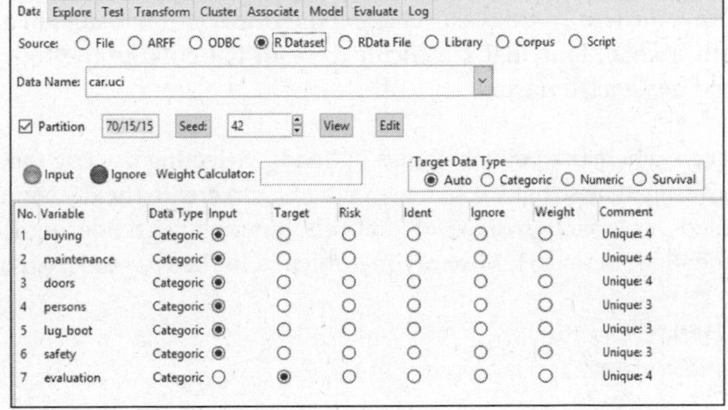

FIGURE 7-7: The Rattle Data tab, after acquiring the car.uci data frame.

Data exploration

Figure 7-8 shows the result of using the Explore tab to show the distribution of the evaluations in car.uci. The vast majority of the cars, as you can see, are "unacceptable." The Explore tab allows a variety of data explorations, and I encourage you to examine other aspects of the data.

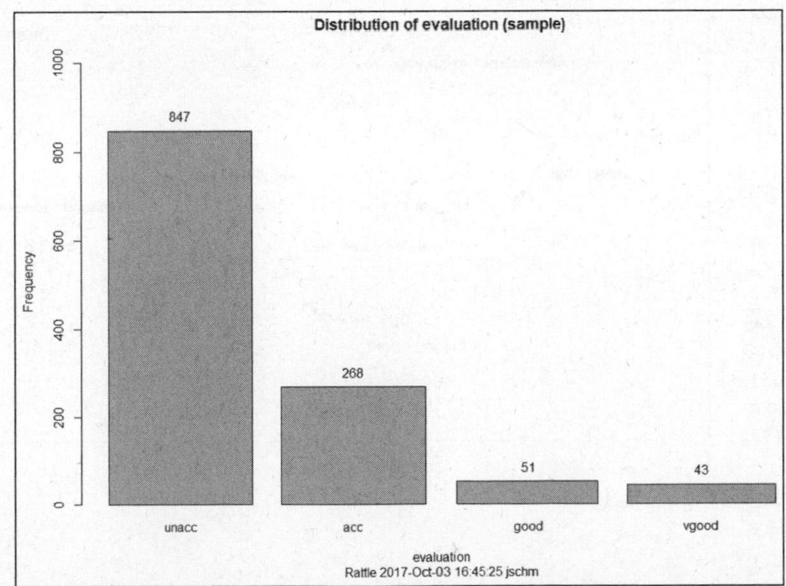

FIGURE 7-8: The distribution of evaluations in the car.uci data frame.

Building and drawing the tree

On the Model tab, clicking Execute harnesses the `rpart()` function to create the decision tree. I use the default values in the boxes on this tab. The main panel shows the resulting description of the nodes, as shown in Figure 7-4 for `iris.uci`.

It's all quite detailed, and sifting through all the minutia would be a chore. Instead, I draw the tree. In this case, clicking the Draw button results in a lot of nodes, each with a small font that's difficult to read. If I enlarge the font, the whole thing becomes a mishmash.

Here's where the Log tab comes in handy. Selecting the Log tab and doing a bit of scrolling shows that `Rattle` uses `rpart()` to create the decision tree in a variable called `crs$rpart`. Instead of `Rattle`'s function for rendering the tree (it's called `fancyRpartPlot()`), I use `prp()`, which is in the `rpart.plot` package:

```
library(rpart.plot)
prp(crs$rpart, cex=1,varlen=0,branch=0)
```

The result is shown in Figure 7-9.

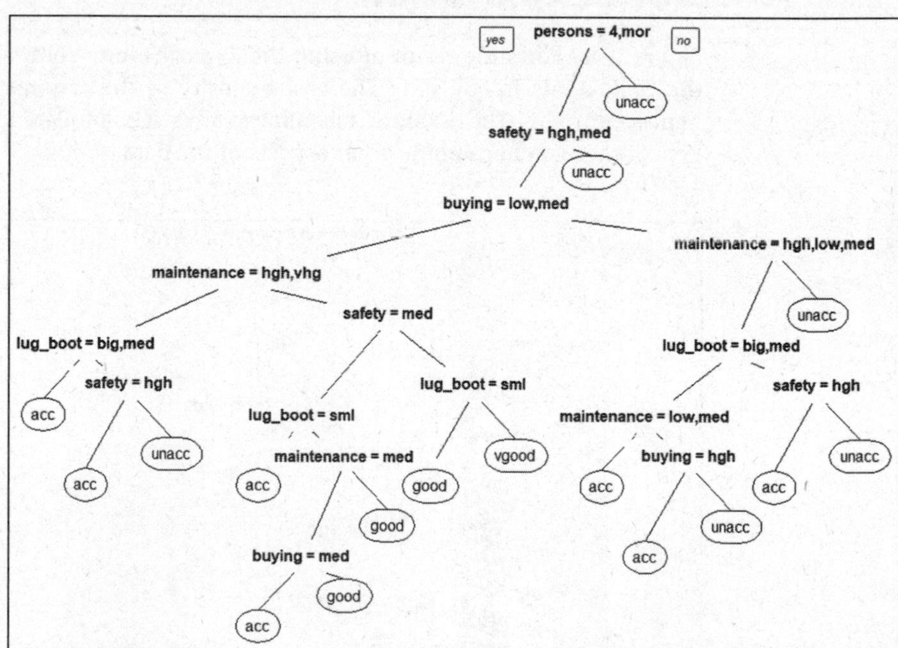

FIGURE 7-9: The decision tree for `car.uci`, rendered in `rpart()`.

This is a plainer-looking tree than the Rattle function renders, with no colors and little information in the nodes, but everything is easier to see. The first argument to prp() is the Rattle-created decision tree, and the second enlarges the font. The third argument, varlen = 0, prints the full name of each attribute and value (rather than truncating), and branch = 0 provides the branch style shown in the figure.

Evaluating the tree

On the Evaluate tab, click the Testing radio button to evaluate the decision tree against the Testing dataset. Clicking Execute produces the error matrices shown in Figure 7-10.

```
Error matrix for the Decision Tree model on car.uci [test] (counts):

       Predicted
Actual  acc good unacc vgood Error
  acc    57    2     1     0   5.0
  good    0    8     0     3  27.3
  unacc   9    0   169     0   5.1
  vgood   3    0     0     8  27.3

Error matrix for the Decision Tree model on car.uci [test] (proportions):

       Predicted
Actual   acc good unacc vgood Error
  acc   21.9  0.8   0.4   0.0   5.0
  good   0.0  3.1   0.0   1.2  27.3
  unacc  3.5  0.0  65.0   0.0   5.1
  vgood  1.2  0.0   0.0   3.1  27.3

Overall error: 6.9%, Averaged class error: 16.175%

Rattle timestamp: 2017-10-04 10:33:42 jschm
======================================================================
```

FIGURE 7-10: Error matrices for the car.uci decision tree.

The numbers in the first matrix are counts; the numbers in the second are proportions of the sample. The numbers on the main diagonal are correct classifications, and the others are errors.

The tree does a nice job with the most frequent categories (unacceptable and acceptable), and not quite as well on the other two (good and very good). The overall error rate is 6.9 percent.

Quick suggested project: Understanding the complexity parameter

Rattle is a terrific teaching tool. In this little two-part project, you can use Rattle to help wrap your brain around the complexity parameter (cp) and what it entails.

The default value of the cp is .01. To tell you how to calculate cp is beyond the scope of this book. To paraphrase what I say earlier in this chapter, just think of cp as the "minimum benefit" that a split must add to the tree. If the split doesn't yield at least that much benefit (the value of cp), rpart( ) doesn't add it.

What happens if you set cp to .00? You get no restrictions on what a split must add. Hence, you wind up with the most complex tree possible. So here's the first part of this quick project: Set cp to .00 and Execute, and then use

```
library(rpart.plot)
prp(crs$rpart, cex=1,varlen=0,branch=0)
```

to draw the tree. Compare it with Figure 7-9. More complex, right? Evaluate this tree against the Testing set, and look at the overall error rate. Compared to the original error rate (6.9 percent), is the extra complexity worth adding?

The second part of this project is to move in the other direction. Set cp to a higher value, like .10. This makes it restrictive to add a split. Click Execute. Then draw the tree. It looks way less complex than with cp = .01, doesn't it? Evaluate against the Testing set. How about that overall error rate?

REMEMBER

On a live tree that grows outdoors in your garden, what do you call the process of cutting branches to make the tree look better? Does *pruning* sound familiar? That's also the name for eliminating splits to make a decision tree less complex (which is what increasing the cp does).

Suggested Project: Titanic

A dataset that's often used to illustrate ML concepts is the information about passengers on the *Titanic*'s disastrous voyage in 1912. The target variable is whether the passenger survived. You can use this data to create a decision tree.

The data resides in an R package called titanic. If it's not already on the Packages tab, click Install. In the Install Packages dialog box, type **titanic** and click the Install button. After the package downloads, find it on the Packages tab and select its check box.

In the titanic package, you'll find titanic_train and titanic_test. Don't be tempted to use one as the training set and the other as the test set for this particular application of Rattle. The titanic_test set doesn't include the Survived variable, so it's not usable for testing a decision tree the way I lay out the process here.

Instead, create the data frame like this:

```
library(titanic)
titanic.df <- titanic_train
```

Then use `Rattle`'s Data tab to read in the dataset. Figure 7-11 shows what the Data tab looks like after a few modifications.

No.	Variable	Data Type	Input	Target	Risk	Ident	Ignore	Weight	Comment
1	PassengerId	Ident	○	○	○	◉	○	○	Unique: 891
2	Survived	Numeric	○	◉	○	○	○	○	Unique: 2
3	Pclass	Numeric	◉	○	○	○	○	○	Unique: 3
4	Name	Ident	○	○	○	◉	○	○	Unique: 891
5	Sex	Categoric	◉	○	○	○	○	○	Unique: 2
6	Age	Numeric	◉	○	○	○	○	○	Unique: 88 Missing: 177
7	SibSp	Numeric	◉	○	○	○	○	○	Unique: 7
8	Parch	Numeric	◉	○	○	○	○	○	Unique: 7
9	Ticket	Categoric	○	○	○	○	◉	○	Unique: 681
10	Fare	Numeric	◉	○	○	○	○	○	Unique: 248
11	Cabin	Categoric	○	○	○	○	◉	○	Unique: 148
12	Embarked	Categoric	◉	○	○	○	○	○	Unique: 4

FIGURE 7-11: The `Rattle` Data tab, after modifying the `titanic.df` dataset.

What are those modifications? First, a rule of thumb: If a variable is categoric and has a lot of unique values (and if it's not already classified as an Ident (identifier)), click its Ignore radio button. Also, when first encountering this dataset, `Rattle` thinks `Embarked` is the target variable. Use the radio buttons to change `Embarked` to `Categoric` and to change `Survived` to `Target`.

Good luck!

IN THIS CHAPTER

» Looking at random forests

» Growing a random forest for irises

» Developing a random forest for glass identification

Chapter 8 Into the Forest, Randomly

In Chapter 7, I help you explore decision trees. Suppose a decision tree is an expert decision-maker: Give a tree a set of data, and it makes decisions about the data. Taking this idea a step further, suppose you have a panel of experts — a group of decision trees — and each one makes a decision about the same data. One could poll the panel to come up with the best decision.

This is the idea behind the *random forest* — a collection of decision trees that you can poll, and the majority vote is the decision.

Growing a Random Forest

So how does all this happen? How do you create a forest out of a dataset? Well, randomly.

Here's what I mean. In Chapter 7, I discuss the creation of a decision tree from a dataset. I use the `rattle` package to partition a data frame into a training set, a validation set, and a test set. The partitioning takes place as a result of random sampling from the rows in the data frame. The default condition is that `rattle` randomly assigns 70 percent of the rows to the training set, 15 percent to the validation set, and 15 percent to the test set.

The random row selection proceeds from a seed value, whose `Rattle` default is 42. This produces the 70 percent of the observations for creating the decision tree. What happens if I change the seed value? The result is a different 70 percent of the sample and (potentially) a different tree. If I change the seed again and again and produce a decision tree each time (and save each tree), I create a forest.

Figure 8-1 illustrates this concept. The trees provide decision rules for the `iris.uci` data frame, which I show you in Chapter 6. To refresh your memory, the data are measurements of the length and width of petals and sepals in 150 irises. They consist of 50 each of the *setosa, versicolor,* and *virginica* species. Given a flower's measurements, a tree uses its decision rules to determine the flower's species. I added `.uci` to the data frame's name to indicate that I downloaded it from the Machine Language Repository of the University of California-Irvine. A little data clean-up was necessary, which is a topic you can find in Chapter 6.

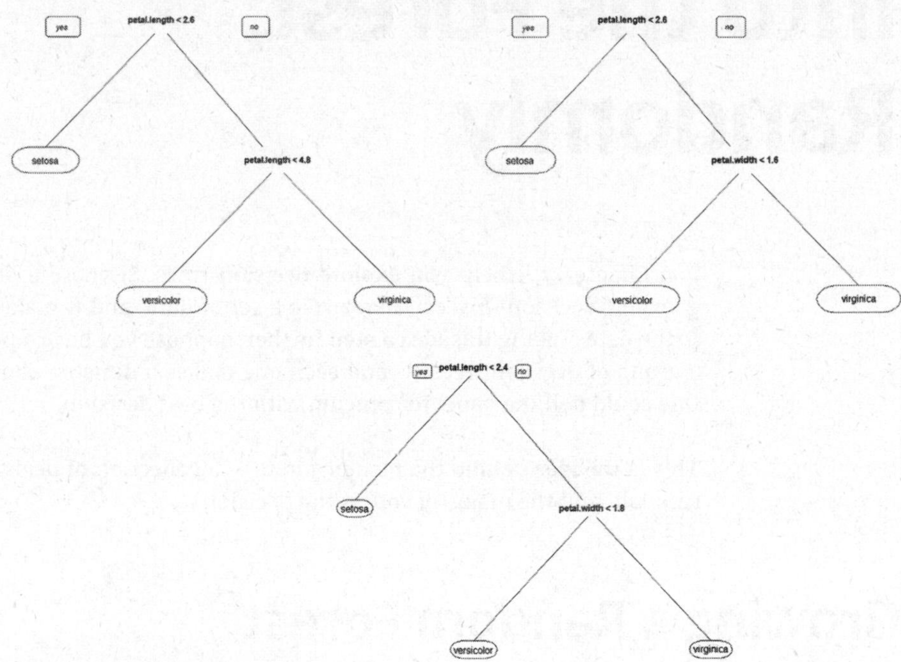

FIGURE 8-1: Three `Rattle`-produced decision trees for the `iris.uci` data frame.

Notice that each tree has its own decision rules, and that the splits aren't all based on the same variables. Instead of having only one tree decide a flower's species, I can have all three of them make the determination. If they don't all reach the same decision, the majority rules.

Now imagine hundreds of these trees, all created from the same data frame. In this setup, though, I randomly sample rows from the 70 percent of the rows designated as the training set, rather than create a new training set each time, as in the preceding example.

And then I add one more dimension of randomness: In addition to random selection of the data frame rows, suppose I add random selection of the variables to consider for each split of each decision tree.

So, here are two things to consider each time I grow a tree in the forest:

- For the data, I randomly select from the rows of the training set.
- For each split, I randomly select from the columns. (How many columns do I randomly select each time? A good rule of thumb is the square root of the number of columns.)

That's a huge forest, with a lot of randomness! A technique like this one is useful when you have a lot of variables and relatively few observations (lots of columns and not so many rows, in other words).

R can grow a random forest for you.

Random Forests in R

R has a package for creating random forests. If you guessed that it's called `randomForest`, you're right. Its function for creating the random forest is called . . . wait for it . . . `randomForest()`.

If this package is already on the Packages tab, select its check box and you're in business. If it isn't on the tab, select the Install tab, and in the Install Packages dialog box, type **randomForest** and click the Install button. When the package finishes downloading, find its check box on the Packages tab and click it.

Building the forest

With the `randomForest` check box selected, here's how to create a 500-tree forest for the `iris.uci` data frame. First, you create a training set consisting of 70 percent of the rows randomly selected from the data frame. For this task, you use the `sample()` function. First, however, you set the *seed* for the randomization, like this:

```
set.seed(810)
```

The seed is the number that starts off the randomization in sample(). You don't have to do this, but if you want your numbers to come out like mine, set the seed to the same number as mine.

TIP

If you want the randomization to take place the same way each time you use sample(), you have to set the seed every time.

Now for the sampling:

```
training.set = sample(nrow(iris.uci),0.7*nrow(iris.uci))
```

The first argument of sample() is the number of rows in the data frame; the second argument is how many of the rows to randomly sample.

TIP

You can use sample() with or without replacement. "Without replacement" is the default condition. This means that once you randomly select an item for the sample, you don't put it back ("replace it") into the set of items you're sampling from. "With replacement" means that you put it back and you can possibly select it again and again for this sample. For this to happen, add replacement = TRUE as an argument.

Then use randomForest():

```
iris.forest <- randomForest(formula =
 species ~ petal.length + petal.width + sepal.length + sepal.width,
             data = iris.uci, ntree = 500, subset=training.set,
             importance = TRUE)
```

In this straightforward example, the first argument is a formula indicating that species depends on the other four variables, the second is the data frame, and the third is the number of trees to create. The next-to-last one is the subset of the data for creating each tree. And the last argument, importance, tells the function that you want to examine the importance of each variable in creating the forest. (I talk about importance a bit more in the upcoming section "A closer look.")

TIP

As is the case with many R functions, this is only the bare minimum. Lots of other arguments are available for randomForest().

Evaluating the forest

Let's take a look at how well the forest does its job. The line

```
print(iris.forest)
```

produces this result:

```
Call:
 randomForest(formula = species ~ petal.length + petal.width +       sepal.length +
   sepal.width, data = iris.uci, ntree = 500,       importance = TRUE, subset =
   training.set)
Type of random forest: classification
                     Number of trees: 500
No. of variables tried at each split: 2

        OOB estimate of  error rate: 6.67%
Confusion matrix:
           setosa versicolor virginica class.error
setosa         36          0         0  0.00000000
versicolor      0         32         2  0.05882353
virginica       0          5        30  0.14285714
```

The first few lines, of course, echo the function call and then present descriptive information about the tree. Notice that the default number of variables tried at each split is the square root of the number of independent variables. In this case, that happens to be 2. You can vary this by setting a value for a `randomForest()` argument called `mtry` (for example, `mtry = 3`).

Finally, the confusion matrix (see Chapter 7) shows the actual species of each iris (in the rows) and the species as identified by the forest (in the columns). The numbers of correct identifications are in the main diagonal, and errors are in the off-diagonal cells. The forest mistakenly identified 2 *versicolor* as *virginica* and 5 *virginica* as *versicolor*. The error rate is 6.67 percent. This is the off-diagonal total (5 + 2 = 7) divided by the total number of observations (36 + 32 + 30 + 5 + 2 = 105, and the 105 is 70 percent of 150). So the forest is accurate 93.33 percent of the time — which is pretty good!

Um, what does the `OOB` represent? OOB stands for *o*ut *o*f *b*ag. In the random forest world, a *bag* is the part of the training set that went into creating the decision tree.

The OOB (out of bag) estimate, then, is based on testing the forest on data not included in the bag.

A closer look

The product of `randomForest()` is an object, and it has a set of attributes. Here are the attribute names:

```
> names(iris.forest)
 [1] "call"  "type" "predicted" "err.rate" "confusion" "votes"
 [7] "oob.times"  "classes" "importance"  "importanceSD" "localImportance"
   "proximity"
[13] "ntree"  "mtry" "forest" "y" "test"  "inbag"
[19] "terms"
```

Some, like `ntree`, are short and sweet and identify inputs to `randomForest()`. Others provide a huge amount of information: `err.rate`, for example, shows the error rates for every tree in the forest. Still others, for this example, are `NULL`.

It's instructive to examine `importance`:

```
> round(iris.forest$importance,2)
             setosa versicolor virginica MeanDecreaseAccuracy MeanDecreaseGini
petal.length   0.31       0.29      0.28                 0.29            30.31
petal.width    0.34       0.30      0.27                 0.30            30.91
sepal.length   0.03       0.01      0.04                 0.03             6.17
sepal.width    0.01       0.00      0.01                 0.01             1.83
```

I rounded to two decimal places so that this example could all fit nicely on the printed page. The first three columns show the relative importance of each variable for identifying each species. Without going into exactly how this is calculated, *relative importance* means how much each variable contributes to accuracy for identifying a species. Consistent with the overall impression of the iris data (refer to Chapter 6), the two petal variables add the most.

The measure in the fourth column is based on rearranging the values of a variable and seeing how the rearrangement affects performance. If the variable is not important, rearranging its values does not decrease the forest's accuracy. If it is important, the accuracy does decrease — hence the name, `MeanDecreaseAccuracy`. Again, the two petal variables are the most important.

The fifth column looks at importance in a different way: If you don't use the forest, what are the chances that you misclassify an iris if you just select a species for it at random? That's called the *gini* index. The numbers in the fifth column represent the reduction in the gini (that is, in the misclassification) by using the row variable in a split; `randomForest()` measures this for each variable over all the trees in the forest, resulting in the numbers in the fifth column. Once again, the petal variables are the most important: Using them in splits (as variables in a tree, in other words) provides the largest decreases in misclassification.

REMEMBER

You get this entire set of importance statistics only if you set `importance=TRUE` when you use `randomForest()`.

Plotting error

With random forests, one useful plot is to show how the error rates change as the forest encompasses progressively more trees. Sometimes, this plot can give you an idea of the optimal number of trees.

First, I used `plot()`:

```
plot(iris.forest, col = "black")
```

Had I not added `col = black` to `plot()`, the default colors would have been too light and too difficult to distinguish from one another on this black-and-white page.

Then I added `legend()`:

```
legend("topright", legend=c(levels(iris.uci$species),"OOB"),
       lty = c("dashed","dotted","dotdash","solid"),
       cex=.8,bty = "n")
```

To differentiate among the levels of `species`, I maintained the `plot()` default linetypes (`lty`) and included them as part of the legend. I used the output of `print(iris.tree)` as a guide to match `lty` with `species` (and with `OOB`).

The last two arguments deal with the legend's overall appearance. `cex = .8` contracts the text size and with it the entire legend so that the legend doesn't obstruct the top line in the plot. `bty = "n"` removes the border from the legend, which also contributes to the ease of seeing the top line.

The result is shown in Figure 8-2.

With fewer than 100 trees, the plot looks something like a forkful of angel hair pasta. To turn the magnifying glass on the graph between 1 and 100 trees, I added the `xlim` argument to `plot()`:

```
plot(iris.forest, col = "black",xlim = c(1,100))
```

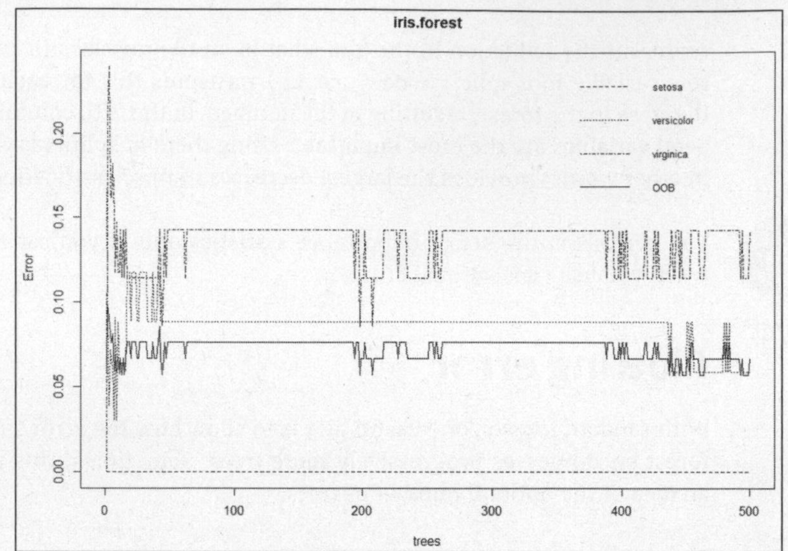

FIGURE 8-2: `iris.forest` error rates as a function of the number of trees in the forest.

And the result is shown in Figure 8-3.

TIP

To examine the data behind these plots, take a look at the 500 rows of `iris.forest$err.rate`.

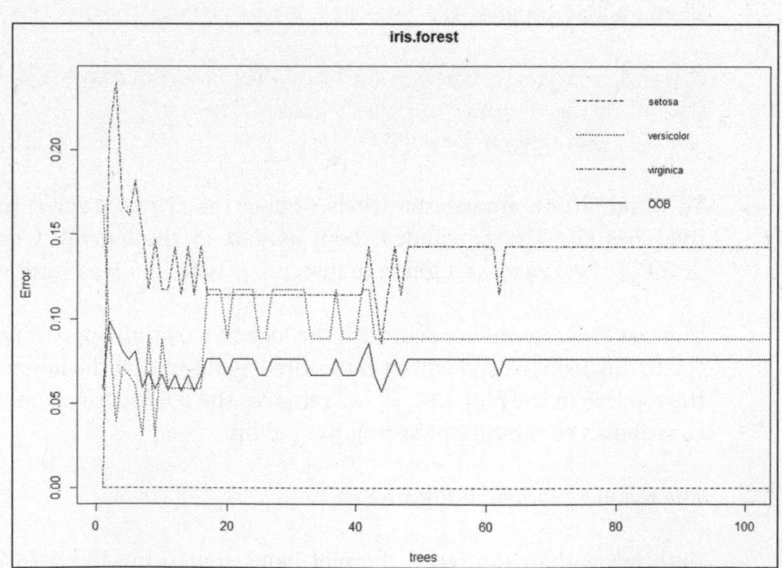

FIGURE 8-3: `iris.forest` error rates for 1 to 100 trees.

Plotting importance

Another useful plot visualizes the `MeanDecreaseAccuracy` and `MeanDecreaseGini` of the variables. A `ggplot2`-based `Rattle` function called `ggvarImp()` does this for you:

```
library(ggplot2)
library(rattle)
ggVarImp(iris.forest)
```

The result of this function is the good-looking graph shown in Figure 8-4, and it reflects the importance-related numbers I discuss in the earlier section "A closer look."

TIP

In the projects in this chapter and in Chapter 7, the target is a categorical variable. It's also possible for the target to be a numeric variable, (in which case regression is involved), but I don't get into that topic in this book.

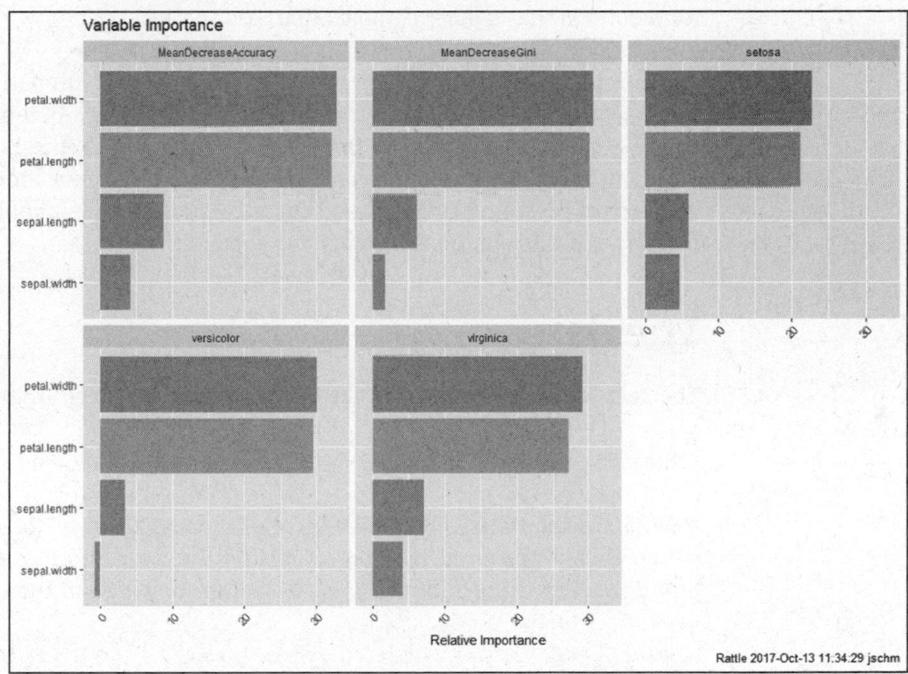

FIGURE 8-4: The plot of importance of the variables in `iris.forest`.

LOOKING AT THE RULES

If you want to look at the decision rules for individual trees, a function called `printRandomForests()` is the one for you. This function lives in the `rattle` package. With `rattle` downloaded, these two lines:

```
library(rattle)
printRandomForests(iris.forest, models=c(1,500))
```

print the rules that the first tree and the 500th tree use to decide an iris's species. I don't print the rules here because each tree uses a lot of them. Give it a try!

Project: Identifying Glass

In this section, I show you how to use the `rattle` package to grow a random forest for a domain that's more complex than iris species.

In criminological investigations, it's often important to properly identify glass at crime scenes so that it can serve as evidence. So this random forest identifies where a glass fragment came from (building window, vehicle window, or headlamp, for example), based on a physical property (refractive index — how much it bends light passing through it) and chemical properties (amount of sodium, magnesium, and aluminum it contains, for example).

The data

The data are in a dataset from the UCI ML Repository. You'll find the data set at

```
https://archive.ics.uci.edu/ml/datasets/glass+identification
```

Navigate to the Data Folder and click `glass.data`, a text file of comma-separated variables. My preferred method of putting the data into R is to press Ctrl+A to highlight everything and then press Ctrl+C to copy it all to the clipboard. Then

```
glass.uci <- read.csv("clipboard",header = FALSE)
```

creates a data frame, and

```
colnames(glass.uci)<-c("ID","RI","Na","Mg","Al","Si","K","Ca","Ba","Fe","Type")
```

assigns the names to the columns. The first of these names, ID, is an identifier for the piece of glass, and the second is the glass fragment's refractive index. The last one, Type, is the target variable. All the ones in between are the chemical elements that constitute the glass.

I have one more thing to do before I get down to business. At the moment, the levels of Type (the target variable) are numbers. Instead, I want to give them informative names. To do this, I use mapvalues(), which lives in the plyr library:

```
library(plyr)
glass.uci$Type <- mapvalues(glass.uci$Type,
          from = c(1,2,3,5,6,7),
                              to = c("bldg_windows_float","bldg_windows_non_float",
                                   "vehicle_windows_float","containers","table
   ware","headlamps"))
```

The terms float and non_float refer to the process for making a window. The "float" process produces near-optical quality glass; "non-float" glass is lower quality.

Notice that the from vector does not include 4. This is because the corresponding type (vehicle_windows_non_float) is not in the dataset.

TIP

The names for the columns and for the Type levels are at the URL for this dataset.

Getting the data into Rattle

Rattle is a graphical user interface (GUI) to many R machine learning functions. With the rattle package downloaded, entering

```
library(rattle)
rattle()
```

opens the Rattle Data tab. First, I load the glass.uci data frame into Rattle and click the R Dataset radio button, which opens the Data Name box. Then I click the down arrow next to the Data Name box and select glass.uci from the drop-down menu. Next, I click the Execute icon in the upper left corner. Figure 8-5 shows the appearance of the Data tab after I complete these steps.

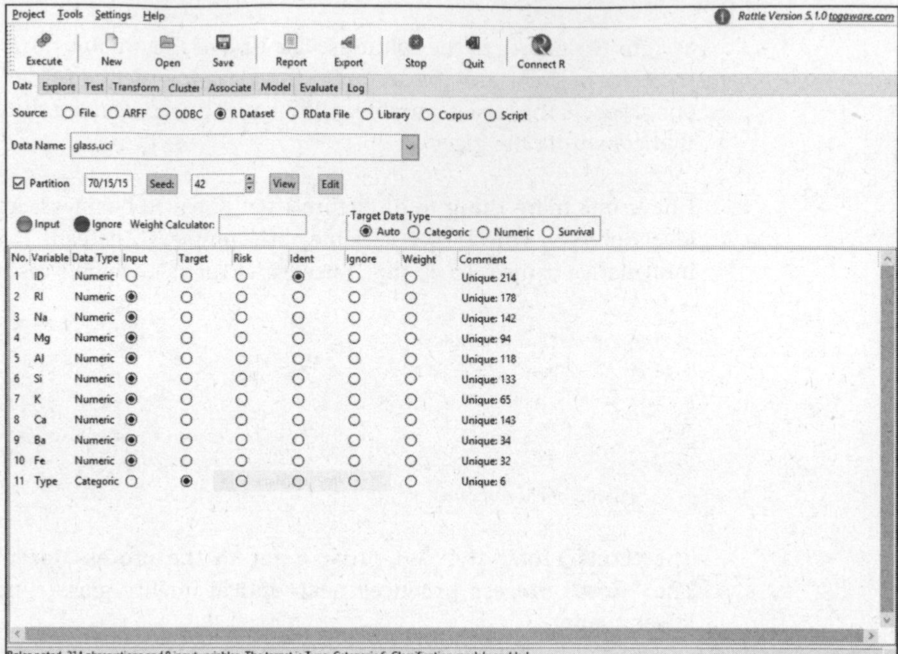

FIGURE 8-5: The `rattle` Data tab after selecting `glass.uci` and clicking Execute.

Exploring the data

Next, a little data exploration. To examine the distribution of `Type`, I click the Explore tab and clear the Group By box (whose default selection is `Type`). Then I click the Bar Plot check box next to Type, toward the bottom of the window. Figure 8-6 shows how the Explore tab looks after I do this.

Clicking Execute produces the bar plot shown in Figure 8-7. As you can see, one of the `Type`-names (`bldg_windows_float`) got crowded out of the x-axis. The figure shows that the two building window types are the most frequent in the data frame.

The summary indicates that the random forest has an OOB error rate of 25.5 percent. It identifies headlamps most accurately and does a so-so job on the two types of building windows. The vehicle windows? Not so much. So it would be a good idea to exercise some caution if you use this random forest for glass identification, because its overall accuracy is 74.5 percent. If you select the Evaluate tab and evaluate against the Validation set and then against the Test set, you'll find similar results.

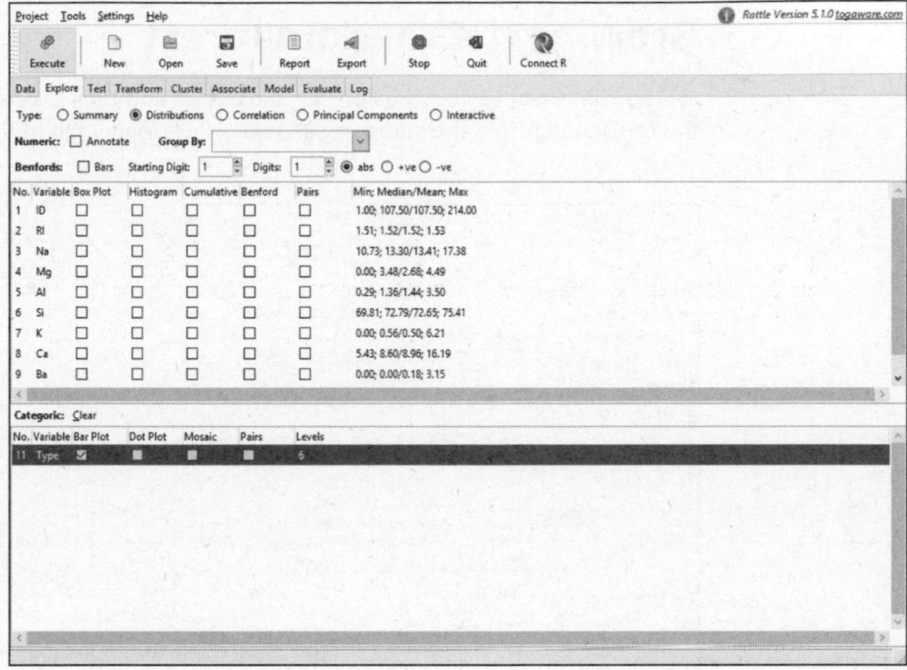

FIGURE 8-6: The `Rattle` Explore tab, after clearing the Group By box and selecting the Bar Plot check box for Type.

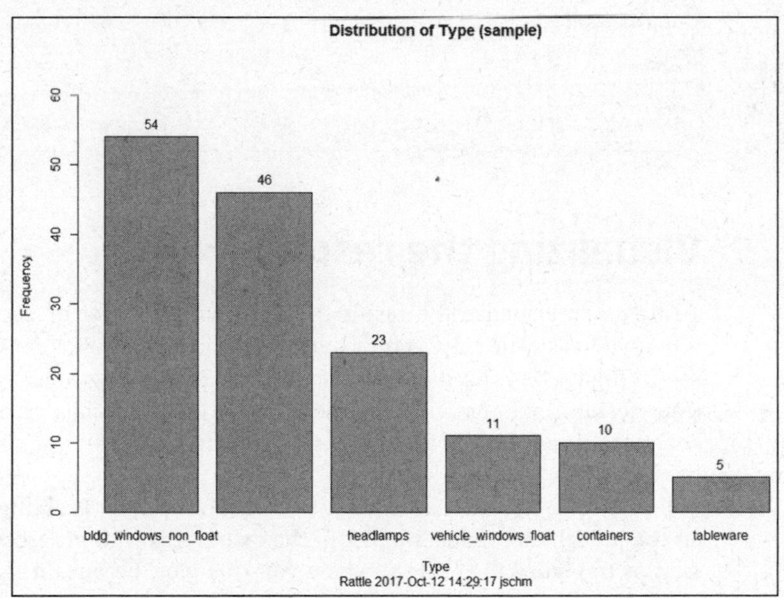

FIGURE 8-7: The distribution of Type in the `glass.uci` data frame.

Growing the random forest

On the Model tab, I select the Forest radio button and click Execute. `Rattle` creates the forest and prints the summary shown on the Model tab in Figure 8-8.

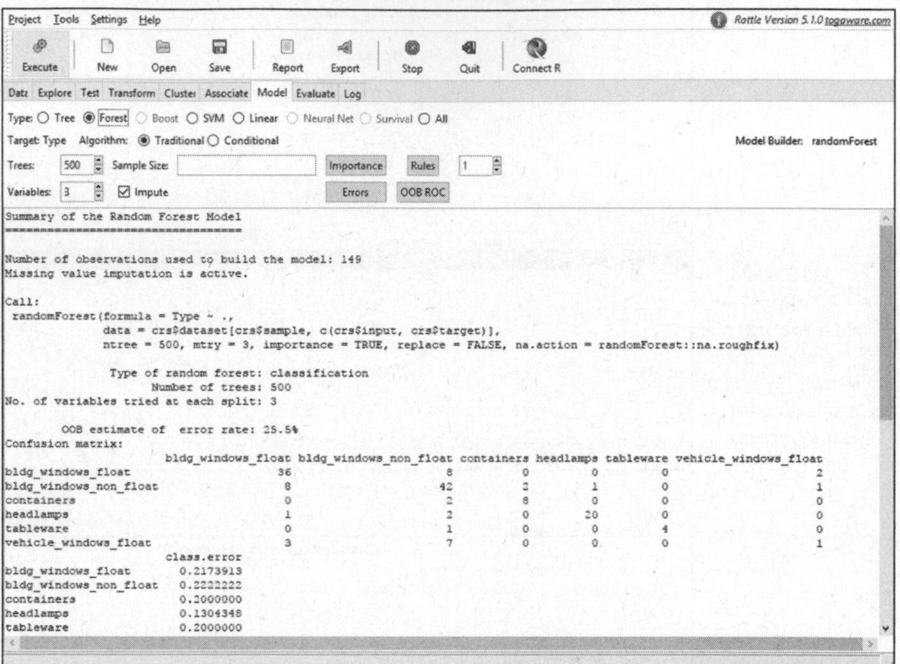

FIGURE 8-8: Summary of the random forest for `glass.uci`.

Visualizing the results

To help you visualize the results, I begin with the plot of variable importance. When you click the Importance button on the Model tab, `Rattle` plots what you see in Figure 8-9. As the figure shows, for identifying most types of glass, Mg (Magnesium) content is the most important variable, as is the case for `MeanDecreaseAccuracy` and for `MeanDecreaseGini`.

The plot of error rates isn't nearly as easy on the eyes. Pressing the Error button on the Model tab produces a plot of the error rates with progressively more trees, similar to Figure 8-2. I don't show you this plot, because it's a mishmash. The legend won't help you decipher it, because the legend's linetype colors don't appear to match up with the legend's text colors.

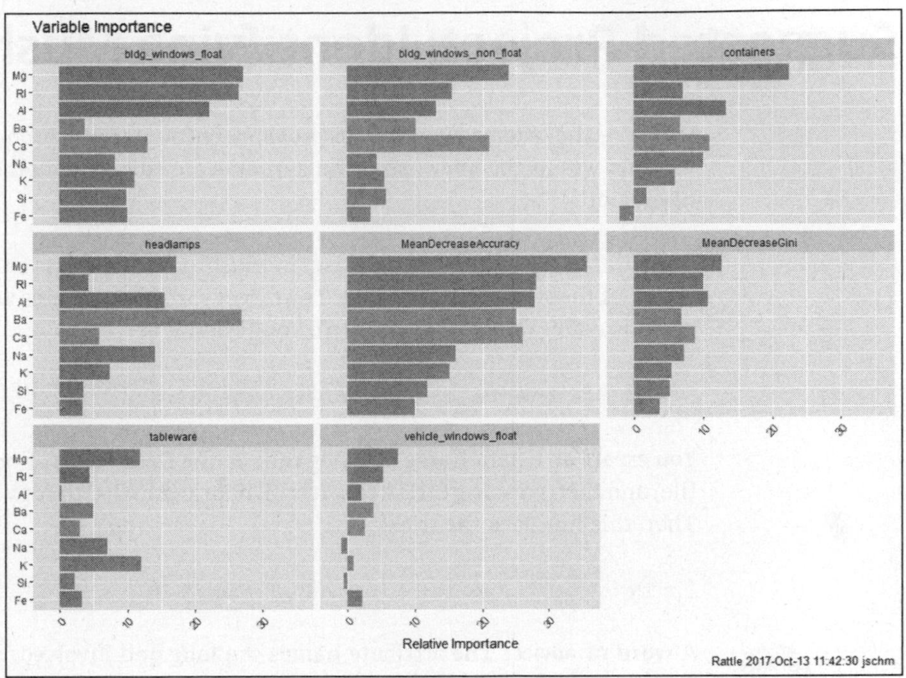

FIGURE 8-9: The plot of variable importance for `glass.forest`.

This is one of those extremely rare occasions when looking at the data might be more helpful than looking at a graph. Let's say I want to examine the error rates for the OOB and for the first three variables in the 30th through 35th trees. (Why not all the variables? Because I want the output to fit neatly on this page!)

The `Rattle` Log tells you that the random forest is in an object called `crs$rf`. As I mention earlier in this chapter, the error rates for a random forest are in an attribute called `err.rate`. For all error rates for all trees, I use `crs$rf$err.rate`. To round them to two decimal places, it's `round(crs$rf$err.rate, 2)`. For the 30th to 35th trees, the function call becomes `round(crs$rs$err.rate[30:35,],2)`. And, to limit the output to just the OOB and the first three variables, I use:

```
> round(crs$rf$err.rate[30:35,1:4],2)
      OOB bldg_windows_float bldg_windows_non_float containers
[1,] 0.28               0.22                   0.28        0.2
[2,] 0.29               0.24                   0.26        0.2
[3,] 0.27               0.24                   0.24        0.2
[4,] 0.28               0.24                   0.22        0.2
[5,] 0.29               0.26                   0.26        0.2
[6,] 0.30               0.26                   0.28        0.2
```

Suggested Project: Identifying Mushrooms

If you're the outdoorsy type, you probably encounter mushrooms growing in the wild. As you might know, some mushrooms are edible, and others are most definitely not(!)

The UCI ML repository has a dataset of mushrooms with lots and lots of instances (8,124 of them) and 22 attributes. The target variable indicates whether the mushroom is edible (e) or poisonous (p). You'll find it at

```
https://archive.ics.uci.edu/ml/datasets/mushroom
```

You create an R data frame by navigating to the Data Folder, finding the `.csv` data file, and then pressing Ctrl+A to select all data and Ctrl+C to copy it to the clipboard. Then this line does the trick:

```
mushroom.uci <- read.csv("clipboard", header=FALSE)
```

TIP

A word of advice: The attribute names are long and involved, so for this project *only,* don't bother naming the columns unless you really and truly want to. Instead, use the default V1, V2, and so on that R provides. Also, and this is important, after you put the data into `Rattle`, you'll see that `Rattle` makes a guess about the target variable. Its guess, V23, is wrong. The real target variable is V1. So click the appropriate radio buttons to make the changes.

Finally, unlike the datasets I've used so far, this one has missing values. They're all in V12 (2,480 of them), denoted by a question mark. To deal with this, select the `Rattle` Transform tab and click the radio button for Impute and the radio button for Zero/Missing. Click V12 and then Execute. This substitutes *Missing* for the question mark. (***Spoiler alert:*** With this data frame, it doesn't make much difference whether you do this or not.)

When you create the forest, you should have a confusion matrix with just two rows and two columns. You'll be pleasantly surprised by the OOB error rate!

IN THIS CHAPTER

» Working with a support vector machine (SVM)

» Using SVMs in R

» An SVM for congressional voting

Chapter 9

Support Your Local Vector

Classification is an important part of machine learning (ML). One important classifying technique is the *support vector machine* (SVM). So, what exactly is an SVM and how does it work?

Some Data to Work With

To introduce the SVM, I use the `iris` data set, which I first discuss in Chapter 6. It provides four measurements on each of 150 irises, with 50 flowers in each of three species.

This data set is useful for examples whose objective is to use the measurements (petal width and length, sepal width and length) as a means of identifying a flower's species. Though one species *(setosa)* is distinct from the other two (*versicolor* and *virginica*), those other two aren't completely distinct from one another.

TIP

In preceding chapters, I tell you how to work with `iris.uci`, a data set downloaded from the UCI ML repository and subsequently cleaned up. In this chapter, I describe how to work with the `iris` data set that comes with R.

Using a subset

To make things a bit easier to follow, I start with a subset of the `iris` data set. I call it `set.vers` because it consists of only the *setosa* and *versicolor* species — in other words, everything except *virginica:*

```
set.vers <-subset(iris, Species != "virginica")
```

Figure 9-1 shows a scatterplot of `set.vers` with `Petal.Length` on the *x*-axis and `Petal.Width` on the *y*-axis. Black circles represent *setosa,* and white circles represent *versicolor.* If you want to know how to use `ggplot` to create a graph like this one, see the following sidebar, "Plotting (two-thirds of) the irises."

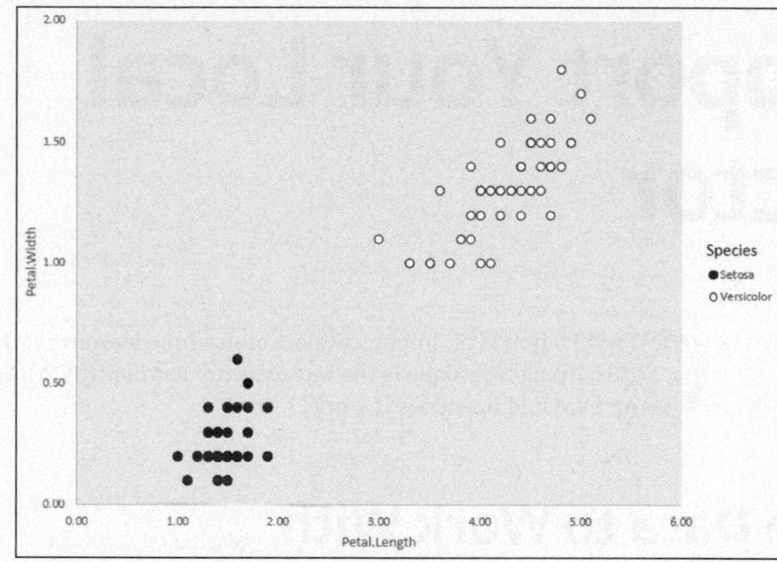

FIGURE 9-1: `Petal.Width` versus `Petal.Length` in the `set.vers` data frame.

Defining a boundary

The two species shown in Figure 9-1 occupy quite different areas in the plot, don't they? Apparently, it's pretty easy to tell them apart. In fact, you could add a boundary line between the two areas, as shown in Figure 9-2, that nicely divides the plot. Any flower to the right and above the line is a *versicolor,* and any flower to the left and below the line is a *setosa.* The line is called a *separation boundary.*

When you can draw a line like this one for the separation boundary, the data are said to be *linearly separable.*

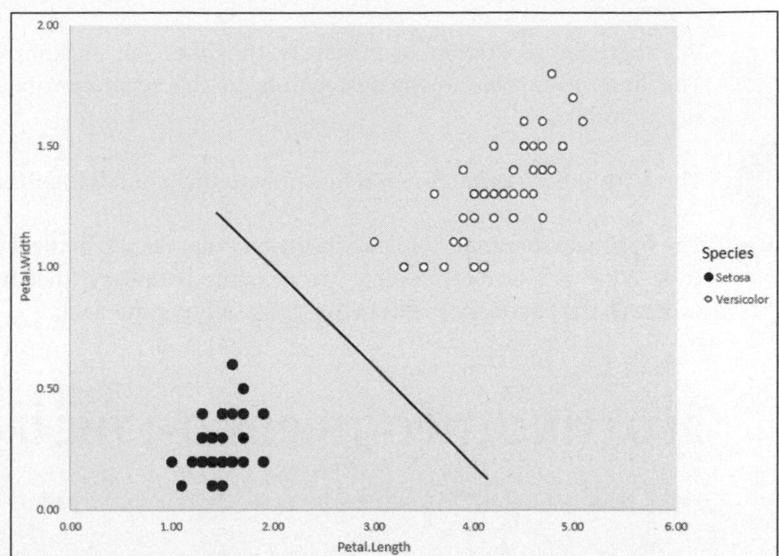

FIGURE 9-2: `Petal.Width` versus `Petal.Length` with a separation boundary.

Understanding support vectors

Having an infinite number of separation boundaries is possible. Truthfully, I eyeballed this one. But Figure 9-3 shows what the separation boundary is supposed to do. The two dotted lines in the figure represent the *margin*, which is the distance between the separation boundary and its nearest points.

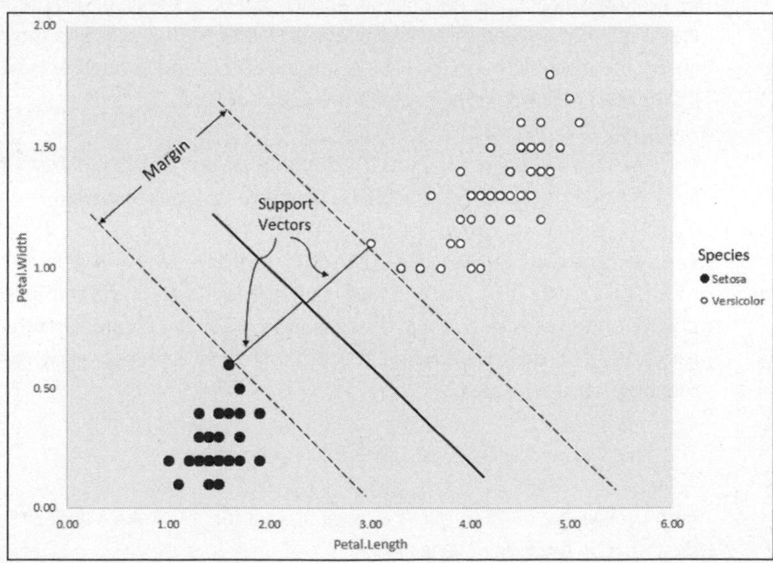

FIGURE 9-3: Margin and support vectors for the separation boundary.

The optimal separation boundary is the one that maximizes that distance. The lines from the two nearest points to the separation boundary are called *support vectors*.

REMEMBER

The term *support vectors* often refers only to the points rather than the lines.

The optimal separation boundary is the one that results in the fewest support vectors. Why? If fewer data points are near the boundary (meaning fewer support vectors), the boundary works better at classifying the data.

PLOTTING (TWO-THIRDS OF) THE IRISES

Here's how to use ggplot to create a graph like the one shown earlier, in Figure 9-1:

```
library(ggplot2)
ggplot(set.vers, aes(x=Petal.Length,y=Petal.Width,color=Species)) +
  geom_point(size=4) +
  scale_color_manual(values = c("black","white"))+
  geom_point(shape=1,size=4,color="black")+
  theme(panel.grid.major = element_blank(), panel.grid.minor =
   element_blank())
```

Let's look at these lines one by one. The first line, of course, supplies the ggplot2 package. The second, the ggplot() function, lays the foundation for the whole thing. Its first argument is the data frame, and its second is the aesthetic mapping of the data elements to the graphical elements: the variables for the axes and the variable for the color. The next line, geom_point(), specifies the graphical elements to add to the plot (along with their size).

The next, scale_color_manual(), changes the point fill-colors from the default colors (which wouldn't be distinguishable on this page) to black and white.

The next line is yet another geom_point() function. Why another one? That's a little trick. The second geom_point() function overlays a graphical character with a black border on top of each one that the first geom_point() created. In other words, this trick adds a border to each circle in the plot. It's a bit unnecessary when the fill is black, too, but you get the idea.

The final line removes the grid lines from the plot.

Think you've got it? Then here's a quick project for you: Take a shot at Figure 9-4, described in the following section.

In the simple 2-variable case I present here, the separation boundary is a straight line. With more variables, it's a *hyperplane*.

Whether it's a line or a hyperplane, how do you find this all-important separation boundary, which separates the data into classes? Support vectors get the job done. The idea is to find points, like the two shown earlier, in Figure 9-3, that result in support vectors and then use the support vectors to define the separation boundary.

So you have to have something that, in effect, searches for support vectors. That something is the support vector machine. Before I discuss SVMs, I have to tell you a little more about separability, as described in the following section.

Separability: It's Usually Nonlinear

How many data sets are perfectly linearly separable, like `set.vers`? Not many. In fact, here's `vers.virg`, the two-thirds of the irises that aren't *setosa*:

```
vers.virg <- subset(iris, Species !="setosa")
```

Figure 9-4 shows the plot of `Petal.Width` versus `Petal.Length` for this data frame. You can clearly see the slight overlap between species, and the resulting nonlinear separability.

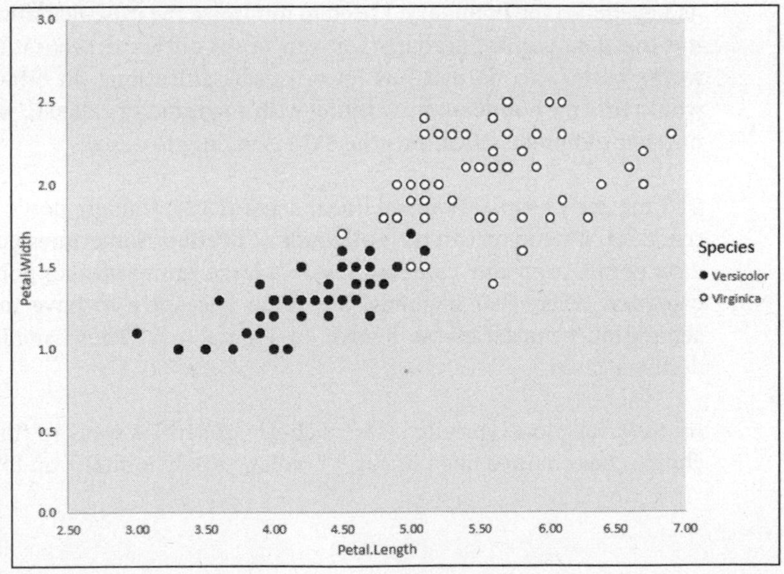

FIGURE 9-4: `Petal.Width` versus `Petal.Length` in the `vers.virg` data frame, showing nonlinear separability.

How can a classifier deal with overlap? One way is to permit some misclassification — some data points on the wrong side of the separation boundary.

Figure 9-5 shows what I'm talking about. I've eyeballed a separation boundary with the *versicolor* on the left and (most) *virginica* on the right. The figure shows five *virginica* to the left of the boundary. This is called *soft margin classification.*

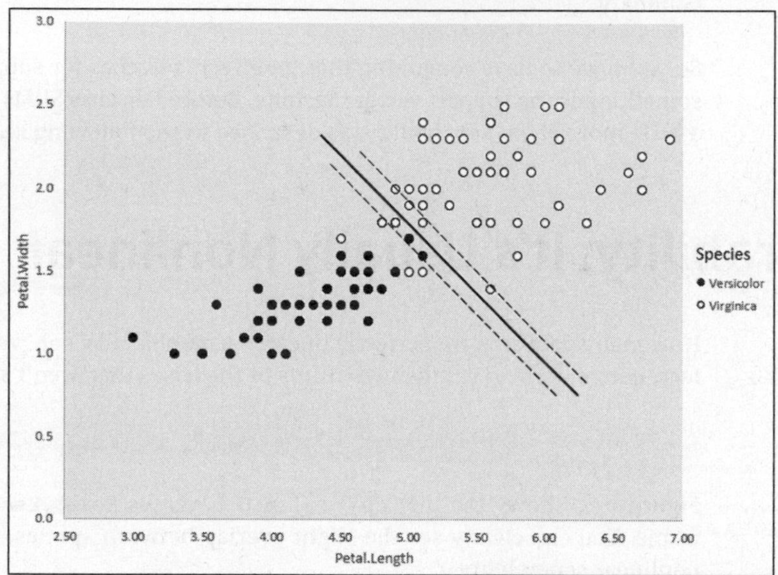

FIGURE 9-5: Soft margin classification in the `vers.virg` data frame.

As I eyeballed the boundary, I tried to minimize the miscalculations. As you examine the data points, perhaps you can see a different separation boundary that works better — one that has fewer misclassifications, in other words. An SVM would find the boundary by working with a parameter called C, which specifies the number of misclassifications the SVM is willing to allow.

Soft margin classification and linear separability, though, don't always work with real data, where you can have all kinds of overlap. Sometimes you find clusters of data points from one category inside a large group of data points from another category. When that happens, it's often necessary to have multiple nonlinear separation boundaries, as shown in Figure 9-6. Those nonlinear boundaries define a *kernel.*

An SVM function typically offers a choice of several ways to find a kernel. These choices have names like "linear," "radial," "polynomial," and "sigmoid".

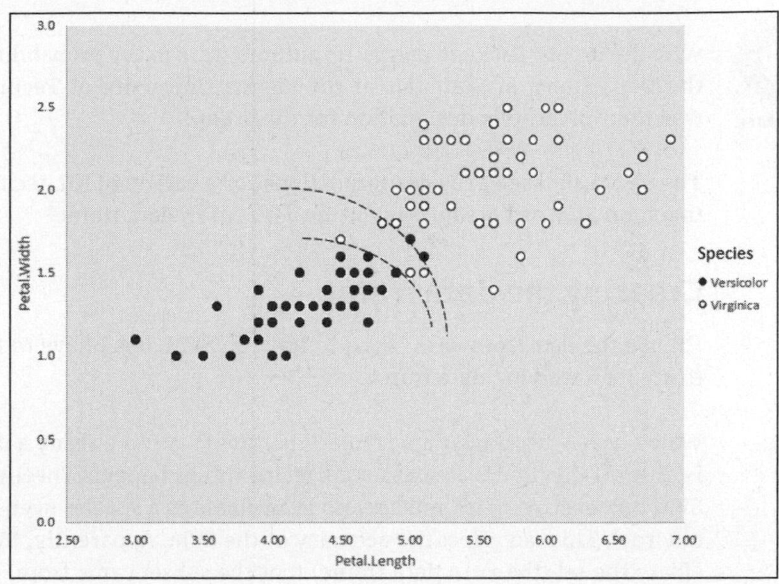

FIGURE 9-6: A kernel in the `vers.virg` data frame.

The underlying mathematics is pretty complicated, but here's an intuitive way to think about kernels: Imagine Figure 9-4 as a page torn from this book and lying flat on the table. Suppose that you could separate the data points by moving them in a third dimension above and below the page — say, the *versicolor* above and the *virginica* below. Then it would be easy to find a separation boundary, wouldn't it? Think of *kerneling* as the process of moving the data into the third dimension. (How far to move each point in the third dimension? That's where the complicated mathematics comes in.) And the separation boundary would then be a plane, not a line.

Support Vector Machines in R

Two prominent R packages deal with SVM. One is called e1071, and the other is `kernlab`. I show you how to work with both of them in this section.

Working with e1071

To get going with the `e1071` package, click the Install button on the Packages tab in RStudio. In the Install Packages dialog box, type **e1071** and click Install. After the package downloads, click its check box on the Packages tab.

REMEMBER

Why the cryptic package name? Its authors were in the probability theory group in the Department of Statistics at the Vienna University of Technology, and e1071 was the University's designation for the group.

The `e1071` package provides R functions for a variety of ML techniques, but I only touch on SVM as I create one for the `vers.virg` data frame.

Creating the data frame

I'll use the data from `vers.virg` to train an SVM, but I have to take an extra step to create a working data frame.

Wait a sec. A "working data frame?" Isn't `vers.virg` already a data frame? Yes, it is. But if I don't take an extra step, weird things happen. Specifically, if I train an SVM on `vers.virg`, it thinks *setosa* is available as a species even though it's not in any row. This can affect the accuracy of the SVM. Apparently, SVM software considers the set (the `iris` data frame) that the subset came from.

So the plan here is to create a `.csv` (comma-separated variable) text file and then read that text file back into R and convert it to a data frame. That way, the new data frame has exactly the same data as `vers.virg`, but it's not the product of `subset()`.

The first step is

```
write.csv(vers.virg,"vvcsv")
```

The second argument is the name of the newly created `.csv` file.

Next, you navigate to the file, open it, and then press Ctrl+A to highlight everything in it. Then you press Ctrl+C to copy it all to the clipboard. This code reads it back into a new data frame called `vvx`:

```
vvx <-read.csv("clipboard",header=TRUE,sep=",")
```

Here are the first six rows:

```
   X Sepal.Length Sepal.Width Petal.Length Petal.Width      Species
1 51          7.0         3.2          4.7         1.4 versicolor
2 52          6.4         3.2          4.5         1.5 versicolor
3 53          6.9         3.1          4.9         1.5 versicolor
4 54          5.5         2.3          4.0         1.3 versicolor
5 55          6.5         2.8          4.6         1.5 versicolor
6 56          5.7         2.8          4.5         1.3 versicolor
```

Separating into training and test sets

The first thing to do when training an SVM is to split the data frame into a training set and a test set. A neat little function called `sample.split()` takes care of this, but you first have to install its package, which is called `catools`. Once it's downloaded and installed, here's how to split the data:

```
set.seed(810)
svm_sample = sample.split(vvx$Species,SplitRatio = .75)
```

If you'd like to reproduce my results, set the seed to the same number I did. I set `sample.split()` so that 75 percent of the observations in `vvx` are in `svm_sample`, and 25 percent are not. So the training set is

```
training.set = subset(vvx,svm_sample == TRUE)
```

and the test set is

```
test.set = subset(vvx,svm_sample == FALSE)
```

Training the SVM

Now I show you how to use `svm()` to train the SVM on the training set:

```
svm_model <- svm(Species ~ Petal.Width + Petal.Length, data=training.set,
              method="C-classification", kernel="linear")
```

The first argument shows that `Species` depends on `Petal.Width` and `Petal.Length`. I did this to stay consistent with Figures 9-1 through 9-6. The next argument specifies the data to use.

The third argument, `method`, says that this is a classification. The final argument specifies the type of `kernel`. I mention earlier in this chapter that several types are possible. The one I use here is the simplest.

After running this code, you examine the SVM:

```
> svm_model

Call:
svm(formula = Species ~ Petal.Width + Petal.Length, data = training.set, method =
   "C-classification",
    kernel = "linear")
```

```
Parameters:
   SVM-Type:  C-classification
 SVM-Kernel:  linear
       cost:  1
      gamma:  0.5

Number of Support Vectors:  16
```

The important item is the last line, which tells you that the SVM found 16 support vectors in its quest to find a boundary that classifies each iris as *versicolor* or *virginica.*

Plotting the SVM

At this point, it's a good idea to visualize the SVM. You can use `plot()` to do that:

```
plot(svm_model, data = training.set[, c(4, 5, 6)]
                formula= Petal.Width ~ Petal.Length)
```

The first argument is the SVM, and the second supplies the data for the plot: the last three columns of the training set. The last argument, `formula`, specifies the variables to include in the plot. This formula puts `Petal.Width` on the *y*-axis and puts `Petal.Length` on the *x*-axis.

The code produces a nice-looking plot, as you can see when you run it. To make everything look nicer on this page, though, I added a couple of touches, and the result is shown in Figure 9-7. (If you're interested, see the following sidebar, "The extra touches for the SVM plot.")

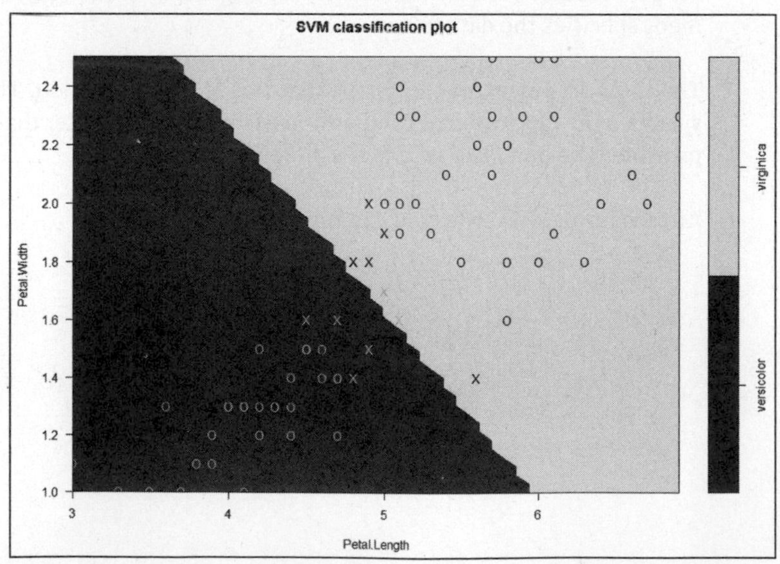

FIGURE 9-7: Plotting the SVM for the vvx training set, e1071 version.

THE EXTRA TOUCHES FOR THE SVM PLOT

Here's the code that produced what you see in Figure 9-7:

```
plot(svm_model, data = training.set[, c(4, 5,6)],     formula=Petal.
    Width~Petal.Length,
           dataSymbol = "O", svSymbol = "X",
          symbolPalette = palette(c("gray95","gray0")), color.palette = gray.
    colors)
```

The `dataSymbol` argument specifies an uppercase *O* as the character for the data points, and the `svSymbol` argument specifies an uppercase *X* as the character for the support vectors. (The defaults are these letters in lowercase.) The `symbolPalette` argument renders the colors for the symbols, and `color.palette` renders the colors for the category areas.

In the figure, *O* represents a data point, and *X* represents a support vector. Points in the darker gray area represent irises classified as *versicolor*, and points in the lighter gray area are irises classified as *virginica*.

The nonlinear separation boundary, as you can see, is a jagged edge. Black points (*virginica*) are predominantly in the lighter area, and gray points (*versicolor*) are predominantly in the darker area. *Predominantly*, of course, doesn't mean "always." Some of the support vector points are misclassified — a few gray *X*s are in the lighter area, and a few black *X*s are in the darker area.

Testing the SVM

How does this SVM perform? A function called `predict()` provides a vector of predicted classifications based on the SVM. First, use `predict()` to test its classifications of the flowers in the training set:

```
pred.training <-predict(svm_model,training.set)
```

The overall average performance is the mean of the vector of predictions:

```
> mean(pred.training==training.set$Species)
[1] 0.9473684
```

Notice that you have to specify `Species` in the `mean()` function.

How about on the flowers in the test set?

```
> pred.test <-predict(svm_model,test.set)
> mean(pred.test==test.set$Species)
[1] 0.9583333
```

It's highly accurate on both sets.

Quick suggested project 1: Using all the variables

In the earlier section "Training the SVM," the formula I use in the `svm()` function is

```
Species ~ Petal.Width + Petal.Length
```

What happens if you include `Sepal.Width` and `Sepal.Length`? The formula then would be

```
Species ~ .
```

The period, as I point out in Chapter 7, means "include all the variables."

How many support vectors result? What's the effect on performance?

Quick suggested project 2: Working with kernels

In the earlier section "Separability: It's Usually Nonlinear," I talk about kernels and try to give you an intuitive understanding of what they're about. To get a little more of a feel for kernels, train the SVM with the Polygon, Radial, and Sigmoid options, test each SVM, and then plot the results for each one.

Quick suggested project 3: Classifying all the irises

To simplify the discussion of SVMs, I limited the examples to two classes by taking subsets of the `iris` data frame. SVMs, however, are not limited to two classes.

Instead of `vers.virg`, use the entire `iris` data frame. Remember to split `iris` into a training set and a test set and then train the SVM on the training set. How many support vectors result? How does the SVM perform on the test set?

Working with kernlab

On the Packages tab, click the Install button. In the Install Packages dialog box, type **kernlab** and click Install. When the package has downloaded, click its check box on the Packages tab.

The kernlab SVM function is called ksvm(). I show you how to use it here on the training set and then on the test set I already created. Here's the code to train an SVM:

```
kern_svm <-ksvm(Species ~ Petal.Width + Petal.Length, training.set,
   kernel="vanilladot")
```

The first argument is the formula that indicates Species is dependent on Petal.Width and Petal.Length (again, to stay consistent with Figures 9-1 through 9-6). The second argument shows the source of the data (the training set you create in the preceding section). In the third argument (kernel), "vanilladot" is kernlab's name for a linear kernel.

Running kern_svm results in:

```
> kern_svm
Support Vector Machine object of class "ksvm"

SV type: C-svc  (classification)
 parameter : cost C = 1

Linear (vanilla) kernel function.

Number of Support Vectors : 16

Objective Function Value : -12.3997
Training error : 0.065789
```

The results (16 support vectors) match up with e1071's svm() function.

With respect to performance on the training set, running predict() yields this:

```
> pred.test <- predict(kern_svm,training.set)
> mean(pred.test == training.set$Species)
[1] 0.9342105
```

which corresponds to 1-kern_sym$error (that is, to 1 minus the Training error of 0.065789 in the output of kern_sym).

The accuracy on the test set is

```
> pred.test <- predict(kern_svm,test.set)
> mean(pred.test == test.set$Species)
[1] 0.9583333
```

You use `plot()` to visualize the SVM:

```
plot(kern_svm,data=training.set, formula=Petal.Width ~ Petal.Length)
```

Figure 9-8 shows the resulting plot. The triangles are *versicolor*, the circles are *virginica*, and the filled-plot characters are the support vectors. Unlike in the `e1071` plot, no legend explains the classification.

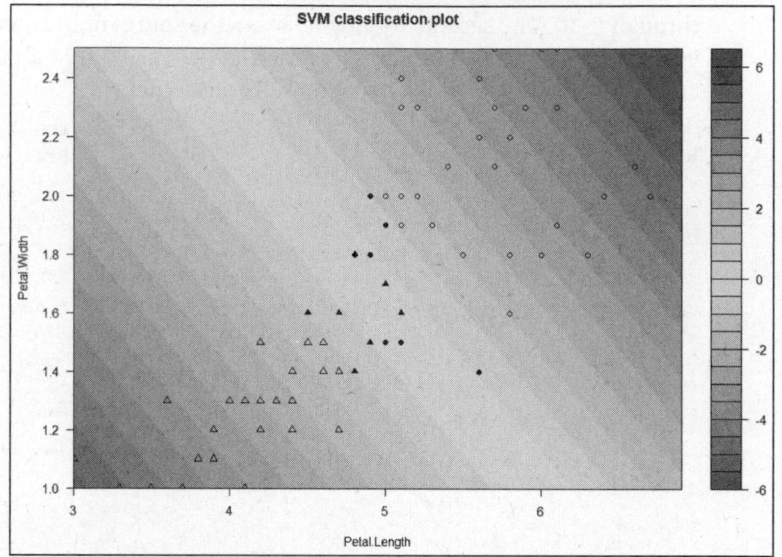

FIGURE 9-8: Plotting the SVM for the vvx training set, `kernlab` version.

Project: House Parties

SVMs work well when you have to classify individuals on the basis of many features — usually, way more than in the `iris` data frame. In this section, I tell you how to create an SVM that identifies the party affiliations of members of the 1984 U.S. House of Representatives. The target variable is whether the congressperson is a Republican or a Democrat, based on their votes on 16 issues of that time. The issues range from water-project cost sharing to education spending.

Nine votes are possible, but they are aggregated into the three classes y (yea), n (nay), or ? (vote not registered). (Usually, a question mark (?) signifies missing data, but not in this case.)

Here are a couple of cautions to bear in mind:

- » The name of each issue does not provide enough information to understand the entirety of the issue. Sometimes the associated bill has such convoluted wording that it's hard to tell what a y or n vote means.
- » Nothing here is intended as an endorsement or a disparagement of any position or of either party. This is just a machine learning exercise.

You'll find the `Congressional Voting Records` data set in the UCI ML repository. The URL is

`https://archive.ics.uci.edu/ml/datasets/congressional+voting+records`

From this page, navigate to the Data Folder and then to the data. Press Ctrl+A to highlight all the data, and then press Ctrl+C to copy it all to the clipboard. Then this code

```
house <- read.csv("clipboard",header=FALSE)
```

turns the data into a data frame. At this point, the first six rows of the data frame are

```
> head(house)
          V1 V2 V3 V4 V5 V6 V7 V8 V9 V10 V11 V12 V13 V14 V15 V16 V17
1 republican  n  y  n  y  y  y  n  n   n   y   ?   y   y   y   n   y
2 republican  n  y  n  y  y  y  n  n   n   n   n   y   y   y   n   ?
3   democrat  ?  y  y  ?  y  y  n  n   n   n   y   n   y   y   n   n
4   democrat  n  y  y  n  ?  y  n  n   n   n   y   n   y   n   n   y
5   democrat  y  y  y  n  y  y  n  n   n   n   y   ?   y   y   y   y
6   democrat  n  y  y  n  y  y  n  n   n   n   n   n   y   y   y   y
```

A look at the variable names (in the data set description) shows that most of them are pretty long (like `anti-satellite-test-ban`). Typing them takes a lot of time, and assigning them short abbreviations might not be much more informative than `V15` or `V16`. So just change `V1` to `Party`:

```
colnames(house)[1] = "Party"
```

I use the `kernlab` package to create the SVM. More specifically, I use the `rattle` package, which provides a GUI to `kernlab`.

Reading in the data

With the `rattle` package installed,

```
rattle()
```

opens the Data tab. To read in the data, follow these steps:

1. **Click the R Dataset radio button to open the Data Name box.**
2. **Click that box's down arrow and select House from the menu that appears.**
3. **Click to select the check box next to Partition, and then click the Execute button in the upper left corner of the window.**
4. **Click the Target radio button for Party and the Input radio button for V17, and then click the Execute icon again.**

The `Rattle` Data tab should now look like Figure 9-9.

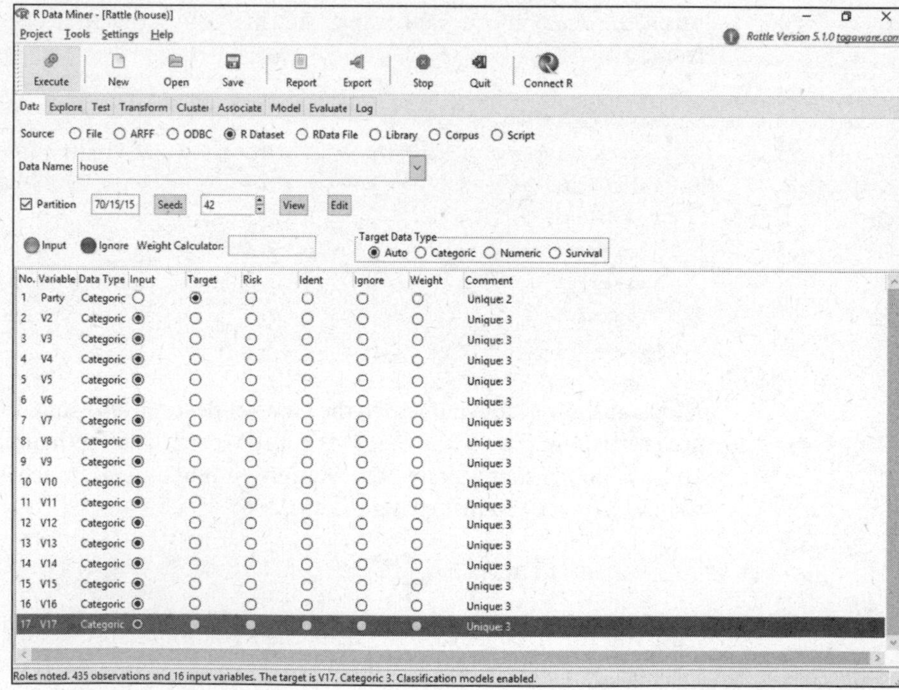

FIGURE 9-9: The `rattle` Data tab, after selecting and modifying the house data frame.

Exploring the data

Next, you'll want to explore the data. The first thing to look at is a distribution of party affiliation. Here's how:

1. **On the Explore tab, click the Distributions radio button and the check box next to Party.**
2. **In the Group By box, select blank (the first choice) so that this box is empty.**

   Figure 9-10 shows what the Explore tab looks like after all this takes place.

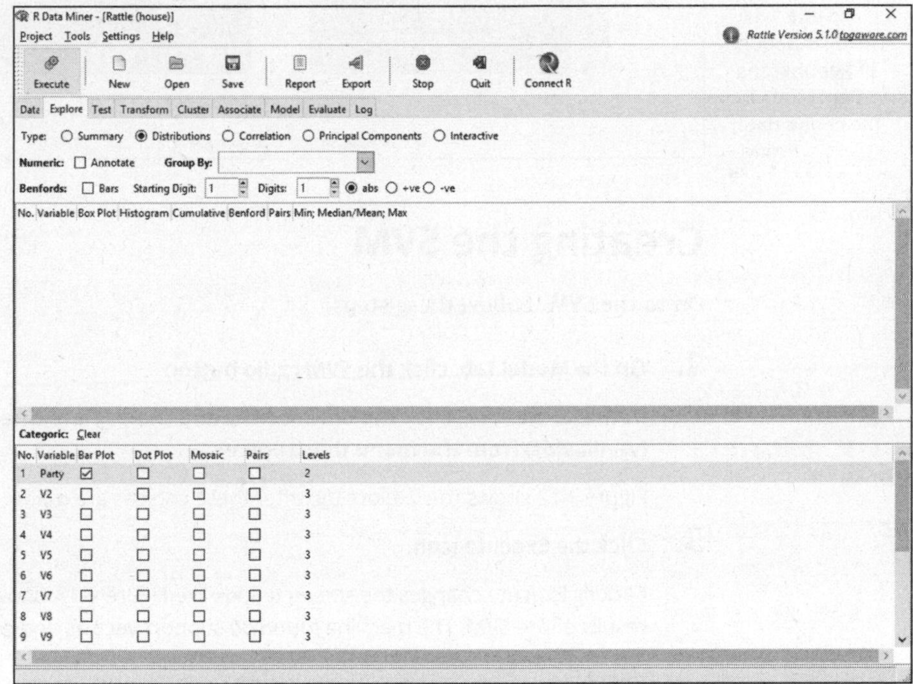

FIGURE 9-10: The `rattle` Explore tab, set up to plot a distribution of party affiliation.

3. **Click Execute.**

   That last step produces what you see in Figure 9-11, which shows the distribution of Republicans and Democrats in the data frame.

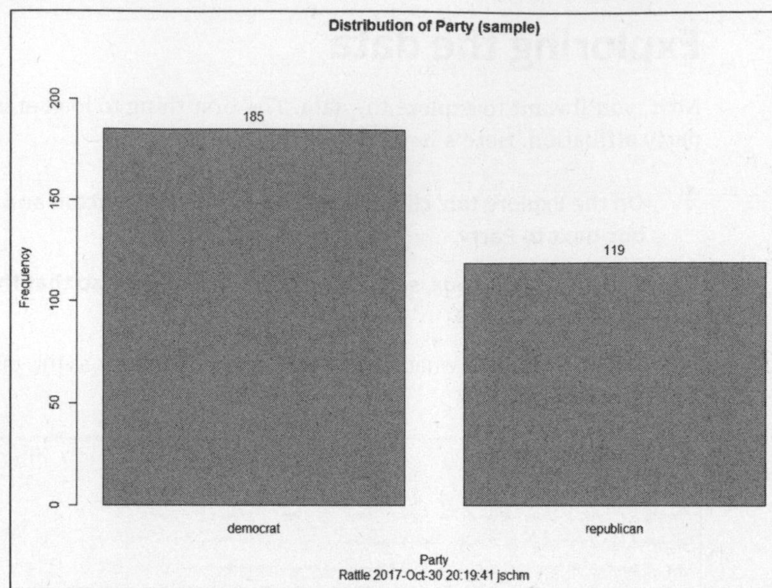

FIGURE 9-11: The distribution of Republicans and Democrats in the house data frame.

Creating the SVM

On to the SVM. Follow these steps:

1. **On the Model tab, click the SVM radio button.**
2. **In the Kernel box, click the down arrow and then select Linear (vanilladot) from the menu that appears.**

   Figure 9-12 shows the Explore tab after these choices are made.
3. **Click the Execute icon.**

   Clicking Execute changes the screen to look like Figure 9-13, showing the results of the SVM. The machine found 34 support vectors and produced a Training error of .016447.

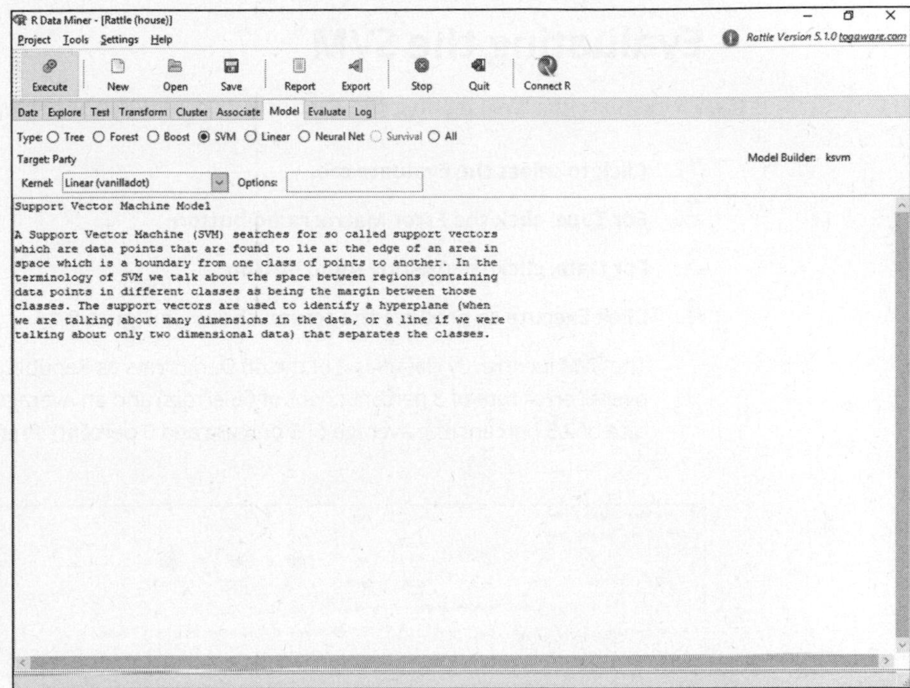

FIGURE 9-12: The `rattle` Model tab, set up to create an SVM for the house data frame.

R Data Miner - [Rattle (house)]

Project Tools Settings Help — Rattle Version 5.1.0 togaware.com

Execute New Open Save Report Export Stop Quit Connect R

Data Explore Test Transform Cluster Associate Model Evaluate Log

Type: Tree Forest Boost SVM Linear Neural Net Survival All

Target: Party — Model Builder: ksvm

Kernel: Linear (vanilladot) Options:

```
Summary of the SVM model (built using ksvm):

Support Vector Machine object of class "ksvm"

SV type: C-svc  (classification)
 parameter : cost C = 1

Linear (vanilla) kernel function.

Number of Support Vectors : 34

Objective Function Value : -18.4298
Training error : 0.016447
Probability model included.

Time taken: 0.04 secs

Rattle timestamp: 2017-10-30 20:30:09 jschm
======================================================================
```

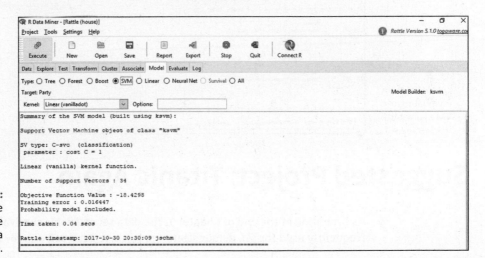

FIGURE 9-13: The results of the SVM for the house data frame.

Evaluating the SVM

To evaluate the SVM against the Testing set, complete these steps:

1. **Click to select the Evaluate tab.**
2. **For Type, click the Error Matrix radio button.**
3. **For Data, click the Testing radio button.**
4. **Click Execute to produce the screen shown in Figure 9-14.**

   The SVM incorrectly classifies 2 of the 40 Democrats as Republicans, for an overall error rate of 3 percent (2 out of 66 errors) and an average class error rate of 2.5 percent (the average of 5 percent and 0 percent). Pretty impressive.

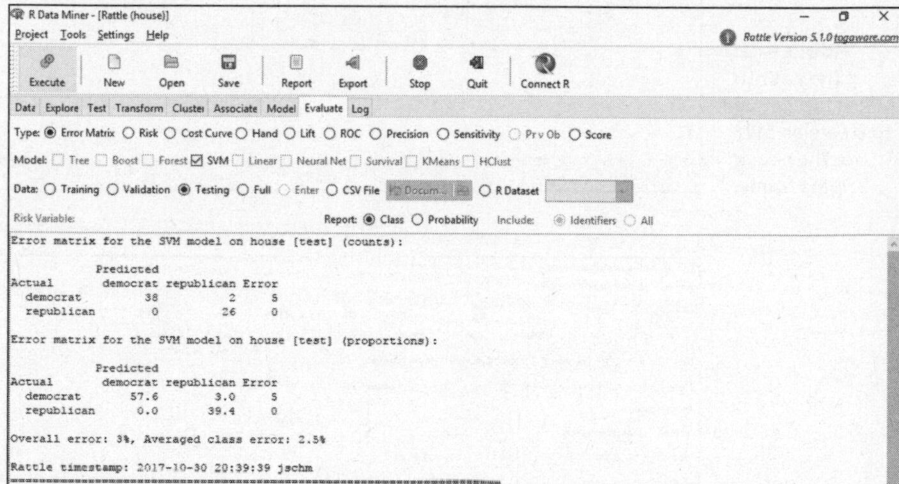

FIGURE 9-14: Evaluating the SVM against the Testing set.

Suggested Project: Titanic Again

As I mention at the end of Chapter 7, the data set of *Titanic* survival information is frequently used for ML demonstrations. It's a pretty good one for SVM.

For the details on using the data, take a look at the final section of Chapter 7. Pay close attention to the modifications I lay out in that section.

When you get to the Model tab, try creating the SVM with different kernel types and note the effect on training error.

IN THIS CHAPTER

» Mastering *k*-means clustering

» *k*-means clustering irises in R

» *k*-means clustering the `glass` data set

Chapter 10

K-Means Clustering

In unsupervised learning, a machine learning (ML) process looks for structure in a data set. The objective is to find patterns, not make predictions. One way to structure a data set is to put the data points into subgroups called *clusters*. The trick is to find a recipe for creating the clusters. One such recipe is called *k-means clustering*.

How It Works

To introduce k-means clustering, I show you how to work with the `iris` data frame, as I have in previous chapters. This is the `iris` data frame that's in the base R installation. Fifty flowers in each of three iris species (*setosa, versicolor,* and *virginica*) make up the data set. The data frame columns are `Sepal.Length`, `Sepal.Width`, `Petal.Length`, `Petal.Width`, and `Species`.

For this discussion, you're concerned with only `Petal.Length`, `Petal.Width`, and `Species`. That way, you can visualize the data in two dimensions.

Figure 10-1 plots the `iris` data frame with `Petal.Length` on the *x*-axis, `Petal.Width` on the *y*-axis, and `Species` as the color of the plotting character. (For the `ggplot` details, see the later sidebar "Plotting the irises".)

In k-means clustering, you first specify how many clusters you think the data fall into. In Figure 10-1, a reasonable assumption is 3 — the number of species.

The next step is to randomly assign each data point (corresponding to a row in the data frame) to a cluster. Then find the central point of each cluster. ML honchos refer to this center as the *centroid*. The x-value of the centroid is the mean of the x-values of the points in the cluster, and the *y*-value of the centroid is the mean of the y-values of the points in the cluster.

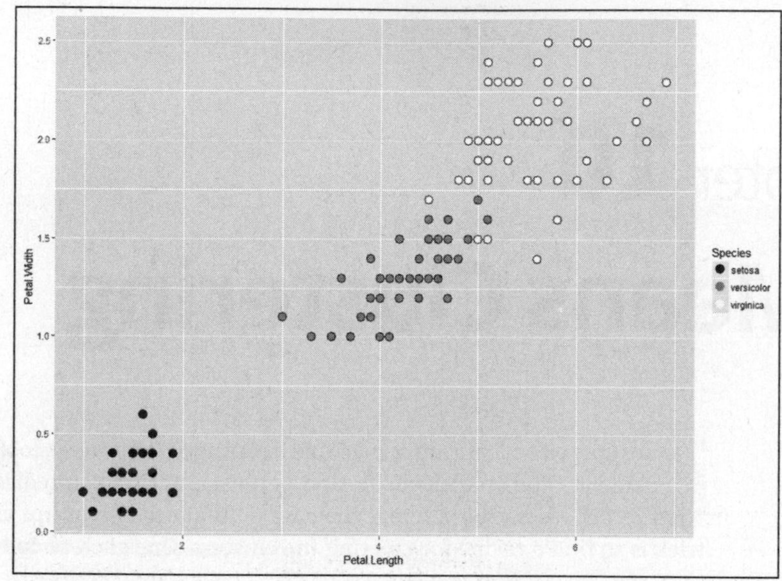

FIGURE 10-1: Two dimensions of the `iris` data frame.

The next order of business is to calculate the distance between each point and its centroid, square that distance, and add up the squared distances. This sum-of-squared-distances-within-a-cluster is better known as the *within sum of squares*.

Finally, and this is the crucial part, the process repeats until the within sum of squares for each cluster is as small as possible: in other words, until each data point is in the cluster with the closest centroid.

It's also possible to calculate a centroid for the entire set of observations. Its x-coordinate is the average of every data point's x-coordinate (`Petal.Length`, in this example), and its y-coordinate is the average of every data point's y-coordinate (`Petal.Width`, in this example). The sum of squared distances from each point to this overall centroid is called the *total sum of squares*. The sum of squared distances from each cluster centroid to the overall centroid is the *between sum of squares*.

The ratio *(between sum of squares)/(within sum of squares)* is a measure of how well the k-means clusters fit the data. A higher number is better.

THAT DISTANCE THING

"The distance between each point and its centroid"? How do you calculate that?

The most common way to do this is called *Euclidean distance*, and just because you asked, here's how to find it. If the coordinates of a point are *xp* and *yp* and the coordinates of the centroid are *xc* and *yc*, the distance *d* between them is

$$d = \sqrt{\left(x_p - x_c\right)^2 + \left(y_p - y_c\right)^2}$$

With more than two dimensions, the equation gets a little hairier, but the principle is the same. And non-Euclidean distance measures (with names like *Minkowski* and *city-block*) are variations on this theme.

TECHNICAL STUFF

If these sum-of-squares ring a bell, you've most likely heard of a statistical analysis technique called *analysis of variance*. If the ratio of those two sums of squares sounds familiar, you might remember that, in another context, that ratio's square root is called the *correlation coefficient*.

K-Means Clustering in R

The R function `kmeans()` handles k-means clustering. It comes with the base R installation, so no additional package download is necessary.

Setting up and analyzing the data

For k-means clustering with the iris dataset (using `Petal.Length` and `Petal.Width`), here's the code:

```
set.seed(810)
```

If you want to replicate my results, set the seed (for the random selection of sets that kicks off the whole thing) to the same number I did:

```
kmi <- kmeans(iris[,3:4],centers=3,nstart=15)
```

The first argument to `kmeans()` is the data (Columns 3 and 4 of the `iris` data frame). The second argument specifies the number of clusters, and the third indicates the number of random sets to choose at the beginning of the process.

Understanding the output

Here are the results:

```
> kmi
K-means clustering with 3 clusters of sizes 52, 50, 48

Cluster means:
  Petal.Length Petal.Width
1     4.269231    1.342308
2     1.462000    0.246000
3     5.595833    2.037500

Clustering vector:
  [1] 2 2 2 2 2 2 2 2 2 2 2 2 2 2 2 2 2 2 2 2 2 2 2 2 2 2 2 2 2 2 2 2 2 2 2 2 2 2
   2 2 2 2 2 2 2 2 2 2 2 2 1 1 1 1 1 1 1 1
 [59] 1 1 1 1 1 1 1 1 1 1 1 1 1 1 1 1 1 1 1 3 1 1 1 1 1 3 1 1 1 1 1 1 1 1 1 1 1
   1 1 1 1 1 3 3 3 3 3 3 1 3 3 3 3 3 3 3 3
[117] 3 3 3 1 3 3 3 3 3 3 1 3 3 3 3 3 3 3 3 3 3 1 3 3 3 3 3 3 3 3 3 3 3

Within cluster sum of squares by cluster:
[1] 13.05769  2.02200 16.29167
 (between_SS / total_SS =  94.3 %)

Available components:

[1] "cluster"      "centers"      "totss"        "withinss"     "tot.withinss"
   "betweenss"    "size"
[8] "iter"         "ifault"
```

The first output line tells you the number of flowers in each cluster. Because they're not all 50, they don't match up perfectly with the species.

The `Cluster means` show you the centroid coordinates for each cluster. The ordering of the clusters is arbitrary: It's based on the random selection at the start of the process. For example, as Figure 10-1 shows, the *setosa* are in the leftmost region of the plot, leading to the expectation that they might be Cluster 1. `kmeans()` has assigned *setosa* to Cluster 2, however.

You can verify the centroids for Cluster 2 (and that Cluster 2 is the *setosa*) by calculating

```
mean(iris$Petal.Length[iris$Species == "setosa"])
mean(iris$Petal.Width[iris$Species == "setosa"])
```

This doesn't work for the other two species because they don't perfectly correspond to Clusters 1 and 3. (Pretty close, though.)

The next output section, `Clustering vector`, shows the cluster assigned to each flower in the data frame.

The next-to-last section shows the within sum of squares for each cluster and the ratio of the between sum of squares to the total sum of squares. The ratio, 94.3 percent, indicates that the clustering scheme is a good fit with the data.

The final section is a bit more important than it looks at first glance. It shows the names of attributes that are available as a result of the k-means clustering. This list tells you how to retrieve the attributes. If, for some reason, you want to retrieve the `Clustering vector` (as mentioned in the later sidebar "Plotting the irises"), that's `kmi$cluster`. Try it, if you don't believe me. Another important one, as you'll see, is `tot.withinss`, which is the sum of the `withinss` for each cluster:

```
> kmi$tot.withinss
[1] 31.37136
> sum(kmi$withinss)
[1] 31.37136
```

How, exactly, do the clusters match up with the species? To answer this question, you have to sum up the data points in each cluster and the data points in each species and cross-tabulate. (For example, how many *versicolor* are in each cluster?) The `table()` function does all this:

```
> table(kmi$cluster,iris$Species)

    setosa versicolor virginica
  1      0         48         4
  2     50          0         0
  3      0          2        46
```

So `kmeans()` put 2 *versicolor* in Cluster 3, and 4 *virginica* in Cluster 1.

Visualizing the clusters

How does the clustering look? Figure 10-2 shows you. (For the coding details on how to create this figure, see the later sidebar "Plotting the irises".)

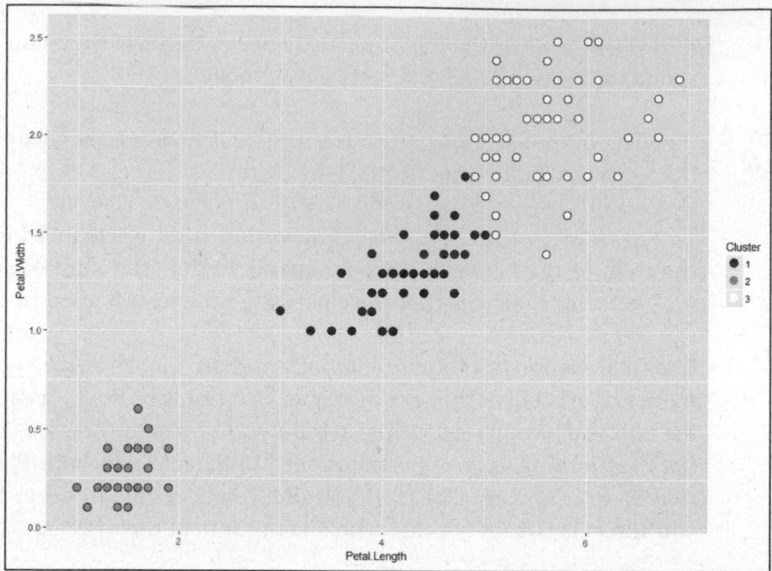

FIGURE 10-2: K-means clustering the `iris` data frame, with three clusters.

It's pretty close to the plot in Figure 10-1, but it's not exact. If you're sharp-eyed, perhaps you can see the six flowers in Figure 10-1 that are classified differently in Figure 10-2. Notice in this figure that no flowers are intermingled with others: The cluster boundaries are pretty clear.

Finding the optimum number of clusters

At the beginning of this discussion, you might have just assumed that 3 was the "best" number of clusters. Three species, three clusters — short and sweet. But is this really the case?

Remember that k-means clustering minimizes the within sum of squares for each cluster. Another way to say this is that k-means clustering minimizes the total of the within sums of squares. So one way to select the optimum number is to use `kmeans()` for a range of different values for `centers` (the number of clusters), retrieve the associated `tot.withinss` for each one, and compare. (The trivial solution, of course, is to have as many clusters as data points. If each data point has its own, personal cluster, the within sums of squares are all zero.)

To help with the comparison, I'll draw a graph. I'll put the number of clusters on the *x*-axis and the total within sum of squares on the *y*-axis. A statistician looking at that graph would look for an "elbow," or a drop in the `tot.withinss` followed by a leveling-out in which further reduction in the `tot.withinss` is minimal. That elbow represents the optimum number of clusters.

To run `kmeans()` on 2 to 15 clusters, you use a `for`-loop. You begin by creating an empty vector that will eventually hold all `total.withinss` values:

```
totwss <- NULL
```

The `for` loop is

```
for (i in 2:15){
   totwss <- append(totwss,kmeans(iris[,3:4],centers=i)$tot.withinss)
            }
```

The loop adds *(appends)* each new `tot.withinss` value to the end of the `totwss` vector.

The code for the plot is

```
plot(x=2:15, y=totwss, type="b", xlab="Clusters", ylab= "Total Within SS")
```

The `type =` "b" argument specifies that both lines and points appear in the graph. The plot appears in Figure 10-3.

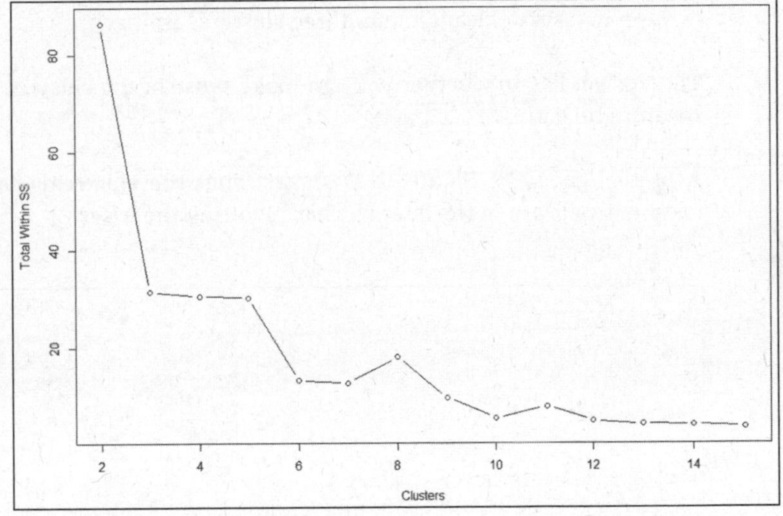

FIGURE 10-3: Total within sum of squares versus Clusters for k-means clustering of the `iris` data frame.

The graph does show an elbow with three clusters, but after five clusters the graph shows another drop-off. What looks like another elbow appears with six clusters and then total within sum of squares looks pretty stable.

So here's the clustering with six clusters:

```
set.seed(810)
kmi6 <-kmeans(iris[,3:4],centers=6,nstart=15)
```

Here are some selected results:

```
K-means clustering with 6 clusters of sizes 11, 50, 27, 19, 21, 22

Cluster means:
  Petal.Length Petal.Width
1     6.354545    2.127273
2     1.462000    0.246000
3     4.485185    1.407407
4     3.773684    1.152632
5     5.028571    1.766667
6     5.559091    2.145455

Within cluster sum of squares by cluster:
[1] 1.689091 2.022000 1.232593 2.224211 1.449524 2.407727
 (between_SS / total_SS =  98.0 %)
```

Most of the time, analysts look for the solution with the fewest clusters. Is the almost 4 percent improvement in the between/total ratio (over three clusters) enough to justify the additional three clusters? Hmm . . . .

The answer lies in whether you can make sense of the clusters. Can you attach a meaningful name to each one?

A plot might help. Figure 10-4 shows what the clustering looks like. (Again, coding details are in the later sidebar "Plotting the irises".)

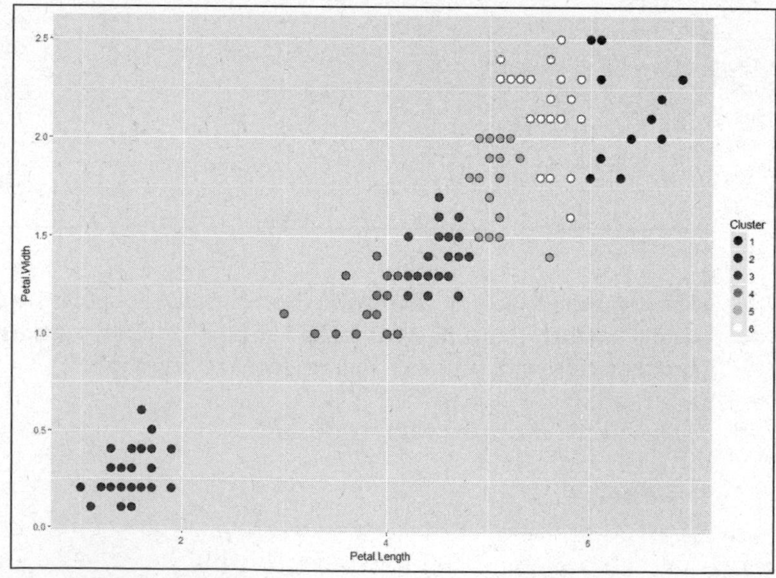

FIGURE 10-4: K-means clustering the `iris` data frame, with six clusters.

The clusters are pretty distinct. The *setosa,* as always, form their own group in the lower left area. The cluster in the upper right area consists of *virginica,* but not all the *virginica.* Are these "large" *virginica?* How about the next cluster to the left? Are they "small" *virginica?* Large *versicolor?* A mixture of the two? What about the other three clusters?

A table can be helpful:

```
> table(kmi6$cluster,iris$Species)

   setosa versicolor virginica
  1      0          0        11
  2     50          0         0
  3      0         26         1
  4      0         19         0
  5      0          5        16
  6      0          0        22
```

Most of the *versicolor* are in Clusters 3 and 4, and most of the *virginica* are in 1, 5, and 6. And so . . .?

The bottom line: Numbers and graphs don't tell the entire story. We can use statistical techniques to suggest possible explanations, but that takes us only so far. Nothing can substitute for knowledge of the content area. A botanist would be able to tell you how to name these clusters in a meaningful way, and perhaps come up with a sensible way of deciding on the number of clusters in the first place.

In my humble opinion, then, this technique works best if you have some knowledge about an area and want to understand more about the structure of a data set in that area.

Quick suggested project: Adding the sepals

In the examples so far in this chapter, I've confined the variables to just `Petal.Length` and `Petal.Width`. What happens if the k-means clustering also includes `Sepal.Length` and `Sepal.Width`? (To make this happen, change `iris[,3:4]` to `iris[,1:4]` in the arguments to `kmeans()`. And don't forget that first comma in the brackets!)

How does adding the sepal variables affect the clustering for the 3-cluster case? For the 6-cluster case? How about the optimum number of clusters? What do the plots of the 3-cluster case and the 6-cluster case look like with the sepal variables included?

PLOTTING THE IRISES

If you've read the first sidebar in Chapter 9, "Plotting (two-thirds of) the irises," you're familiar with the ideas explained in *this* sidebar. In fact, this sidebar is that one on steroids. Here, I show you how to plot Figures 10-1, 10-2, and 10-4. For all of them, assume that the package ggplot2 is installed.

Figure 10-1 plots the `iris` data frame with `Petal.Length` on the *x*-axis, `Petal.Width` on the *y*-axis, and `Species` as the color of the data points. Here's the code:

```
ggplot(iris, aes(x=Petal.Length,y=Petal.Width,color=Species))+
  geom_point(size=4)+
  scale_color_manual(values=c("grey0","grey65","grey100"))+
  geom_point(shape=1,size=4,color="black")
```

The first line, `ggplot()`, specifies the data and maps variables in the data to aspects of the plot. The second line, `geom_point()`, adds the data points to the plot and specifies their size. If I just stop here, I get a nice-looking graph whose default colors wouldn't show up well on this black-and-white page.

Instead of the default colors, the third line indicates the colors to use in the data points. The first species is colored in `grey0`, which is black. The second is in `grey65`, which is a shade of gray. The third is in `grey100`, which is white.

The final line, another `geom_point()`, is a trick that adds a border to each data point. It superimposes an unfilled data point with a border onto each data point already in the graph.

Figure 10-2 plots the `iris` data frame in the same way, but this time the data-point colors represent the three clusters stored in `kmi`. So I have to change the `color` mapping in the `ggplot()` statement. How do I retrieve each flower's cluster from the clustering results? As I point out in the earlier "Output" section, `kmi$cluster` returns the `Clustering vector`, which is exactly what I need here.

Does this mean that I just change `color=Species` to `color=kmi$cluster`? Not quite. The clusters, remember, are numbers (1, 2, 3). The species are names ("setosa," "virginica," "versicolor"). `ggplot()` thinks that the numbers represent values of a continuous numeric variable, not names, like the species. This doesn't fly with `scale_color_manual()`, which maps colors onto category names, not numbers. So I have to somehow turn the cluster numbers into categories. Fortunately, the `as.factor()` function does just that. The change to the code, then, is `color = as.factor(kmi$cluster)`.

One more change: If I change only `color` and nothing else, the title of the legend is `as.factor(kmi$cluster)`, and no one wants that. So I add the argument name="Cluster" to the scale_color_manual() function to retitle the legend. Here's the code, with the changes in bold:

```
ggplot(iris, aes(x=Petal.Length,y=Petal.Width,color=as.factor(kmi$cluster)))+
  geom_point(size=4)+
  scale_color_manual(name="Cluster",values=c("grey0","grey65","grey100"))+
  geom_point(shape=1,size=4,color="black")
```

You can probably figure out how to plot Figure 10-4. The code is the same as for Figure 10-2, but for Figure 10-4 the results of the 6-cluster *k*-means clustering are in kmi6. Change the color argument in ggplot() accordingly. The values argument in scale_color_manual() is

```
values=c("grey0","grey20","grey40","grey60","grey80","grey100")
```

Project: Glass Clusters

In this section, I show you a project that's more complex than clustering irises. The basis for this project is a data set I use in Chapter 8, in the section "Project: Identifying Glass." As a refresher, the data are measurements of chemical and physical properties of 149 pieces of glass. Each piece comes from one of six types (windows or headlamps, for example). Correctly identifying the source of a glass fragment can be a crucial part of a criminal investigation.

The objective here, however, is not identification. The idea is to find structure within the data set: What types of glass are similar to one another? What types are different?

REMEMBER

The distinction between "learning to correctly identify" and "learning the structure of" is the distinction between *supervised* learning and *unsupervised* learning.

The data

As in previous ML projects, the data comes from the UCI ML repository. You'll find this data set at https://archive.ics.uci.edu/ml/datasets/glass+identification.

Navigate to the Data Folder. Then click glass.data, which is a text file of comma-separated variables. Press Ctrl+A to highlight everything, and press Ctrl+C to put it all on the clipboard.

The following command brings the data into R as a data frame:

```
glass.uci <- read.csv("clipboard",header = FALSE)
```

I still need the header, and that's

```
colnames(glass.uci)<-c("ID","RI","Na","Mg","Al","Si","K","Ca","Ba","Fe","Type")
```

The first column, ID, is an identifier for the piece of glass, and the second is the glass fragment's refractive index (how much it bends light that passes through it). The last one, Type, is unsurprisingly, the type of glass. All the ones in the middle are the chemical elements in the glass.

The levels of Type are numbers. To give them informative names, I use a plyr function called mapvalues():

```
library(plyr)
glass.uci$Type <- mapvalues(glass.uci$Type,
          from = c(1,2,3,5,6,7),
                              to = c("bldg_windows_float","bldg_windows_non_float",
                                        "vehicle_windows_float","containers","tabl
   eware","headlamps"))
```

float and non_float are processes for making a window: "float" produces near-optical-quality glass, and "non-float" glass is lower-quality.

The from vector does not include 4, because the corresponding type (vehicle_windows_non_float) is not in the data set.

REMEMBER

I didn't make up the names for the columns and for the Type levels. They're at the URL for this data set.

Starting Rattle and exploring the data

If you've read Chapter 8, you've already seen this part of the movie: Rattle provides a GUI (graphical user interface) to ML-related functions and enables you to work with those functions in a convenient way. kmeans() is one of those functions.

With the rattle package downloaded,

```
library(rattle)
rattle()
```

opens the `Rattle` Data tab. From here on, I summarize the steps. For a fuller exposition, including figures, see the section "Getting the data into `Rattle`" in Chapter 8.

1. **To load the data set into `rattle`, click the R Dataset radio button and select `glass.uci` from the Data Name box's drop-down list.**
2. **Click the Execute button in the upper left corner of the window.**
3. **Click the Explore tab to take a look at the data.**

   As in Chapter 8, one way to start is to look at the distribution of glass types.
4. **Clear the Group By box, and check the box next to Type.**
5. **Click Execute for the bar plot shown in Figure 8-7 (over in Chapter 8).**

Preparing to cluster

Should I show you how to use all nine numeric variables to form the clusters? I'm going to cheat a bit and ask you to look at the analysis in Chapter 8. Figure 8-9 (refer to Chapter 8) shows how much each variable contributes to the random forest in that example. The plot for `MeanDecreaseAccuracy` shows that Mg (Magnesium content), RI (refractive index), and Al (Aluminum content) are the three most prominent variables. That sounds like a good starting point.

So, back to the Data tab. After you make the appropriate selections among the radio buttons to ignore all but RI, Mg, and Al, the Data tab looks like Figure 10-5. You click Execute to register these selections.

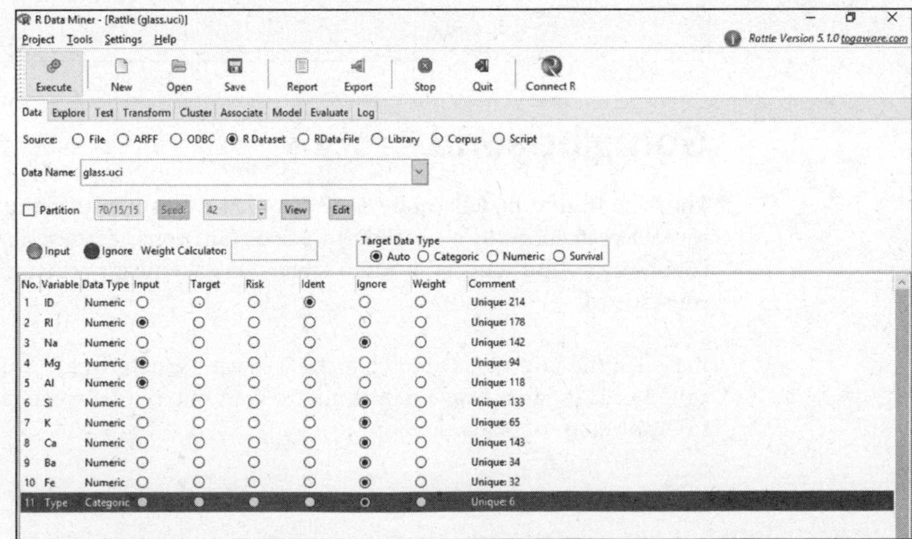

FIGURE 10-5: Setting up the variables for k-means clustering of the `glass.uci` data frame.

Doing the clustering

On to the Cluster tab. In the Clusters box, I used the arrows to select 6, and I typed **810** into the Seed box just to be consistent with what I did earlier in this chapter. (Type the same number in that box if you want the same results as mine.) In the Runs box, I used the arrows to select 15 (again, for consistency with what I did earlier). After I made these selections and clicked Execute, the Data tab looks like Figure 10-6. `rattle` shows you the cluster sizes (how many observations are in each cluster), the mean of each variable, the cluster centers (the coordinates of each cluster's centroid), and the within sum of squares for each cluster.

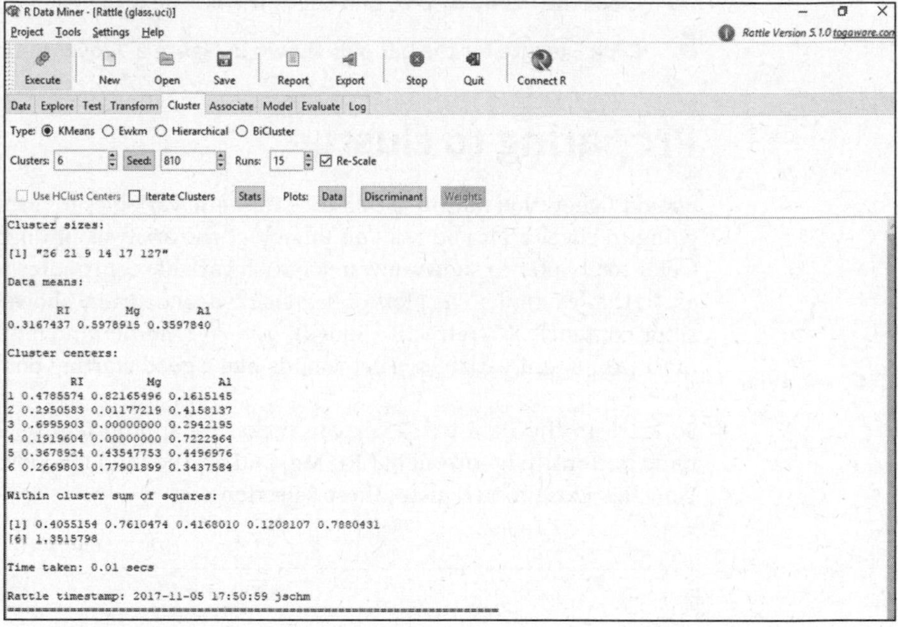

FIGURE 10-6: Setting up the k-means clustering for the `glass.uci` data frame.

Going beyond `Rattle`

The `Rattle` output tells quite a bit about the clusters. Clicking the Data button reveals even more. It's possible to use R functions, as described earlier in this chapter, to find out still more about the k-means clustering that `rattle` constructed.

If I click the Log tab, I find that the k-means clustering is stored in a variable called `crs$kmeans`. This enables me to find out the between-sum-of-squares-to-total-sum-of-squares ratio:

```
> crs$kmeans
```

The relevant line of the output is

```
(between_SS / total_SS =  87.6 %)
```

which is a pretty high ratio.

How about the amounts of the different types of glass in each cluster? That's the province of the `table()` function. Set the first argument to the cluster vector, and the second argument to the glass type:

```
> table(crs$kmeans$cluster,glass.uci$Type)

   bldg_windows_float bldg_windows_non_float containers
  1                17                      3          0
  2                 0                      1          5
  3                 0                      8          1
  4                 0                      0          2
  5                 0                      4          5
  6                53                     60          0

   headlamps tableware vehicle_windows_float
  1        1         0                     5
  2       11         4                     0
  3        0         0                     0
  4       12         0                     0
  5        3         5                     0
  6        2         0                    12
```

Cluster 6 looks like a `windows` cluster; clusters 2 and 4, like `headlamps` clusters. I can't see any other explanatory labels jumping out, but if I knew more about glass, perhaps I could. Maybe you can.

Suggested Project: A Few Quick Ones

Three quick projects suggest themselves, as described next.

Visualizing data points and clusters

Want to sharpen your `ggplot` skills? Take a look at the earlier sidebar "Plotting the irises" and use the code ideas to create a graph of the `glass.uci` data frame: Put `RI` on the *x*-axis, `Mg` on the *y*-axis, and `Type` as the color. Then create the same kind of plot but with the k-means clusters (stored in `crs$kmeans$cluster`) as the color.

TIP

If you don't feel like using `ggplot` to create the second graph, you can have `Rattle` do it for you: On the Cluster tab, click the Data button. `Rattle` plots a matrix that contains all possible pairwise plots, including `RI` versus `Mg`.

The optimum number of clusters

Six glass types, six clusters. Seems like a natural, right? Maybe, maybe not. Modify the code in the earlier section "Finding the optimum number of clusters" to plot the total within sum of squares versus clusters to find the "right" number for this data frame. (Don't forget to reset `totwss` to `NULL`!)

Is the optimum number really 6? If not, retry with the number the plot suggests and then complete the two analyses (ratio and table) from earlier in this section, and note any changes from using six clusters.

Adding variables

The preceding two projects stress R functions rather than `Rattle`. But `Rattle` makes it quick and easy to modify the clustering process. For example, `Ca` (calcium content) is another variable that shows up prominently in Figure 8-9 (refer to Chapter 8). Use the `Rattle` Data tab to add that variable. (Don't forget to click Execute.) How does that affect the k-means clustering?

IN THIS CHAPTER

» Neural networks defined

» Why and when to use neural networks

» A neural network for the `iris` dataset

» The `nnet` package

» Neural networks in `Rattle`

Chapter 11
Neural Networks

Neural networks are a popular form of supervised machine learning. They're popular because they're widely applied in an array of areas, like speech recognition and image processing. Investors rely on these networks to recognize patterns in the stock market and decide whether to buy or sell. As the name indicates, their design reflects the structure and function of the nervous system.

Networks in the Nervous System

The nervous system consists of cells called *neurons*. Figure 11-1 shows a neuron on the left connected to three neurons on the right. The neuron on the left receives, through its dendrites, messages from other neurons. This neuron processes what it receives, and the result becomes a signal it sends along its axon. Through connections called *synapses* (yes, each one is a tiny gap), the signal passes to the neurons on the right.

Each right-side neuron can receive inputs from several neurons. Each one puts together all its inputs and in turn passes a signal to still other neurons. Ultimately, a message arrives in the brain. The brain interprets the message.

One theory holds that if one neuron continually sends messages to another, the connection between them grows stronger. According to this theory, the adjustment of the connection strengths among neurons is what learning is all about.

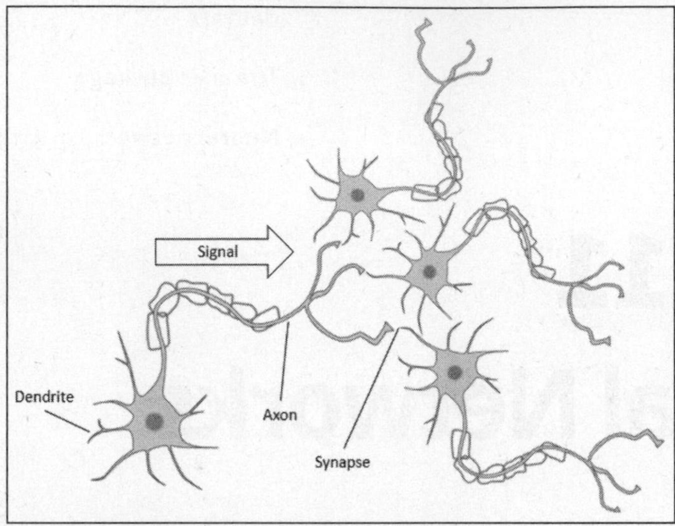

FIGURE 11-1: Neurons in the nervous system.

Artificial Neural Networks

I've oversimplified the workings of the nervous system. Discovering exactly how the neurons process inputs and send messages has sometimes been the basis for winning the Nobel prize.

My description, though, does sketch out the basis for the artificial neural networks in the world of machine learning (ML).

Overview

An ML neural network consists of simulated neurons, often called *units*, or *nodes*, that work with data. Like the neurons in the nervous system, each unit receives input, performs some computation, and passes its result as a message to the next unit. At the output end, the network makes a decision based on its inputs.

Imagine a neural network that uses physical measurements of flowers, like irises, to identify the flower's species. The network takes data like the petal length and petal width of an iris and learns to classify an iris as either *setosa*, *versicolor*, or *virginica*. In effect, the network learns the relationship between the inputs (the petal variables) and the outputs (the species).

Figure 11-2 shows an artificial neural network that classifies irises. It consists of an *input layer*, a *hidden layer*, and an *output layer*. Each unit connects with every unit in the next layer. Numerical values called *weights* are on each connection. Weights can be positive or negative. To keep the figure from getting cluttered, I only show the weights on the connections from the input layer to the hidden layer.

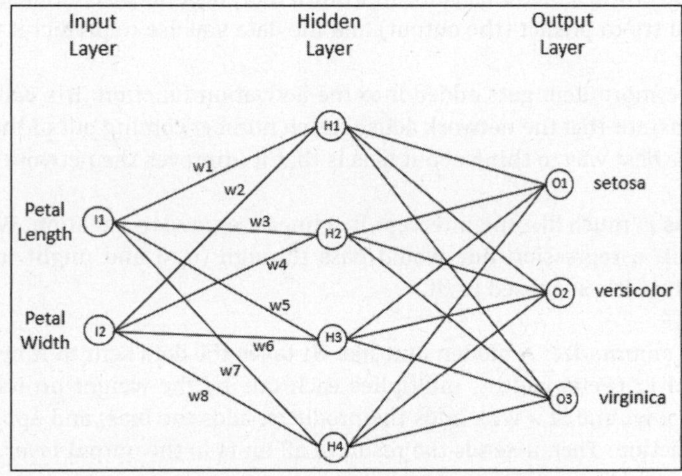

FIGURE 11-2: An artificial neural network that learns to classify irises.

Input layer and hidden layer

The data points are represented in the input layer. This one has one input unit (I1) that holds the value of petal length and another (I2) that holds the value of petal width (refer to Figure 11-2). The input units send messages to another layer of four units, called a *hidden layer*. The number of units in the hidden layer is arbitrary, and picking that number is part of the art of neural network creation.

Each message to a hidden layer unit is the product of a data point and a connection weight. For example, H_1 receives I1 multiplied by w1 along with I2 multiplied by w2. H1 processes what it receives.

What does "processes what it receives" mean? H1 adds the product of I1 and w1 to the product of I2 and w2. H1 then has to send a message to O1, O2, and O3.

What is the message it sends? It's a number in a restricted range, produced by H1's *activation function*. Three activation functions are common. They have exotic, math-y names: *hyperbolic tangent*, *sigmoid*, and *rectified linear unit*.

Without going into the math, I'll just tell you what they do. The hyperbolic tangent (known as *tanh*) takes a number and turns it into a number between −1 and 1. Sigmoid turns its input into a number between 0 and 1. Rectified linear unit (ReLU) replaces negative values with 0.

By restricting the range of the output, activation functions set up a nonlinear relationship between the inputs and the outputs. Why is this important? In most real-world situations, you don't find a nice, neat linear relationship between what you try to predict (the output) and the data you use to predict it (the inputs).

One more item gets added into the activation function. It's called bias. *Bias* is a constant that the network adds to each number coming out of the units in a layer. The best way to think about bias is that it improves the network's accuracy.

TECHNICAL STUFF

Bias is much like the intercept in a linear regression equation. Without the intercept, a regression line would pass through (0,0) and might miss many of the points it's supposed to fit.

To summarize: A hidden unit like H1 takes the data sent to it by I1 (Petal length) and I2 (Petal width), multiplies each one by the weight on its interconnection (I1 × w1 and I2 × w2), adds the products, adds the bias, and applies its activation function. Then it sends the result to all units in the output layer.

Output layer

The output layer consists of one unit (O1) for *setosa*, another (O2) for *virginica*, and another (O3) for *versicolor*. Based on the messages they receive from the hidden layer, the output units do their computations just as the hidden units do theirs. Their results determine the network's decision about the species for the iris with the given petal length and petal width. The flow from input layer to hidden layer to output layer is called *feedforward*.

How it all works

Where do the interunit connection weights come from? They start out as numbers randomly assigned to the interunit connections. The network trains on a data set of petal lengths, petal widths, and the associated species. On each trial, the network receives a petal length and a petal width and makes a decision, which it then compares with the correct answer. Because the initial weights are random, the initial decisions are guesses.

Each time the network's decision is incorrect, the weights change based on how wrong the decision was (on the amount of error, in other words). The adjustment (which also includes changing the bias for each unit) constitutes "learning." One way of proceeding is to adjust the weights from the output layer back to the hidden layer and then from the hidden layer back to the input layer. This is called *backpropagation* because the amount of error "backpropagates" through the layers.

A network trains until it reaches a certain level of accuracy or a preset number of iterations through the training set. In the evaluation phase, the trained network tackles a new set of data.

REMEMBER

This three-layer structure is just one way of building a neural network, and it is what I cover in this chapter. Other types of networks are possible.

Neural Networks in R

R has a couple of packages that enable you to create neural networks like the one I describe in the preceding section. In *this* section, however, I deal with the `nnet` package.

On the Packages tab, click Install to open the Install Packages dialog box. In the dialog box, type **nnet** and click the Install button. When the package finishes downloading, click its check box on the Packages tab.

Building a neural network for the iris data frame

To introduce `nnet`, I begin with the `iris` data frame, which comes with R. This data frame consists of 150 rows and 5 columns. Each row provides measurements of sepal length, sepal width, petal length, and petal width of an iris whose species is either *setosa*, *versicolor*, or *virginica*. Fifty of each species are in the data frame.

In this section, I use the `nnet()` function to build a neural network that does what I describe in the preceding section: It learns to identify an iris's species based on its petal length and petal width.

The first thing to do is create a training set and a test set. I do this with a function called `sample.split()`, which is part of the `caTools` package. So, on the Packages tab, click Install to open the Install Packages dialog box. Type **caTools** in the dialog box and click the Install button. After the package downloads, click its check box on the Packages tab.

Set the seed to this number if you want to reproduce my results:

```
set.seed(810)
```

With caTools installed, this line partitions the iris data frame into a 70-30 split, maintaining the original proportions of the Species in each piece:

```
sample = sample.split(iris$Species, SplitRatio = .70)
```

sample is a vector of 150 instances of TRUE (the data frame row is in the 70 percent) or FALSE (the data frame row is not in the 70 percent).

To create the training set and the test set, use the following:

```
iris.train = subset(iris, sample == TRUE)
iris.test  = subset(iris, sample == FALSE)
```

One of the things I like most about R is its consistency. To create a model, whether it's linear regression, analysis of variance, k-means clustering — or whatever — the general format is

```
object.name <- function.name(dependent.variable ~ independent.variable(s), data,
                              other stuff)
```

And that's the way to create a neural network with the nnet package's nnet() function:

```
nni <- nnet(Species ~ Petal.Length + Petal.Width, iris.train, size=4)
```

The first argument to nnet() is the formula that relates Species to Petal.Length and Petal.Width. The second argument is the training data, and the third is the number of units in the hidden layer. (Many more arguments are available for this function.)

After running the nnet() function, what are the final adjusted weights? To find out, I use the summary() function:

```
> summary(nni)
Neural Network build options: softmax modelling.

In the following table:
   b  represents the bias associated with a node
   h1 represents hidden layer node 1
```

```
  i1 represents input node 1 (i.e., input variable 1)
  o  represents the output node

Weights for node h1:
 b->h1 i1->h1 i2->h1
-17.92   6.14   6.67

Weights for node h2:
 b->h2 i1->h2 i2->h2
  0.59  -0.09  -0.50

Weights for node h3:
 b->h3 i1->h3 i2->h3
-32.96   1.98  24.58

Weights for node h4:
 b->h4 i1->h4 i2->h4
 11.95  -5.01  -2.53

Weights for node o1:
 b->o1 h1->o1 h2->o1 h3->o1 h4->o1
 20.62 -19.43  39.61 -30.52  27.84

Weights for node o2:
 b->o2 h1->o2 h2->o2 h3->o2 h4->o2
  1.01   2.16  54.41 -13.16   3.25

Weights for node o3:
 b->o3 h1->o3 h2->o3 h3->o3 h4->o3
-20.63  15.79 -93.39  45.34 -30.47
```

Take a look at h1 (H1 in Figure 11-2). Its bias is −17.92, the weight on its connection from I1 (shown in Figure 11-2 as w1) is 6.14, and the weight on its connection from I2 (w2 in the Figure) is 6.67.

Plotting the network

To visualize all this, I could go back to Figure 11-2 and add all the weights. Or, I could let R do all the work. A terrific package called `NeuralNetTools` provides `plotnet()`, which does the job quite nicely. To install it, follow the procedure I describe earlier in this chapter: On the Packages tab, click Install to open the Install Packages dialog box. In the dialog box, type **NeuralNetTools** and click the Install button. After the package downloads, click its check box on the Packages tab.

With NeuralNetTools installed, this line produces what you see in Figure 11-3.

```
plotnet(nni)
```

The figure doesn't show the weights explicitly, but instead represents them graphically. A black line represents a positive weight; a gray line represents a negative weight. The thicker the line, the higher the numerical value. Notice also that the diagram shows B1, which applies the biases to the Hidden units, and B2, which applies the biases to the Output units. (To omit those from the plot, I would add the argument bias=FALSE to plotnet()).

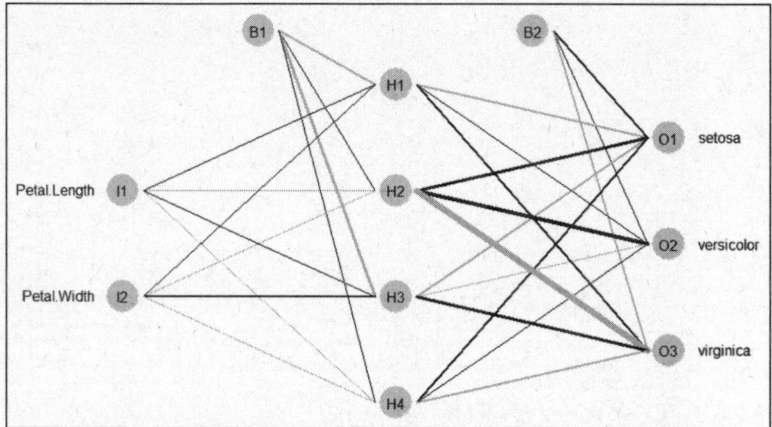

FIGURE 11-3: The neural net for iris.train, rendered by plotnet().

Evaluating the network

How well does the network perform? I use the predict() function (which is in the nnet package) to find out. The line

```
predictions <- predict(nni,iris.test,type = "class")
```

creates a vector of predictions based on the neural network nni, one prediction for each row of the iris.test data frame I created earlier. The type= "class" argument indicates that the neural network decided on a classification for each iris.

Now I use the table() function to set up a *confusion matrix* — a table that shows actual values versus predicted values:

```
table(iris.test$Species,predictions)
```

The first argument is the species of the irises in the test set; the second is the vector of predictions. Here's the matrix:

```
           predictions
            setosa versicolor virginica
setosa          15          0         0
versicolor       0         14         1
virginica        0          2        13
```

The columns are the predicted species, and the rows are the correct species. The numbers in the main diagonal are the correct classifications, and the numbers off the main diagonal are errors. The network misclassified one *versicolor* as a *virginica,* and two *virginica* as *versicolor.* The overall error rate is 6.7 percent (3/45), which is quite accurate.

Quick suggested project: Those sepals

As in previous chapters where I use the `iris` data frame, I used just the two petal variables in the example. And, as in previous chapters, I suggest that you include the sepal variables and create the neural network again. All you have to do is change the formula in the first argument to `nnet()`. Any effect on the network's performance? How about if you change the maximum number of iterations? What happens to the confusion matrix? What happens if you do it all over again with just the sepal variables?

Project: Banknotes

One popular application of neural networks is image classification. The idea is to represent an image as a set of mathematical characteristics, and each image is a member of a category. The characteristics are inputs to a network; the categories are the outputs. The network learns the relationship between the image characteristics and the image categories and can then classify new images it hasn't trained on.

The data

One area for image classification is the detection of counterfeit currency. A data set in the UCI ML repository provides the opportunity to try out a neural network for just that purpose. It's the banknote+authentication data set, and you'll find it at

```
https://archive.ics.uci.edu/ml/datasets/banknote+authentication
```

The data are four measures of digital images of 1,372 authentic and fraudulent banknotes.

Three of the four measures are based on some complicated mathematics, called *wavelet transformation*, applied to each image. The transformation produces a distribution of "wavelets." The three measures are the variance, skewness, and kurtosis of each image's wavelet distribution. The fourth measure is called *entropy*, which is a measure of how "busy" an image is. A solid black square is a low-entropy image, my cluttered-up desk is a high-entropy image.

Navigate to the Data Folder and click on the link to the text file. When the text file opens, press Ctrl+A to highlight the entire file, and then press Ctrl+C to copy it all to the clipboard.

These lines of code produce a data frame:

```
banknote.uci <- read.csv("clipboard",header=FALSE)
colnames(banknote.uci) <- c("Variance","Skewness","Kurtosis","Entropy","Class")
```

The last column, `Class`, indicates whether the banknote is real or fraudulent. The possible values are `0` and `1`. The data set's web page doesn't say which is which. (I assume `1` = real, but I could be wrong.)

Taking a quick look ahead

In the `iris` example, the output layer has three units, one for each species. In this example, two outcomes are possible: `0` and `1`. Does this mean two units in the output layer for this neural network? Nope. In this example, I'll have one output unit that returns a value, and that value represents the network's decision.

At this point, I visualize the data set to get a feel for the numbers I'll be dealing with. I use `ggplot` techniques that I outline in Chapter 10. (Go back and take a look at the "Plotting the irises" sidebar.) Picking two input variables arbitrarily — `Kurtosis` and `Entropy` as the x- and y-variables, respectively, and `Class` as the color — creates the result shown in Figure 11-4. From this viewpoint, the classes don't appear to be highly separable. Other viewpoints are possible. (As an exercise, plot other pairs of variables to see these other viewpoints.)

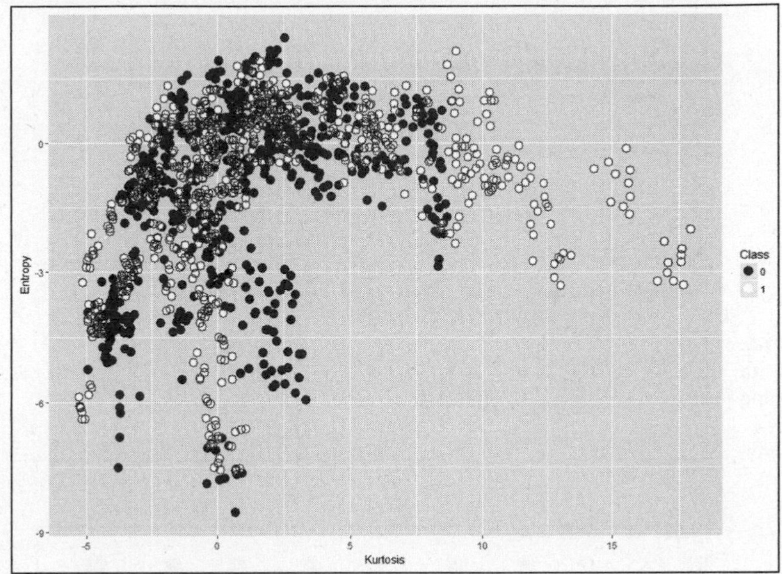

FIGURE 11-4: Entropy and Kurtosis in the banknote.uci data frame.

Setting up Rattle

Rattle provides a GUI to the nnet package and is useful for creating neural networks of the type I deal with in this example: two possible outputs mapped into one output unit. This is the optimum type of output layer for rattle. Follow these steps:

1. **With the rattle package installed, type** rattle().

   Doing so opens the rattle Data tab.

2. **To read the** banknote.uci **data frame into rattle, click the R Dataset radio button and then select** banknote.uci **in the Data Name box.**

3. **Click the check box next to Partition and change the accompanying box from 70/15/15 to** 70/30.

   This creates a training set of 70 percent of the data and a test set of the remaining 30 percent.

4. **Click Execute.**

   The Data tab now looks like Figure 11-5.

5. **On the Model tab, click the Neural Net radio button.**

6. **In the Hidden Layer Nodes box, I type** 3.

   You can pick a different number, if you like.

7. **Click Execute.**

   The Model tab looks like Figure 11-6.

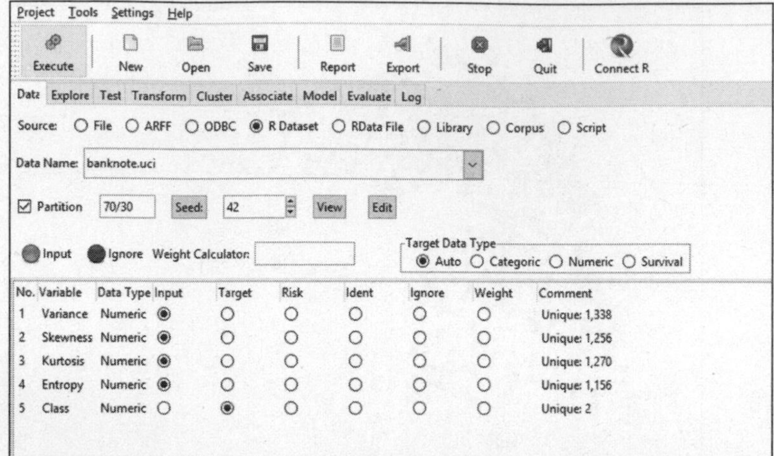

FIGURE 11-5: The `rattle` Data tab, after reading in the `banknote.uci` data frame.

```
Summary of the Neural Net model (built using nnet):

A 4-3-1 network with 23 weights.
Inputs: Variance, Skewness, Kurtosis, Entropy.
Output: as.factor(Class).
Sum of Squares Residuals: 0.0000.

Neural Network build options: skip-layer connections; entropy fitting.

In the following table:
   b  represents the bias associated with a node
   h1 represents hidden layer node 1
   i1 represents input node 1 (i.e., input variable 1)
   o  represents the output node

Weights for node h1:
 b->h1 i1->h1 i2->h1 i3->h1 i4->h1
 38.11 -26.60 -13.74 -26.10   8.99

Weights for node h2:
 b->h2 i1->h2 i2->h2 i3->h2 i4->h2
  3.55 -29.92 -32.27 -52.27 -22.05

Weights for node h3:
 b->h3 i1->h3 i2->h3 i3->h3 i4->h3
 16.81 -44.89 -23.22 -26.49 -13.86

Weights for node o:
  b->o  h1->o  h2->o  h3->o  i1->o  i2->o  i3->o  i4->o
-20.50  40.32  47.39  22.71  -9.26  -5.65  -3.75   9.52
```

FIGURE 11-6: The `rattle` Model tab, after creating the neural network for the `banknote.uci` data frame.

I show you this kind of output earlier, in the section "A neural network for the `iris` data frame." The table shows the weights for the connections to the Hidden units and to the Output unit, as well as the biases. The exceptionally low Sum of Squares Residual tells you that the network is exceptionally accurate, as you can see in the next section.

Evaluating the network

I click the Evaluate tab and ensure that the Error matrix radio button is selected and that the Testing radio button is selected. Clicking Execute creates a confusion matrix based on the Testing set. The output looks like this:

```
Error matrix for the Neural Net model on banknote.uci [test] (counts).

      Predicted
Actual   0   1 Error
     0 225   0   0.0
     1   1 186   0.5

Error matrix for the Neural Net model on banknote.uci [test] (proportions):

      Predicted
Actual    0    1 Error
     0 54.6  0.0   0.0
     1  0.2 45.1   0.5

Overall error: 0.3%, Averaged class error: 0.25%
```

As you can see, the network misclassified just one case. Looks like a pretty good network!

Going beyond Rattle: Visualizing the network

My version of `Rattle`, 5.1.0, does not have a way to plot the network. Perhaps by the time you read this book, a newer version will have that capability.

But that's okay. Designer Graham Williams had the foresight to enable users to tailor `Rattle`'s outputs for their own purposes. To find what I need, I click the Log tab.

Scrolling through the tab reveals that `Rattle` has stored the neural network in an object called `crs$nnet`. To see what the network looks like, I use the `plotnet()` function from the `NeuralNetTools` package:

```
plotnet(crs$nnet)
```

This code produces the neural network shown in Figure 11-7.

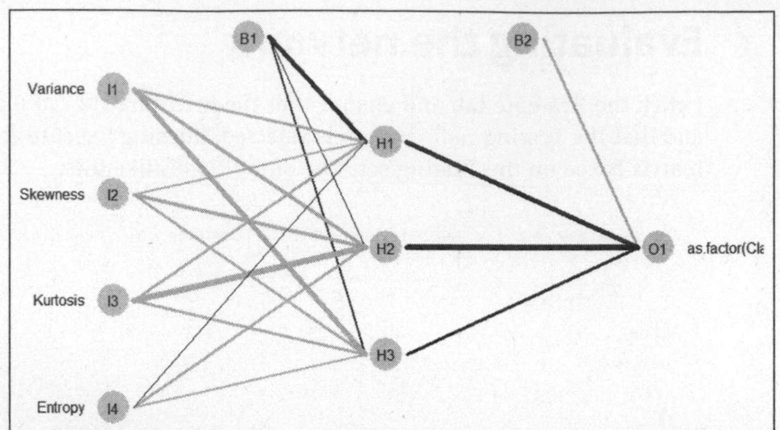

FIGURE 11-7: The neural network for the `banknote.uci` data frame.

As I mention earlier in this chapter, black lines represent positive connection weights, and gray lines represent negative connection weights. The thickness of a line reflects its numerical value. B1 applies biases to the hidden units, and B2 applies biases to the output units.

Another `NeuralNetTools` tool, `olden()`, plots the importance of each variable. Applying this function to the network

```
olden(crs$nnet)
```

produces what you see in Figure 11-8. Apparently, `Kurtosis` and `Variance` are the most important variables for this neural network.

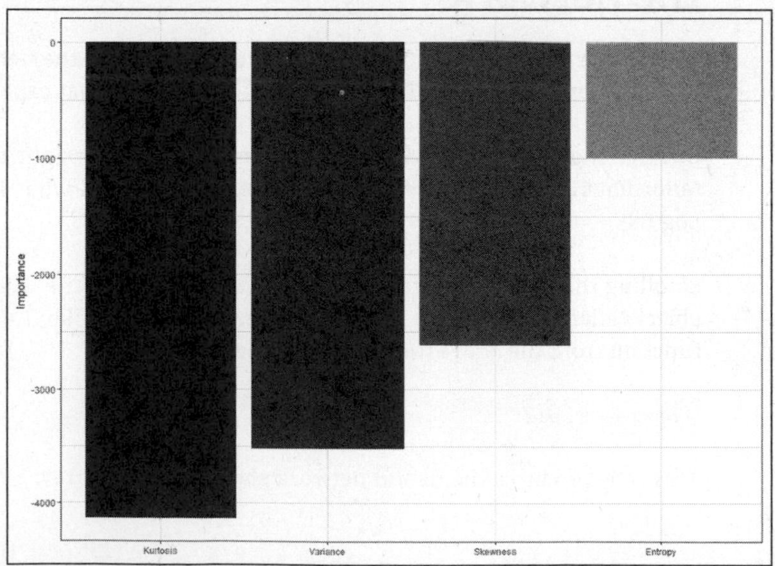

FIGURE 11-8: Bar plot of the importance of each variable in the neural network.

Suggested Projects: Rattling Around

One benefit of Rattle is that it allows you to easily experiment with whatever it helps you create. In the project in the earlier section "Project: Banknotes," try varying the number of hidden units and noting the effect on performance. Another possibility is to vary the inputs. For example, the olden() function showed Kurtosis and Variance as the most important variables. Suppose those are the only two inputs. What happens then?

Here's another little project for you. You'll learn more about neural networks if you can see how the network error rate decreases with the number of iterations through the training set.

So the objective is to plot the error rate for the banknote.uci network as a function of the number of iterations through the training data. You should expect to see a decline as the number of iterations increases.

The measure of error for this little project is *root mean square error* (RMSE), which is the standard deviation of the residuals. Each residual is the difference between the network's decision and the correct answer. You'll create a vector that holds the RMSE for each number of iterations and then plot the vector against the number of iterations.

So the first line of code is

```
rmse <- NULL
```

Next, click the rattle Log tab and scroll down to find the R code that creates the neural network:

```
crs$nnet <- nnet(as.factor(Class) ~ .,
    data=crs$dataset[crs$sample,c(crs$input, crs$target)],
    size=3, skip=TRUE, MaxNWts=10000, trace=FALSE, maxit=100)
```

The values in the data argument are based on Data tab selections. The skip argument allows for the possibility of creating *skip layers* (layers whose connections skip over the succeeding layer). The argument of most interest here is maxit, which specifies the maximum number of iterations.

Copy this code into RStudio.

Set maxit to i, and put this code into a for-loop in which i goes from 2 to 90.

The residuals are stored in `crs$nnet$residuals`. The RMSE is `sd(crs$nnet$residuals)`. Use that to update `rmse`:

```
rmse <-  append(rmse,sd(crs$nnet$residuals))
```

So the general outline for the `for`-loop is

```
for (i in 2:90){crs$nnet <- create the neural net with maxit=i)
                update the rmse vector }
```

(This `for`-loop might take a few more seconds to run than you're accustomed to.)

Finally, use the `plot()` function to plot RMSE on the *y*-axis and to plot iterations on the *x*-axis:

```
plot(x=2:90, y=rmse, type="b", xlab="Iterations", ylab= "Root Mean Square")
```

Your plot should look like the one shown in Figure 11-9.

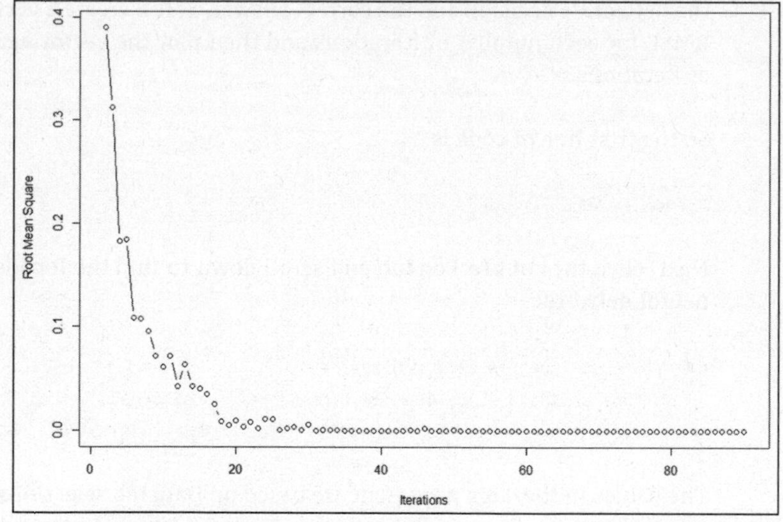

FIGURE 11-9: Root mean square error and iterations in neural networks for the `banknote.uci` data frame.

Here's one more suggested project: Take another look at the code for creating `crs$nnet`. Does anything suggest itself as something of interest that relates to RMSE? Something you could vary in a `for`-loop while holding `maxit` constant? And then plot RMSE against that thing? Go for it!

4

Large(ish) Data Sets

IN THIS PART . . .

Analyze online sales data

Understand RFM (Recency, Frequency, Money) analysis

Apply machine learning to customer segmentation

Analyze flight data

Explore flight departure delays

IN THIS CHAPTER

» Introducing RFM analysis

» Analyzing the data set

» Understanding the results

» Applying machine learning

Chapter 12 Exploring Marketing

If a business can classify its customers according to how frequently they buy, how recently they bought, and how much they spend, its marketers can target those customers and communicate with them appropriately. A recent customer who buys frequently and spends a lot of money would receive a different type of communication than one who rarely buys, spends little, and hasn't bought anything for a long time.

Project: Analyzing Retail Data

First used in the direct mail industry over 40 years ago, a popular type of marketing analysis depends on *recency* (the date of a customer's most recent purchase), *frequency* (how often the customer purchases), and *money* (how much the customer spends).

Named in order of each element's importance, this is called an *RFM analysis*. Recency is the most important because the more recently a customer has bought, the more likely he will again: The longer it takes for him to return to a business, the less likely he will. And customers who buy more frequently are more likely to again, as are customers who spend more.

One way to proceed is to divide the data into quintiles (fifths) for each variable (R, F, and M), and assign a score from 1 (lowest 20 percent) through 5 (highest 20 percent) to each customer for R, for F, and for M.

With a coding scheme like this one, 125 RFM scores are possible (555 through 111). RFM analysis segments these possibilities into five classes, with Class 1 as the least valuable customers and Class 5 the most valuable.

TIP

Dividing the data into fifths is an arbitrary (and, apparently, the most popular) way to proceed. A business can divide its data into fifths, fourths, thirds, or whatever suits its purpose. Also, a business can use business rules to create its segments (defining a *high-frequency* customer as someone who has bought at least four times in the past two weeks, for example).

The data

RFM depends on data for individual transactions. The data have to include, at the very least, an invoice number, customer identification number, purchase date, and purchase amount.

The data set for this project holds information for transactions on a British online retail shopping site. The customers are multinational. The transactions occurred between January 12, 2010, and September 12, 2012. It's on the UCI ML Repository, and you can find it here:

```
http://archive.ics.uci.edu/ml/datasets/online+retail
```

After pointing your browser to this URL, follow these steps to read the data set into R:

1. **Navigate to the Data Folder and download the spreadsheet that contains the data.**
2. **Open the spreadsheet.**

   You see that the column names are `InvoiceNo`, `StockCode`, `Description`, `Quantity`, `InvoiceDate`, `UnitPrice`, `CustomerID`, and `Country`.

   Next, you have to complete a couple of steps to read the data into R. The process is a bit roundabout, but it's reliable and fast, and it gets the job done.
3. **Save the spreadsheet as a CSV (comma-separated values) file.**
4. **Open the CSV file, press Ctrl+A to highlight everything, and then press Ctrl+C to copy to the clipboard.**
5. **In RStudio, use the `read.csv()` function to read the data into R:**

   ```
   retailonline.uci <- read.csv("clipboard",header = TRUE, sep="\t")
   ```

The first argument tells the function to take the data from the clipboard, the second one indicates that the first row contains the column names, and the third one shows that the character that separates values is the tab (not the comma, in this case).

TIP

I prefer this method to `read.xlsx()`.

RFM in R

A package called `didrooRFM` provides the function `findRFM()` that works on data like the Online Retail data set. To download the package, click Install on the Packages tab to open the Install Packages dialog box. Type **didrooRFM** into the dialog box and click the Install button.

After the package downloads, click its check box on the Packages tab.

Preparing the data

The function `findRFM()` requires a data frame that has Invoice Number, Customer ID, Invoice Date, and Amount (in that order). Unfortunately, the `Amount` column is missing from `retailonline.uci`. To create it, I multiply each row's `Quantity` by its `UnitPrice`:

```
retailonline.uci$Amount <- retailonline.uci$Quantity *        retailonline.
  uci$UnitPrice
```

Here are the first six rows of the data frame with columns 2 and 3 omitted so that everything fits neatly on the page:

```
> head(retailonline.uci[,-c(2,3)])
  InvoiceNo Quantity     InvoiceDate UnitPrice CustomerID        Country Amount
1    536365        6 12/1/2010 8:26      2.55      17850 United Kingdom  15.30
2    536365        6 12/1/2010 8:26      3.39      17850 United Kingdom  20.34
3    536365        8 12/1/2010 8:26      2.75      17850 United Kingdom  22.00
4    536365        6 12/1/2010 8:26      3.39      17850 United Kingdom  20.34
5    536365        6 12/1/2010 8:26      3.39      17850 United Kingdom  20.34
6    536365        2 12/1/2010 8:26      7.65      17850 United Kingdom  15.30
```

Next, I create a data frame that holds the required columns. The documentation video for `findRFM()` specifies that `InvoiceNo` should be a unique value for each transaction. In this data frame, however, each row represents a purchased item that can be part of a transaction. Accordingly, the `InvoiceNo` column has duplication: The first six rows, in fact, are all part of the same transaction.

TIP

You can find that `findRFM()` video by typing **?findRFM**. A link to the video appears in the Help documentation.

In the data frame I'm about to show you how to create, each invoice number covers an entire transaction, and the transaction's `Amount` is the total of the amounts for each item in the transaction.

So you create the data frame in two parts and then merge the two parts. The first part is a data frame that has a unique Invoice Number associated with the Customer ID and the Invoice Date. The function `unique()` does the work. It pulls the relevant information from columns 1, 7, and 5 in `retailonline.uci`:

```
firstPart <- unique(retailonline.uci[,c(1,7,5)])

> head(firstPart)
   InvoiceNo CustomerID     InvoiceDate
1     536365      17850 12/1/2010 8:26
8     536366      17850 12/1/2010 8:28
10    536367      13047 12/1/2010 8:34
22    536368      13047 12/1/2010 8:34
26    536369      13047 12/1/2010 8:35
27    536370      12583 12/1/2010 8:45
```

The second part provides the total of all the Amounts in each transaction. For this, you use the helpful `aggregate()` function. The idea is to *aggregate* all the Amounts associated with an Invoice Number by adding them up:

```
secondPart <- aggregate(list(Amount=retailonline.uci$Amount),
   by=list(InvoiceNo=retailonline.uci$InvoiceNo), FUN=sum)
```

The first argument shows what you're aggregating (`Amount`); the second shows what you're aggregating over (`InvoiceNo`); and the third specifies that summation is the way you're aggregating. You use `list()` to create the column names in the aggregation (which is a data frame). Here's what the aggregation looks like:

```
> head(secondPart)
  InvoiceNo Amount
1    536365 139.12
2    536366  22.20
3    536367 278.73
4    536368  70.05
5    536369  17.85
6    536370 855.86
```

To produce the data frame for `findRFM()`, you merge the two parts:

```
dataRFM <- merge(firstPart,secondPart, by = "InvoiceNo")
```

It looks like this:

```
> head(dataRFM)
  InvoiceNo CustomerID      InvoiceDate Amount
1    536365      17850 12/1/2010 8:26 139.12
2    536366      17850 12/1/2010 8:28  22.20
3    536367      13047 12/1/2010 8:34 278.73
4    536368      13047 12/1/2010 8:34  70.05
5    536369      13047 12/1/2010 8:35  17.85
6    536370      12583 12/1/2010 8:45 855.86
```

One issue remains: `InvoiceDate` is not in the proper format for `findRFM()`. It has the date in slash format along with time in hours and minutes. The function prefers R's `date` format without the time information.

The easiest way to reformat `InvoiceDate` appropriately is to use `as.Date()`:

```
dataRFM$InvoiceDate <- as.Date(dataRFM$InvoiceDate, format = "%m/%d/%Y")
```

The second argument to `as.Date()` lets the function know the format of the date it's operating on. The uppercase `Y` indicates that the year appears as four digits. (For two digits, as in 12/1/10, it's a lowercase `y`.)

After the reformat, the data frame looks like this:

```
> head(dataRFM)
  InvoiceNo CustomerID InvoiceDate Amount
1    536365      17850  2010-12-01 139.12
2    536366      17850  2010-12-01  22.20
3    536367      13047  2010-12-01 278.73
4    536368      13047  2010-12-01  70.05
5    536369      13047  2010-12-01  17.85
6    536370      12583  2010-12-01 855.86
```

One more bit of clean-up, and you're done with data prep. It's a good idea to eliminate missing data, so here goes:

```
dataRFM <- na.omit(dataRFM)
```

The data frame is ready for analysis.

Doing the analysis

Now you apply the `findRFM()` function:

```
resultsRFM <-findRFM(dataRFM,recencyWeight = 4, frequencyWeight = 4,
   monetoryWeight = 4)
```

The first argument is the data frame. The next three arguments are the weights (multipliers) to apply to the Recency score, the Frequency score, and the Monetary score. (Yes, I know: The last argument should be `monetary`, not `monetory`. Let it go.) You can use any weights you like to reflect the importance you attach to each variable. I just use the default values (4) here and show you the argument names and their order.

Examining the results

When the `findRFM()` function finishes its work, it produces Figure 12-1, a histogram that shows the distribution of final weighted scores.

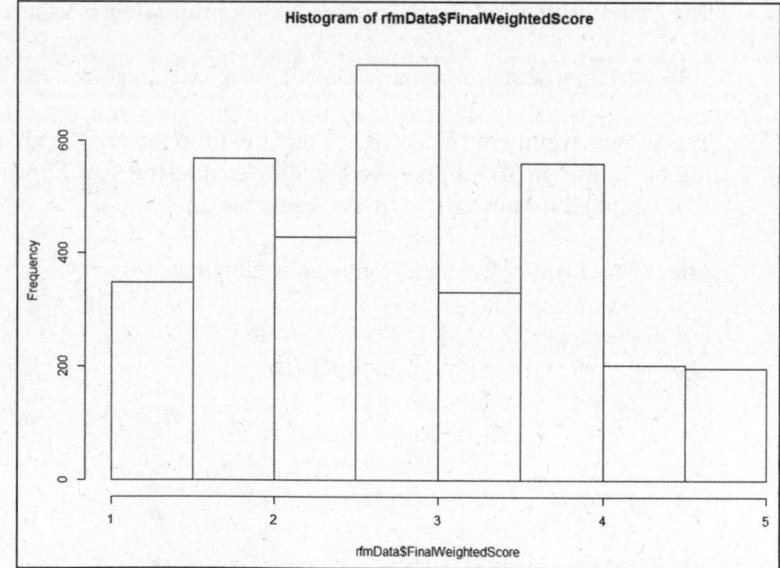

FIGURE 12-1: Distribution of final weighted scores after `findRFM()` analyzes the online retail data.

How about a look at the data frame that the function creates?

Here are the first four columns (and the first six rows):

```
> head(resultsRFM[,c(1:4)])
# A tibble: 6 x 4
  CustomerID MeanValue LastTransaction NoTransaction
       <chr>     <dbl>          <date>         <int>
1      12347  592.3920      2011-12-07             5
2      12352  155.5114      2011-11-03             7
3      12353   89.0000      2011-05-19             1
4      12354 1079.4000      2011-04-21             1
5      12357 6207.6700      2011-11-06             1
6      12358  584.0300      2011-12-08             2
```

This is the `CustomerID` along with the data that lead to the RFM scores: `MeanValue` (the average amount the customer spent per transaction), the `LastTransaction` date, and `NoTransaction` (the number of transactions). The next three columns are the percentiles of each of these pieces of data. I won't show those. (You can take a look, if you like.) These lead in turn to the next three columns: the Monetary, Frequency, and Recency scores. Here they are, along with the `FinalCustomerClass`, which is in the final column:

```
> head(resultsRFM[,c(1,8:10,16)])
# A tibble: 6 x 5
  CustomerID MonetoryScore FrequencyScore RecencyScore FinalCustomerClass
       <chr>         <dbl>          <dbl>        <dbl>              <chr>
1      12347             5              5            5            Class-5
2      12352             2              5            3            Class-3
3      12353             1              1            1            Class-1
4      12354             5              1            1            Class-2
5      12357             5              1            4            Class-3
6      12358             5              2            5            Class-4
```

For this function, the class is apparently the rounded average of the RFM scores.

The classes represent the RFM segmentation of the customers from most valuable (like Customer #12347) to least valuable (like Customer #12353).

One result of interest is the distribution of classes. To visualize this distribution, you first use the `table()` function to tabulate the frequency in each class:

```
tblClass <- table(resultsRFM$FinalCustomerClass)
```

The table is

```
> tblClassss

Class-1 Class-2 Class-3 Class-4 Class-5
    611    1129     973     603      56
```

And then you use `barplot()`:

```
barplot(tblClass)
```

The result is shown in Figure 12-2, a visualization of the RFM segmentation of the customers. As you can see, Class 5 customers are pretty rare.

TIP

In my discussion of `findRFM()`'s output, I left out Columns 5–7 and Columns 11–15. Feel free to examine on your own.

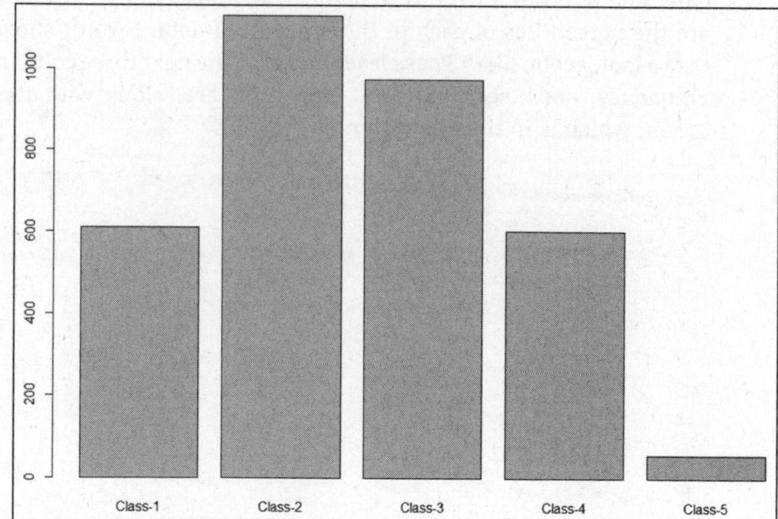

FIGURE 12-2: The distribution of classes in the `retail.uci` data frame.

Taking a look at the countries

Most commercial marketing data sets include demographic information about the customers. Combined with RFM analysis, that information can be the basis for some powerful marketing.

The only demographic data in this data set is the customer's country. It might be instructive to see the distributions of the classes in the countries.

To see how the RFM data connect with the countries, you have to add `Country` into the `resultsRFM` data frame. Remember that the `findRFM()` function assigns RFM scores to each `CustomerID`, so each row in `resultsRFM` holds a unique `CustomerID`. To connect `Country` with this data frame, then, you have to create a data frame that connects each `CustomerID` with its `Country` and then merge that data frame with `resultsRFM`.

To create the data frame that associates each `CustomerID` with its `Country`, you eliminate the duplicated `CustomerID` rows in `retailonline.uci`. You use `!duplicated()` to do that:

```
retail.nondup<- retailonline.uci[!duplicated(retailonline.
   uci$CustomerID),c(7,8)]
```

Specifying Columns 7 and 8 in `c(7,8)` limits the new data frame to just `Customer ID` and `Country`. Here's what the data frame looks like:

```
> head(retail.nondup)
   CustomerID        Country
1       17850 United Kingdom
10      13047 United Kingdom
27      12583         France
47      13748 United Kingdom
66      15100 United Kingdom
83      15291 United Kingdom
```

Next, merge `retail.nondup` with selected columns of `resultsRFM`:

```
RFMCountry <-merge(resultsRFM[,c(1,8:10,16)],retail.nondup, by="CustomerID")
```

I change to shorter column names so that I can show you the data frame on this page:

```
colnames(RFMCountry) <- c("ID","Money","Frequency","Recency","Class","Country")
```

And here it is:

```
> head(RFMCountry)
     ID Money Frequency Recency   Class     Country
1 12347     5         5       5 Class-5     Iceland
2 12352     2         5       3 Class-3      Norway
3 12353     1         1       1 Class-1     Bahrain
4 12354     5         1       1 Class-2       Spain
5 12357     5         1       4 Class-3 Switzerland
6 12358     5         2       5 Class-4     Austria
```

Now you can use `table()` to examine the distribution of `Class` for each `Country`:

```
> table(RFMCountry$Country,RFMCountry$Class)

                       Class-1 Class-2 Class-3 Class-4 Class-5
  Australia                  2       2       1       2       0
  Austria                    2       2       3       2       0
  Bahrain                    1       0       0       0       0
  Belgium                    4       6       4       3       0
  Canada                     1       2       0       0       0
  Channel Islands            0       3       3       2       0
  Cyprus                     2       1       2       0       0
  Czech Republic             0       0       1       0       0
  Denmark                    1       5       2       0       0
  EIRE                       0       0       1       1       1
  European Community         0       1       0       0       0
  Finland                    0       1       2       2       1
  France                     6      17      30      16       3
  Germany                    7      24      16      30       1
  Greece                     0       2       1       0       0
  Hong Kong                  0       0       0       0       0
  Iceland                    0       0       0       0       1
  Israel                     0       1       0       0       0
  Italy                      1       7       2       2       0
  Japan                      2       1       1       1       1
  Lebanon                    0       1       0       0       0
  Lithuania                  1       0       0       0       0
  Malta                      0       2       0       0       0
  Netherlands                2       2       3       0       1
  Norway                     0       0       5       1       0
  Poland                     1       2       1       0       0
  Portugal                   3       4       3       4       0
  Singapore                  0       0       0       1       0
  Spain                      2       6      11       2       0
  Sweden                     0       3       3       0       1
  Switzerland                1       5       9       3       0
  United Kingdom           572    1026     869     530      46
  Unspecified                0       2       0       0       0
  USA                        0       1       0       1       0
```

Obviously, most of the business comes from the United Kingdom. The rest of Europe combines to provide a distant second. It's difficult to make any conclusions from the small non-UK samples, but a quick look shows that the classes seem to be distributed similarly throughout the countries. Perhaps adding post-2011 data would shed some light on intercountry differences.

Enter Machine Learning

Creating classes from RFM scores is one way to segment customers. Another is to use machine learning to discover structure in the data and use that structure as the basis for customer segmentation.

K-means clustering

K-means clustering, which I discuss in Chapter 10, is an applicable machine learning technique. The idea behind k-means clustering is to find subgroups in data. The subgroups are called *clusters*.

Provide a set number of clusters, and a clustering procedure guesses which cluster each data point belongs to. The clustering procedure calculates the distance from each data point to the center of its cluster (known as the *centroid*), squares the distance, and adds up all the squared distances for each cluster. Each cluster thus has its own sum of squared distances, also known as a *within sum of squares*. Adding those up over all the clusters produces a *total within sum of squares*.

The clustering procedure repeats (and potentially reassigns data points to different clusters) until the within sum of squares is as small as possible for each cluster, and the total within sum of squares is a minimum. When this happens, each data point is in the cluster with the closest centroid.

How many clusters should you specify? One way to find out is to carry out the clustering procedure on the data and use a range of possibilities for the number of clusters. After each procedure finishes, calculate the total within sum of squares. Generally, the total within sum of squares decreases as the number of clusters increases. The objective is to find the number of clusters above which little or no reduction in total within sum of squares occurs.

That's what I do with the RFM data. Each data point (corresponding to a customer) appears as a Recency score, a Frequency score, and a Monetary score.

I follow this procedure in Chapter 10. I begin by showing you how to initialize a vector called totwss, which will hold the values of total within sum of squares:

```
totwss <- NULL
```

A for loop carries out the clustering procedure for cluster amounts from 2 to 15, and appends the resulting total within sum of squares to totwss. The kmeans() function does the clustering:

```
for (i in 2:15){
  totwss <- append(totwss,kmeans(resultsRFM[,8:10],centers=i)$tot.withinss)
}
```

Columns 8–10 in resultsRFM hold the variables of interest. The centers = i argument sets the number of clusters, and $totwithinss holds the total within sum of squares for a clustering solution. After each k-means procedure ends, append() puts the total within sum of squares on the end of the totwss vector.

Finally, you plot total within sum of squares against number of clusters:

```
plot(x=2:15, y=totwss, type="b", xlab="Clusters", ylab= "Total Within SS")
```

The plot() function produces Figure 12-3. After 11 clusters, the total within sum of squares seems to not decrease appreciably, suggesting that 11 is a good number of clusters for this data set. This is a judgement call, and you might see it differently. Incidentally, one business analytics website (www.Putler.com/rfm-analysis) advocates for just that many customer segments.

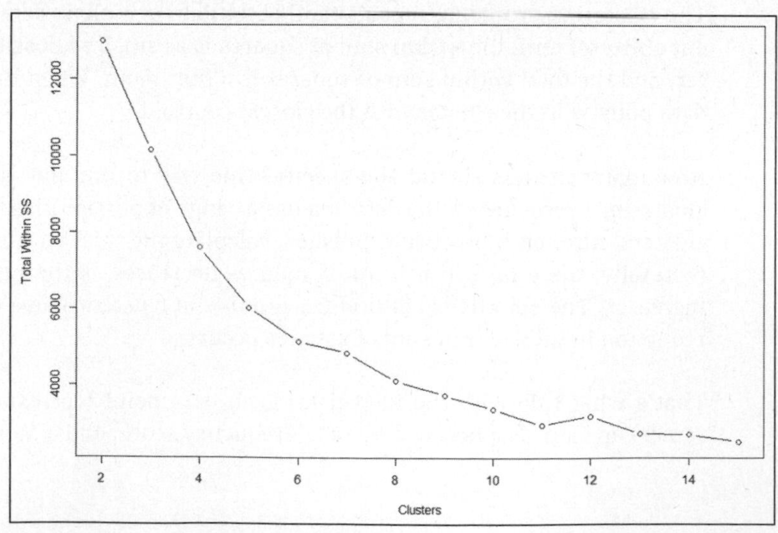

FIGURE 12-3: Total within sum of squares versus number of clusters for k-means clustering of the resultsRFM data frame.

Working with Rattle

`Rattle` provides a GUI to the `kmeans()` function. If you've worked through the chapters in Part 2, you have this package downloaded and all you have to do is click its check box on the Packages tab. If not, click Install on the Packages tab to open the Install Packages dialog box. Type **rattle** into the dialog box and click the Install button. After the package downloads, select its check box on the Packages tab and you're ready to roll.

This command opens the `Rattle` GUI Data tab:

```
rattle()
```

Click the R Dataset radio button and then select `resultsRFM` from the drop-down menu in the Data Name box. You click Execute to read the data frame. When the variable names appear on the Data tab, leave the Ident radio button for `CustomerID` as is, but select the Ignore radio button for all other variables except `MonetoryScore`, `FrequencyScore`, and `RecencyScore`. If the Partition box is selected, deselect it. Because you clicked those radio buttons, click Execute again. After all this, the screen looks like Figure 12-4.

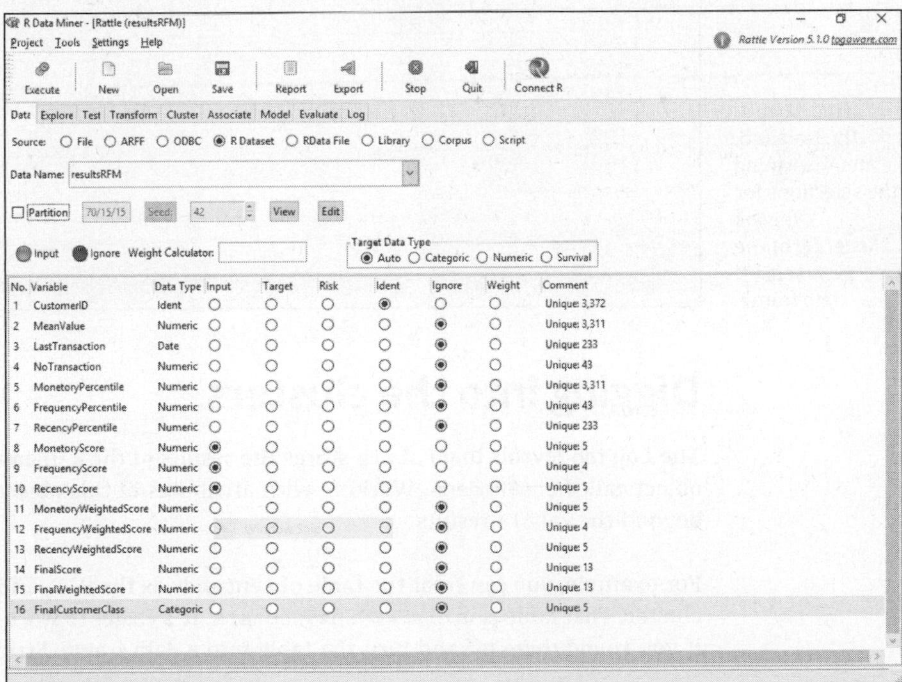

FIGURE 12-4: The `rattle` Data tab, after selecting the variables for k-means clustering.

Next, you open the Cluster tab, and with the KMeans radio button selected, use the arrow in the Clusters box to set 11 as the number of clusters. Make sure that the Rescale box is deselected. Then click Execute. Figure 12-5 shows the appearance of the Data tab after all these actions.

The first couple of lines show the number of data points in each of the 11 clusters. The next lines present the mean for each variable. The table shows the centroids for each cluster.

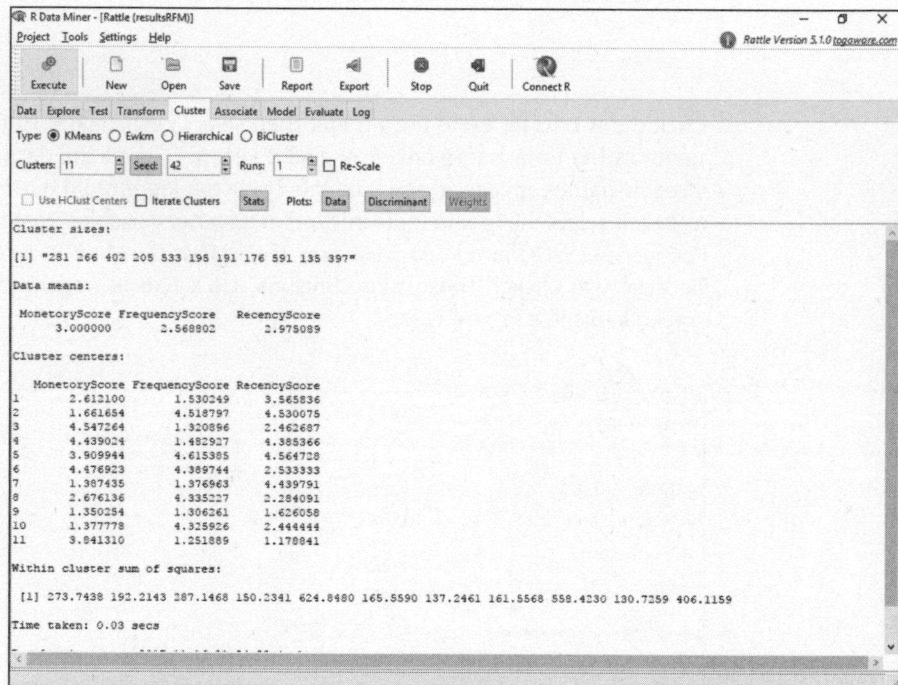

FIGURE 12-5: The Data tab, after executing the selections for k-means clustering of the `resultsRFM` data frame.

Digging into the clusters

The Log tab reveals that `Rattle` stores the results of the k-means clustering in an object called `crs$kmeans`. Working with attributes of this object allows you to go beyond the `Rattle` results.

For example, you can treat the table of centroids as the R, F, and M values of each cluster. That table is in `crs$kmeans$centers`. It's easier to work with those values if you round them off and turn the table into a data frame. Strictly speaking, you first have to turn the table into a matrix and then into a data frame. The function `as.data.frame.matrix()` does all that in one fell swoop:

```
rounded.clusters <- as.data.frame.matrix(round(crs$kmeans$centers))
> rounded.clusters
   MonetoryScore FrequencyScore RecencyScore
1              3              2            4
2              2              5            5
3              5              1            2
4              4              1            4
5              4              5            5
6              4              4            3
7              1              1            4
8              3              4            2
9              1              1            2
10             1              4            2
11             4              1            1
```

With the numbers in a data frame, I can manipulate them and get a sense of what the clusters mean. The cluster numbers are arbitrary: The customers in cluster 1 aren't necessarily more valuable than the customers in cluster 11. So you can use some rules of thumb to reorder them and see what shakes out.

As I mention earlier, experience indicates that recency is most important (a more recent customer is more likely to repeat), followed by frequency (a frequent customer is more likely to repeat), followed by money.

Here's how to sort the clusters by recency, then by frequency, and then by money:

```
with(rounded.clusters, rounded.clusters[order(-RecencyScore,-FrequencyScore,
   -MonetoryScore),])
```

I suggest using `with()` so that in the `order()` function you don't have to use arguments like `rounded.clusters$RecencyScore`. The `order()` function specifies the order of the rows. The minus sign (-) in front of each argument means "in descending order." Running that code produces this:

```
   MonetoryScore FrequencyScore RecencyScore
5              4              5            5
2              2              5            5
1              3              2            4
4              4              1            4
7              1              1            4
6              4              4            3
```

```
8          3          4          2
10         1          4          2
3          5          1          2
9          1          1          2
11         4          1          1
```

With this ordering, the most valuable customers are in Cluster 5, and the least valuable are in Cluster 11. Cluster 5 customers are apparently frequent and recent buyers whose spending is at the second-highest level. Cluster 11 customers spend as much as Cluster 5 customers, but not recently and not frequently. How would marketers communicate with each group?

I leave it to you to interpret the other clusters.

The clusters and the classes

I'm curious to know how the RFM analysis compares with the clustering. How do the clusters line up with the classes?

Each customer's assigned cluster is in `crs$kmeans$cluster`, and the assigned class is in `resultsRFM$FinalCustomerClass`. So this table tells the tale:

```
> table(Cluster=crs$kmeans$cluster,Class=resultsRFM$FinalCustomerClass)
       Class
Cluster Class-1 Class-2 Class-3 Class-4 Class-5
     1        0     214      67       0       0
     2        0       0     205      61       0
     3        0     239     163       0       0
     4        0       0     185      20       0
     5        0       0      47     430      56
     6        0       0     103      92       0
     7        0     169      22       0       0
     8        0      52     124       0       0
     9      528      63       0       0       0
     10       0      78      57       0       0
     11      83     314       0       0       0
```

The table shows Class 5 customers all in Cluster 5, which ranked highest among the clusters. (That they're both "5" is a coincidence.) Cluster 11 (the lowest-ranked) consists entirely of Class 1 and Class 2 customers.

So it looks like the two segmentation schemes are related. To get a definitive answer (instead of "looks like"), you'd need a statistical analysis.

Is this a good time for statistical analysis? It's *always* a good time for statistical analysis! For a table like this, I show you how to use a statistical test to see whether the clusters and the classes are independent of one another. Statisticians call this the *null hypothesis*. A statistical test tells you how likely it is that "independence" can explain the data in the table. If that probability turns out to be very small (less than .05, by convention), you reject the independence explanation.

Here's another way to look at it: If the clusters and the classes were independent of one another, the numbers in the table would look different. They would still add up to the same number of customers and to the same row totals and column totals, but the numbers inside the table would be distributed differently. The question is, does the arrangement we have differ significantly from the independence-based arrangement?

The appropriate statistical test is called *chi squared* ("chi" is pronounced like the first syllable of "kayak"). Here's how to use it:

```
> chisq.test(table(Cluster=crs$kmeans$cluster, Class=resultsRFM$FinalCustomer
   Class))

              Pearson's Chi-squared test

data:  table(Cluster = crs$kmeans$cluster, Class = resultsRFM$FinalCustomer
   Class)
X-squared = 6261.6, df = 40, p-value < 2.2e-16
```

The exceptionally low `p-value` indicates that you can reject the idea that `Cluster` and `Class` are independent of one another. Independence is highly unlikely. (Shameless plug: For the lowdown on statistical testing see *Statistical Analysis with R For Dummies*, written by me and published by Wiley.)

Quick suggested project

If you'd like to explore the Clusters versus Classes table a bit further, download and install the `vcd` (visualizing categorical data) package. One function, `assocstats()`, provides some additional statistics that you can apply. Another function, `assoc()`, produces a nice-looking graphic that spotlights deviations from independence in the table.

Suggested Project: Another Data Set

If you're interested in trying out your RFM analysis skills on another set of data, this project is for you.

The CDNOW data set consists of almost 70,000 rows. It's a record of sales at CDNOW from the beginning of January 1997 through the end of June 1998.

You'll find it at: `https://raw.githubusercontent.com/rtheman/CLV/master/1_Input/CDNOW/CDNOW_master.txt`

Press Ctrl+A to highlight all the data, and press Ctrl+C to copy to the clipboard. Then use the `read.csv()` function to read the data into R:

```
cdNOW <- read.csv("clipboard", header=FALSE, sep = "")
```

Here's how to name the columns:

```
colnames(cdNOW) <- c("CustomerID","InvoiceDate","Quantity","Amount")
```

The data should look like this:

```
> head(cdNOW)
  CustomerID InvoiceDate Quantity Amount
1          1    19970101        1  11.77
2          2    19970112        1  12.00
3          2    19970112        5  77.00
4          3    19970102        2  20.76
5          3    19970330        2  20.76
6          3    19970402        2  19.54
```

It's less complicated than the Online Retail project because `Amount` is the total amount of the transaction. So each row is a transaction, and aggregation is not necessary. The `Quantity` column is irrelevant for our purposes.

TIP

Here's a hint about reformatting the `InvoiceDate`: The easiest way to get it into R date format is to download and install the `lubridate` package and use its `ymd()` function:

```
cdNOW$InvoiceDate <-ymd(cdNOW$InvoiceDate)
```

After that change, here's how the first six rows look:

```
> head(cdNOW)
  CustomerID InvoiceDate Quantity Amount
1          1  1997-01-01        1  11.77
2          2  1997-01-12        1  12.00
3          2  1997-01-12        5  77.00
4          3  1997-01-02        2  20.76
5          3  1997-03-30        2  20.76
6          3  1997-04-02        2  19.54
```

Almost there. What's missing for `findRFM()`? An invoice number. So you have to use a little trick to make one up. The trick is to use each row identifier in the row-identifier column as the invoice number. To turn the row-identifier column into a data frame column, download and install the `tibble` package and use its `rownames_to_column()` function:

```
cdNOW <- rownames_to_column(cdNOW, "InvoiceNumber")
```

Here's the data:

```
> head(cdNOW)
  InvoiceNumber CustomerID InvoiceDate Quantity Amount
1             1          1  1997-01-01        1  11.77
2             2          2  1997-01-12        1  12.00
3             3          2  1997-01-12        5  77.00
4             4          3  1997-01-02        2  20.76
5             5          3  1997-03-30        2  20.76
6             6          3  1997-04-02        2  19.54
```

Now create a data frame with everything but that `Quantity` column and you're ready.

See how much of the Online Retail project you can accomplish in this one.

Happy analyzing!

IN THIS CHAPTER

» Working with the `flights` data frame

» Using `tidyverse` functions

» Joining data frames

» Exploring flight delays

Chapter 13 From the City That Never Sleeps

An airline flight generates a lot of data. The data includes identification of the plane (airline, tail number), identification of the flight (flight number, date, time, origin, destination), characteristics of the flight (distance, time in the air, departure delay, arrival delay), and more. For a budding data analyst, a data set of airline flights presents a treasure trove of opportunities. And that's what I show you how to work with in this chapter.

Examining the Data Set

The data set is called `flights`, and it lives in a package called `nycflights13`. It has the data on all domestic flights out of New York City in 2013. On the Packages tab, click Install to open the Install Packages dialog box. In the dialog box, type **nycflights13** and click the Install button. After the package downloads, select its check box on the Packages tab. Additional data sets are in this package, and I show you how to work with them, too.

A number of other packages are important for data manipulation, and they're part of a bigger package called `tidyverse` (see Chapter 2). If you haven't downloaded it already, follow the procedure in the preceding paragraph (and type **tidyverse** in the dialog box). Click the tidyverse check box on the Packages tab and you're ready for business.

Warming Up

Before I start you out on the project, I walk you through some fundamental skills. Let me begin with a look at the data.

Glimpsing and viewing

The `flights` data set has 19 columns, so `head(flights)` won't be much help. Instead, a `tidyverse` function called `glimpse()` flips the script, by showing you the column names in a column and the first few values of each column in a row:

```
> glimpse(flights,width=50)
Observations: 336,776
Variables: 19
$ year           <int> 2013, 2013, 2013, 2013...
$ month          <int> 1, 1, 1, 1, 1, 1, 1, 1...
$ day            <int> 1, 1, 1, 1, 1, 1, 1, 1...
$ dep_time       <int> 517, 533, 542, 544, 55...
$ sched_dep_time <int> 515, 529, 540, 545, 60...
$ dep_delay      <dbl> 2, 4, 2, -1, -6, -4, -...
$ arr_time       <int> 830, 850, 923, 1004, 8...
$ sched_arr_time <int> 819, 830, 850, 1022, 8...
$ arr_delay      <dbl> 11, 20, 33, -18, -25, ...
$ carrier        <chr> "UA", "UA", "AA", "B6"...
$ flight         <int> 1545, 1714, 1141, 725,...
$ tailnum        <chr> "N14228", "N24211", "N...
$ origin         <chr> "EWR", "LGA", "JFK", "...
$ dest           <chr> "IAH", "IAH", "MIA", "...
$ air_time       <dbl> 227, 227, 160, 183, 11...
$ distance       <dbl> 1400, 1416, 1089, 1576...
$ hour           <dbl> 5, 5, 5, 5, 6, 5, 6, 6...
$ minute         <dbl> 15, 29, 40, 45, 0, 58,...
$ time_hour      <dttm> 2013-01-01 05:00:00, ...
```

The `width` argument controls how much of each row to show. If you leave it out, the output fills out the whole screen (and wouldn't translate well to this page).

Another function, called `View()`, presents a spreadsheet-like (spreadsheetesque?) look at the data in the RStudio Script window:

```
View(flights)
```

It produces what you see in Figure 13-1.

stations × | Untitled2* × | Untitled3* × | Untitled4* × | Untitled5* × | flights ×

Filter

	year	month	day	dep_time	sched_dep_time	dep_delay	arr_time	sched_arr_time	arr_delay
1	2013	1	1	517	515	2	830	819	
2	2013	1	1	533	529	4	850	830	
3	2013	1	1	542	540	2	923	850	
4	2013	1	1	544	545	-1	1004	1022	
5	2013	1	1	554	600	-6	812	837	
6	2013	1	1	554	558	-4	740	728	
7	2013	1	1	555	600	-5	913	854	
8	2013	1	1	557	600	-3	709	723	
9	2013	1	1	557	600	-3	838	846	
10	2013	1	1	558	600	-2	753	745	
11	2013	1	1	558	600	-2	849	851	
12	2013	1	1	558	600	-2	853	856	

Showing 1 to 13 of 336,776 entries

FIGURE 13-1: `View(flights)` puts this view into the RStudio Script window.

Piping, filtering, and grouping

Dealing with a data frame often calls for putting multiple commands and functions together. To make that easy to do, R provides the `pipe` operator, which looks like this: `%>%`. You use it to connect one function to the next.

Suppose that I'm interested in the mean and standard deviation of how long flights from Newark lasted (`air_time`) in the first five days of January. That's

```
Newark_January <- flights %>%
  filter(origin == "EWR" & month == 1 & day <= 5) %>%
  group_by(day)%>%
  summarize(mean=mean(air_time,na.rm=TRUE),
            std_dev=sd(air_time, na.rm=TRUE))
```

The first line, of course, assigns `flights` to `Newark_January`. Read the `%>%` operator as "then."

So *then* the second line uses `filter()` to extract just the flights out of Newark (`"EWR"`) and only in January (`month == 1`) and just the first five days (`day <= 5`).

Then the third line uses `group_by()` to group the data by `day`.

And *then* the fourth line provides the statistics, omitting the missing data.

TIP

The `%>%` operator works a lot like + does in `ggplot`.

To render this little structure nicely onscreen, you use the `kable()` function (which lives in the `knitr` package):

```
> kable(Newark_January,digits=2)


| day|   mean| std_dev|
|---:|------:|-------:|
|   1| 166.89|   97.46|
|   2| 159.20|   93.47|
|   3| 151.36|   83.44|
|   4| 143.39|   84.37|
|   5| 157.10|   95.34|
```

Before going any further, you should know about another statistic: the *standard error of the mean*. It's the standard deviation divided by the square root of the number of scores that go into calculating the mean. Why is the standard error important? Think of the air times in Day 1 as a sample drawn from a large population. The standard error is a measure of how accurately the sample mean estimates the population mean: The larger the sample, the more accurate the estimate.

Given the importance of the standard error of the mean, you'd think that base R would provide a function to calculate it. But it doesn't. A function called `std.error()` is in the `plotrix` package. Follow the usual steps to download and install this package. With `plotrix` installed, you can get the standard error of the mean by adding a line to `summarize()`:

```
Newark_January <- flights %>%
  filter(origin == "EWR" & month == 1 & day <= 5) %>%
  group_by(day)%>%
  summarize(mean=mean(air_time,na.rm=TRUE),
            std_dev=sd(air_time, na.rm=TRUE),
            std_err=std.error(air_time, na.rm=TRUE))
```

and then use `kable()` once again:

```
> kable(Newark_January,digits=2)


| day|   mean| std_dev| std_err|
```

```
|---:|------:|-------:|-------:|
|   1| 166.89|   97.46|    5.63|
|   2| 159.20|   93.47|    5.06|
|   3| 151.36|   83.44|    4.59|
|   4| 143.39|   84.37|    4.60|
|   5| 157.10|   95.34|    6.19|
```

Visualizing

Next, you graph the data, which is always a good thing to do. Figure 13-2 shows the graph of Newark_January, complete with bars for the standard errors.

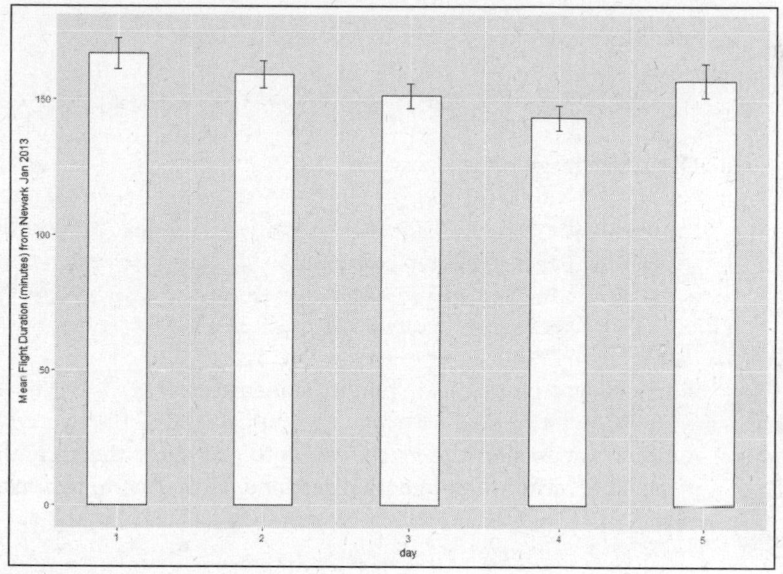

FIGURE 13-2: Mean flight duration versus day in Newark_January.

You use ggplot() to draw this graph. The first line specifies where the data comes from and maps day to the *x*-axis and mean to the *y*-axis:

```
ggplot(Newark_January, aes(x=day, y=mean)) +
```

Next, you add the bars to the plot:

```
geom_bar(stat="identity", color="black", fill = "gray100",width=0.4)+
```

The geom_bar() function usually plots frequency counts. It tries to count frequencies in the data unless you tell it otherwise. Here, the first argument tells geom_bar() to not count frequencies, and instead use the statistic in the table (mapped to *y*) to plot the bars. The color argument sets the border, and fill = "gray100" fills each bar with white. The last argument, unsurprisingly, sets the width of each bar.

Next, you add the bars that represent the standard error of the mean:

```
geom_errorbar(aes(ymax = mean + std_err, ymin = mean - std_err), width=.05)+
```

The aesthetic mappings show how high each error bar ascends and how low it descends.

Finally, you give the y-axis an informative label:

```
labs(y="Mean Flight Duration (minutes) from Newark Jan 2013")
```

The whole megillah is

```
ggplot(Newark_January, aes(x=day, y=mean)) +
  geom_bar(stat="identity", color="black", fill = "gray100",width=0.4)+
  geom_errorbar(aes(ymax = mean + std_err, ymin = mean - std_err), width=.05)+
  labs(y="Mean Flight Duration (minutes) from Newark Jan 2013")
```

REMEMBER

Whenever you plot a mean, plot its standard error.

TIP

Another way to plot the error bars is to just show them coming out of the top of each bar rather than in both directions. To do that in this example, set ymin = mean.

Joining

If you've ever flown in the US and you've checked your baggage, you'll see what might look like a strange abbreviation on your baggage tag. Fly to Chicago's O'Hare International Airport, for example, and the tag says *ORD* (which might confuse you if you've ever been to Fort Ord in California).

Assigned by the Federal Aviation Administration (FAA) and other agencies, some abbreviations are pretty easy to figure out — like JAX, for Jacksonville, Florida, or JFK, for New York's John F. Kennedy International Airport. But would you know off the top of your head that PDL is Hartford, Connecticut? Or that INT is Winston-Salem, North Carolina? Me, neither.

Airport abbreviations are in the origin and dest columns of flights. With only three origins — EWR (Newark), LGA (LaGuardia), and the aforementioned JFK — these are easy to remember. What about the destinations?

```
> glimpse(flights$dest, 60)
 chr [1:336776] "IAH" "IAH" "MIA" "BQN" "ATL" "ORD" ..
```

IAH? BQN? If I have to look up airport abbreviations whenever I want to explore data about origins and destinations, I'd waste a lot of time.

Instead, I can let R do the work. One of the data frames in nycflights13 is called airports, and it holds the abbreviations along with other information about the airports:

```
> glimpse(airports,60)
Observations: 1,458
Variables: 8
$ faa   <chr> "04G", "06A", "06C", "06N", "09J", "0A9",...
$ name  <chr> "Lansdowne Airport", "Moton Field Municip...
$ lat   <dbl> 41.13047, 32.46057, 41.98934, 41.43191, 3...
$ lon   <dbl> -80.61958, -85.68003, -88.10124, -74.3915...
$ alt   <int> 1044, 264, 801, 523, 11, 1593, 730, 492, ...
$ tz    <dbl> -5, -6, -6, -5, -5, -5, -5, -5, -5, -8, -...
$ dst   <chr> "A", "A", "A", "A", "A", "A", "A", "A", "...
$ tzone <chr> "America/New_York", "America/Chicago", "A...
```

The abbreviations are in the faa column, and the corresponding names are in the name column. I don't know about you, but I would have never guessed that 04G refers to Lansdowne Airport (Youngstown, Ohio).

But I digress. To let R do the work of finding out which airports correspond to which abbreviations, you can *join* the flights data frame with the airports data frame. Joining takes place by matching a *key* variable in one data frame with the corresponding *key* variable in the other. (It's something like merge(), which I describe how to use in Chapter 12.) In this case, the key variables have different names (dest in flights, faa in airports).

So here's how to join the flights data frame with the airports data frame. Without belaboring the point, several types of *join* operations are possible, but the *inner join* best suits our purposes:

```
flites_dest_names <- flights %>%
  inner_join(airports, by = c("dest" = "faa")) %>%
  rename(dest_airport=name)
```

The by argument in inner_join() sets up the equivalence between dest and faa. The rename() function substitutes a more informative label for name.

To see the new data frame, use the View() function:

```
View(flites_dest_names)
```

Running this code produces Figure 13-3. I've scrolled to the right so that you can see the relevant information that the join adds.

I use the new data frame to answer the question, "How many flights left JFK for Miami or Orlando in February?" Here's the code:

```
JFK_Miami_Orlando <- flites_dest_names %>%
  filter(origin == "JFK" &
        (dest_airport == "Miami Intl" | dest_airport == "Orlando Intl")
          & month == 2) %>%
  group_by(carrier) %>%
  summarize(number_of_flights = n())
```

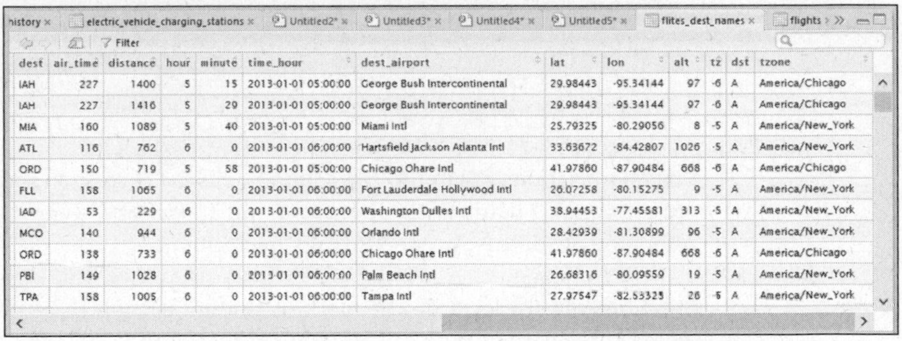

history × | electric_vehicle_charging_stations × | Untitled2* × | Untitled3* × | Untitled4* × | Untitled5* × | flites_dest_names × | flights

Filter

dest	air_time	distance	hour	minute	time_hour	dest_airport	lat	lon	alt	tz	dst	tzone
IAH	227	1400	5	15	2013-01-01 05:00:00	George Bush Intercontinental	29.98443	-95.34144	97	-6	A	America/Chicago
IAH	227	1416	5	29	2013-01-01 05:00:00	George Bush Intercontinental	29.98443	-95.34144	97	-6	A	America/Chicago
MIA	160	1089	5	40	2013-01-01 05:00:00	Miami Intl	25.79325	-80.29056	8	-5	A	America/New_York
ATL	116	762	6	0	2013-01-01 06:00:00	Hartsfield Jackson Atlanta Intl	33.63672	-84.42807	1026	-5	A	America/New_York
ORD	150	719	5	58	2013-01-01 05:00:00	Chicago Ohare Intl	41.97860	-87.90484	668	-6	A	America/Chicago
FLL	158	1065	6	0	2013-01-01 06:00:00	Fort Lauderdale Hollywood Intl	26.07258	-80.15275	9	-5	A	America/New_York
IAD	53	229	6	0	2013-01-01 06:00:00	Washington Dulles Intl	38.94453	-77.45581	313	-5	A	America/New_York
MCO	140	944	6	0	2013-01-01 06:00:00	Orlando Intl	28.42939	-81.30899	96	-5	A	America/New_York
ORD	138	733	6	0	2013-01-01 06:00:00	Chicago Ohare Intl	41.97860	-87.90484	668	-6	A	America/Chicago
PBI	149	1028	6	0	2013-01-01 06:00:00	Palm Beach Intl	26.68316	-80.09559	19	-5	A	America/New_York
TPA	158	1005	6	0	2013-01-01 06:00:00	Tampa Intl	27.97547	-82.53325	26	-5	A	America/New_York

FIGURE 13-3: The result of joining flights with airports: flites_dest_names.

The filter() function is a bit more complicated than the one I show you earlier in this chapter. This is due to the "Miami or Orlando" part. The vertical line inside the parentheses (the ones inside filter(), to be more specific) means *or*. I group the results by carrier. The summarize() function uses n() to count the number of flights.

Here are the results:

```
> kable(JFK_Miami_Orlando)


|carrier | number_of_flights|
```

```
|:-------|----------------:|
|AA      |              228|
|B6      |              252|
|DL      |              196|
```

Quick Suggested Project: Airline names

It would be more helpful to show the names of the airlines instead of the abbreviations in the `carrier` column. The `nycflights13` data set has another data frame called `airlines` that shows each abbreviation along with the full name of the carrier. Join this data frame with `flites_dest_names` and redo what I just did, showing the carrier names instead of the abbreviations.

Project: Departure Delays

I don't know about you, but I'm not a big fan of hustling to the airport to make a flight, only to find that it's delayed. So, in this project, I address my pet peeve (and maybe yours) by taking a look at departure delay data.

Adding a variable: weekday

On which day of the week are the delays longest? To find out, you have to add a variable that indicates the weekday of a departure. The `time_hour` column has the calendar date and the hour for each flight in the data frame. To extract the weekday, you use the `lubridate` package's `wday()` function.

Here's an example of how it works on one entry from `time_hour`:

```
> wday("2013-01-01 05:00:00")
[1] 3
```

This function considers Sunday as Weekday 1, so January 1, 2013, was a Tuesday.

You create a new data frame by adding a variable called `weekday` to `flites_dest_names`. To add the variable, you use the intriguingly named `mutate()` function:

```
flites_day <- flites_dest_names %>%
  mutate(weekday = wday(time_hour))
```

This results in a column of numbers with 1 = Sunday, 2 = Monday, and so forth. To turn those numbers into the appropriate weekdays, you treat the weekday numbers as levels of a factor and provide substitute labels for the numbers:

```
flites_day$weekday <- factor(flites_day$weekday,
                              labels = c("Sunday", "Monday", "Tuesday",
     "Wednesday", "Thursday", "Friday", "Saturday"))
```

TIP

The wday() function takes an argument called label. If you set label=TRUE, the function supplies the weekday names and you don't have to complete this last step. I couldn't get it to work. Maybe you can.

Just to verify:

```
flites_per_weekday <- flites_day %>%
  group_by(weekday) %>%
  summarize(number_of_flights = n())
```

```
> kable(flites_per_weekday)

|weekday   | number_of_flights|
|:---------|-----------------:|
|Sunday    |             45240|
|Monday    |             49626|
|Tuesday   |             49362|
|Wednesday |             49016|
|Thursday  |             49147|
|Friday    |             49221|
|Saturday  |             37562|
```

Quick Suggested Project: Analyze weekday differences

It looks like you have far fewer flights to choose from on Saturday and Sunday than on any other day. Are the differences among days significant? Another way of asking this question: Is number_of_flights independent of weekday? Looking at it still another way: If the two were independent, you would expect an equal number of flights for each weekday. Does the data differ significantly from that pattern?

In Chapter 12, I use chisq.test() to help you answer a similar question. Use that function here. Remember that what you're analyzing is flites_per_weekday$number_of_flights. What can you conclude?

Delay, weekday, and airport

Which weekday has the longest average delays? Does it vary with airport of origin? To find out, you create a data frame called summary_dep_delay:

```
summary_dep_delay <- flites_day %>%
  group_by(origin, weekday) %>%
  summarize(mean = mean(dep_delay, na.rm = TRUE),
            std_dev = sd(dep_delay, na.rm = TRUE),
            std_err = std.error(dep_delay,na.rm=TRUE))
```

Applying kable() gives an okay-looking table (try it!), but a graphic shows the results more clearly. Figure 13-4 shows what I mean.

This bar plot shows that the shortest delays (in 2013) were out of LaGuardia (LGA), and shortest on Saturdays.

Here's how to use ggplot() to draw it. You begin as always by specifying the source of the data and the aesthetic mappings:

```
ggplot(summary_dep_delay, aes(x=weekday, y=mean, fill=origin)) +
```

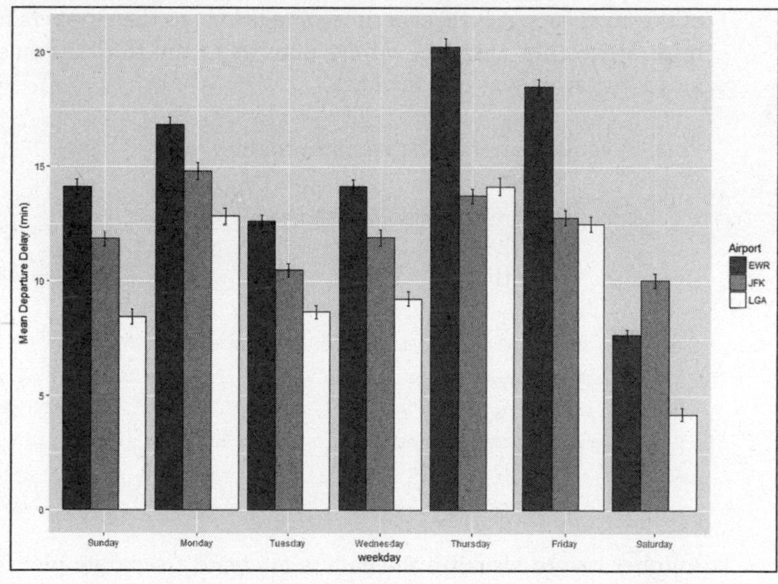

FIGURE 13-4: Mean departure delay (min) versus weekday and airport of origin.

Next, you add the bars:

```
geom_bar(position="dodge", stat="identity", color="black")+
```

`position = "dodge"` means that the bars aren't stacked on top of one another. Instead, they "dodge" each other and line up side by side. As I mention earlier in this chapter, `stat = "identity"` tells `geom_bar()` to use the numbers in the table to plot the bars and to not try to count frequencies in the data. The `color` argument sets the border color of each bar.

Now you add some artistic effects to the bars:

```
scale_fill_manual(name="Airport",values=c("grey40","grey65","grey100"))+
```

The first argument attaches a title to the legend. The second is a vector of colors that associate with each origin.

Next, you add the error-bars:

```
geom_errorbar(aes(ymax=mean+std_err,ymin=mean-std_err), width=.1,
   position=position_dodge(.9))+
```

The first argument, as in the earlier example, sets the upper and lower boundaries of the error bars. A little experimenting led me to the numbers for the second and third arguments. With the wrong number in the third argument, the error bar locations can be way out of whack.

Finally, you add an informative label to the y-axis:

```
labs(y="Mean Departure Delay (min)")
```

Here's the whole thing:

```
ggplot(summary_dep_delay, aes(x=weekday, y=mean, fill=origin)) +
  geom_bar(position="dodge", stat="identity",color="black")+
  scale_fill_manual(name="Airport",values=c("grey40","grey65","grey100"))+
  geom_errorbar(aes(ymax=mean+std_err,ymin=mean-std_err), width=.1,
   position=position_dodge(.9))+
  labs(y="Mean Departure Delay (min)")
```

Another way to visualize the data is to create a separate plot for each airport of origin and show them one above the other. In this kind of arrangement, each plot is called a *facet*. Figure 13-5 is a prime example.

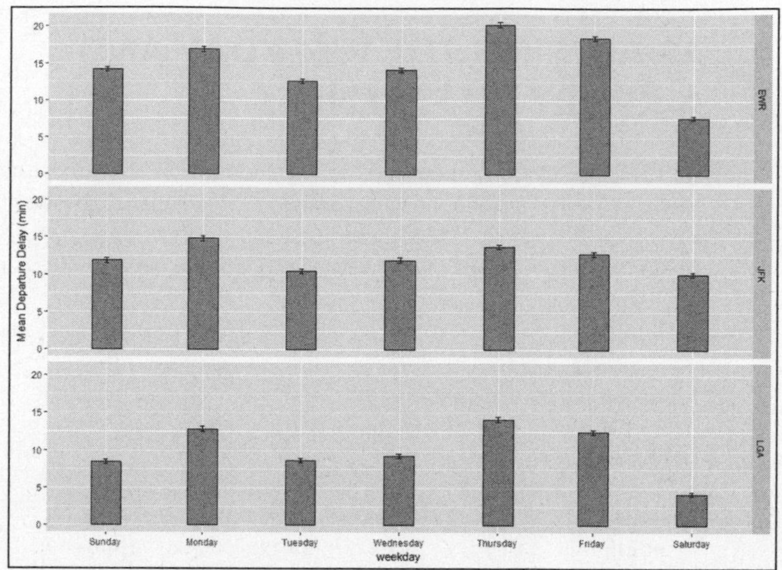

FIGURE 13-5: A facets plot of mean departure delay (min) versus weekday and airport of origin.

No new conclusions, just a different way of plotting the data. The code is

```
ggplot(summary_dep_delay, aes(x=weekday, y=mean)) +
  geom_bar(stat="identity", color="black", fill = "gray65",width=0.3)+
  geom_errorbar(aes(ymax=mean+std_err,ymin=mean-std_err), width=.05)+
  facet_grid(origin ~ .)+
  labs(y="Mean Departure Delay (min)")
```

The code is a bit different from the earlier plot. Color does not differentiate the origins in this plot (facet does), so the `ggplot()` function doesn't need an aesthetic mapping for `color`. The `geom_bar()` function is pretty much the same, except for the addition of a `fill` and a slight change to the `width`. Feel free to modify those, if you like. `geom_errorbar()` is the same as before, but in this plot, you don't have to use the `position` argument. And you change the `width`.

I added the `facet_grid()` function. Its argument arranges the facets vertically. To arrange them horizontally, the argument would be `. ~ origin`, but that would look terrible. Try it, if you don't believe me. As before, the final line adds the label for the y-axis.

Delay and flight duration

Can the duration of the flight (`air_time` in the data frame) somehow influence departure delay? Why might that happen? With a longer flight duration, is departure delay likely to be longer or shorter?

ANALYZING THE WEEKDAY AND AIRPORT DIFFERENCES

Are those differences among weekdays significant? How about those differences among airports of origin? And what about the combination of the two? Does that have any effect? One way to answer these questions is with an *analysis of variance (ANOVA).* The function that performs the ANOVA is called aov(), and here's how to apply it:

```
wkdyorgin <- aov(dep_delay ~ weekday * origin, data=flites_day)
```

To see the results, use summary():

```
> summary(wkdyorgin)
                   Df    Sum Sq Mean Sq F value Pr(>F)
weekday             6   2268319  378053  233.26 <2e-16 ***
origin              2   1310239  655120  404.21 <2e-16 ***
weekday:origin     12    405916   33826   20.87 <2e-16 ***
Residuals      320939 520164045    1621
---
Signif. codes:  0 '***' 0.001 '**' 0.01 '*' 0.05 '.' 0.1 ' ' 1
8214 observations deleted due to missingness
```

The relevant columns here are `F value` and `Pr(>F)`. If it's the case that weekday means are about the same, the F value for weekday would be around `1.00`. As you can see, the F value is way larger than that. It's always possible that in reality all the weekday means are about the same and this data set is a fluke. The `Pr(>F)` value indicates that probability, and that probability is microscopically small. Same story for `origin`.

Figures 13-4 and 13-5 suggest that the pattern of means across weekdays is different from EWR to JFK to LGA. The `weekday:origin` row in the summary table verifies this. The large F value and small `Pr(>F)` in that row tell you that weekday and `origin` are not independent of one another. This non-independence is a statistical characterization of the difference in appearance across the facets of Figure 13-5.

ANOVA has way more to it than I can go into here. For the full story, take a look at a book I'm shamelessly plugging. (Okay, just because you asked, it's *Statistical Analysis with R For Dummies,* published by Wiley.)

First, take a look at some summary statistics for `dep_delay` and for `air_time`:

```
> summary(flites_day$dep_delay)
   Min. 1st Qu.  Median    Mean 3rd Qu.    Max.    NA's
 -43.00   -5.00   -2.00   12.71   11.00 1301.00    8214
```

```
> summary(flites_day$air_time)
   Min. 1st Qu.  Median    Mean 3rd Qu.    Max.    NA's
   20.0    81.0   127.0   149.6   184.0   695.0    9365
```

Looks like they're on two very different playing fields. One way to reduce the discrepancy is to subtract the mean of dep_delay from each dep_delay and then divide by dep_delay's standard deviation. Then follow the same procedure for each air_time. This is called *scaling* the data. (If you've had a statistics course, you might remember z-scores, also known as standard scores.)

The scale() function handles the scaling. I use it in a moment.

To address the questions about air_time and dep_delay, you create a regression line that summarizes the relationship between them (or, more accurately, between their scaled versions). Regression analysis has a lot of ramifications that I don't go into here. That would require a whole separate chapter.

Just for descriptive purposes, I'm concerned about the slope of the regression line. If that line has a positive slope, departure delay increases as flight time increases. It the line has a negative slope, departure delay decreases as flight time increases.

Here's how to construct the regression line between scale(air_time) and scale(dep_delay):

```
dlyat <-lm(scale(dep_delay) ~ scale(air_time), data=flites_day)
```

And here's how to retrieve the slope of the line:

```
> dlyat$coefficients[2]
scale(air_time)
    -0.02165165
```

Yes, it's a small number, but the negative slope suggests that longer flight durations are associated with shorter departure delays.

Why might that be?

Suggested Project: Delay and Weather

It's conceivable that weather conditions could influence flight delays. How do you incorporate weather information into the assessment of delay?

Another nycflights13 data frame called weather provides the weather data for every day and hour at each of the three origin airports. Here's a glimpse of exactly what it has:

```
> glimpse(weather,60)
Observations: 26,130
Variables: 15
$ origin     <chr> "EWR", "EWR", "EWR", "EWR", "EWR", "...
$ year       <dbl> 2013, 2013, 2013, 2013, 2013, 2013, ...
$ month      <dbl> 1, 1, 1, 1, 1, 1, 1, 1, 1, 1, 1, 1, ...
$ day        <int> 1, 1, 1, 1, 1, 1, 1, 1, 1, 1, 1, 1, ...
$ hour       <int> 0, 1, 2, 3, 4, 6, 7, 8, 9, 10, 11, 1...
$ temp       <dbl> 37.04, 37.04, 37.94, 37.94, 37.94, 3...
$ dewp       <dbl> 21.92, 21.92, 21.92, 23.00, 24.08, 2...
$ humid      <dbl> 53.97, 53.97, 52.09, 54.51, 57.04, 5...
$ wind_dir   <dbl> 230, 230, 230, 230, 240, 270, 250, 2...
$ wind_speed <dbl> 10.35702, 13.80936, 12.65858, 13.809...
$ wind_gust  <dbl> 11.918651, 15.891535, 14.567241, 15....
$ precip     <dbl> 0, 0, 0, 0, 0, 0, 0, 0, 0, 0, 0, 0, ...
$ pressure   <dbl> 1013.9, 1013.0, 1012.6, 1012.7, 1012...
$ visib      <dbl> 10, 10, 10, 10, 10, 10, 10, 10, 10, ...
$ time_hour  <dttm> 2012-12-31 19:00:00, 2012-12-31 20:...
```

So the variables it has in common with flites_name_day are the first six and the last one. To join the two data frames, use this code:

```
flites_day_weather <- flites_day %>%
  inner_join(weather, by = c("origin","year","month","day","hour","time_hour"))
```

Now you can use flites_day_weather to start answering questions about departure delay and the weather.

What questions will you ask? How will you answer them? What plots will you draw? What regression lines will you create? Will scale() help?

And, when you're all done, take a look at arrival delay (arr_delay).

5 Maps and Images

IN THIS PART . . .

Tap into geographic data

Map airports in a state

Map U.S. state capitals

Use the `magick` package

Transform images

Combine stationary images with animated images

IN THIS CHAPTER

» Using geographic data

» Mapping a state

» Mapping the country

Chapter 14

All Over the Map

As you might have gathered from glancing at this book's table of contents, one of R's major calling cards is its emphasis on visualization. Beginning with plots of analytic results, R's graphics capabilities have evolved into map development.

R graphics honchos have created several ways of drawing maps. In this chapter, I show you the one that I think is the most straightforward and will get you on the road to Rtography. (See what I did there?)

Project: The Airports of Wisconsin

The map I show you how to draw in this project appears in Figure 14-1. It shows the locations of the major airports in Wisconsin, and includes the cities they serve, the FAA abbreviations, and the number of *enplanements* (commercial passenger boardings) in 2013.

Dispensing with the preliminaries

This project requires a package called `maps` that enables you to draw all kinds of geographic representations. Another necessary package is `ggmap`, which enables you to retrieve geographic information from Google Maps. You also need `ggplot2` to do the plotting.

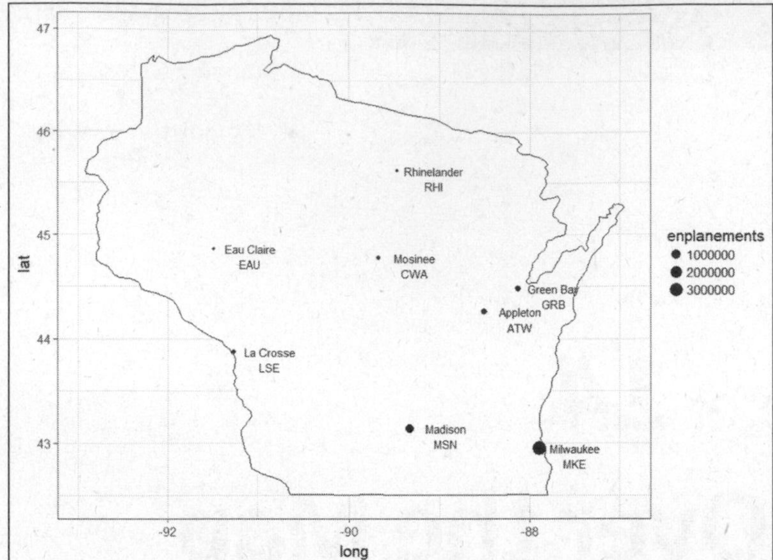

FIGURE 14-1: The major airports of Wisconsin.

On the Packages tab, click Install to open the Install Packages dialog box. In the dialog box, type **maps** and click the Install button. After the package downloads, select its check box on the Packages tab. Follow as many of these steps as necessary for the other two packages.

Getting the state geographic data

First, you have to retrieve the geographic data for Wisconsin. This is a set of latitudes and longitudes for the state map. This happens in two steps. The first step is to retrieve all data for the United States. The information comes from the `maps` package. A `ggplot2` function called `map_data()` puts it in a data frame that `ggplot()` can use to create a map:

```
states <- map_data("state")
```

Here's what this data frame looks like:

```
> head(states)
       long      lat group order  region subregion
1 -87.46201 30.38968     1     1 alabama      <NA>
2 -87.48493 30.37249     1     2 alabama      <NA>
3 -87.52503 30.37249     1     3 alabama      <NA>
4 -87.53076 30.33239     1     4 alabama      <NA>
5 -87.57087 30.32665     1     5 alabama      <NA>
6 -87.58806 30.32665     1     6 alabama      <NA>
```

You can use this data frame to draw a map of the contiguous United States (as in Suggested Project 2, later in this chapter), but right now you should concern yourself only with Wisconsin, and that's the second step:

```
Wisconsin <- subset(states, region == "wisconsin")
```

Getting the airport geographic data

To retrieve the airport geographic data, you start with a list of the airports. Wikipedia does the honors:

```
https://en.wikipedia.org/wiki/List_of_airports_in_Wisconsin
```

Scroll down the Wikipedia page to the list of airports, as Figure 14-2 shows. The figure also shows the rows and columns I selected (the part of the table with the primary airports). Press Ctrl+C to copy the information to the clipboard.

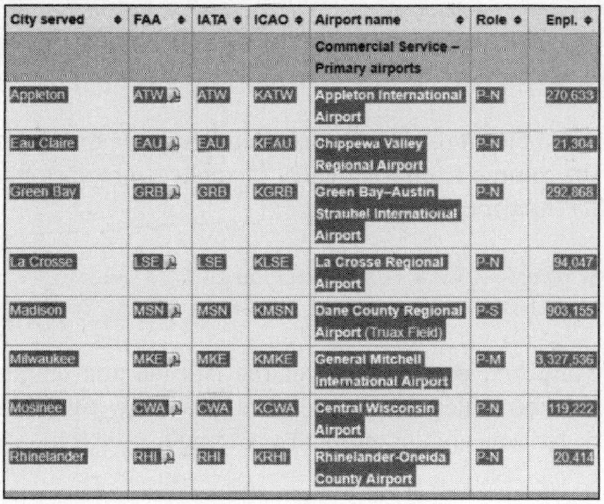

City served	FAA	IATA	ICAO	Airport name	Role	Enpl.
				Commercial Service – Primary airports		
Appleton	ATW	ATW	KATW	Appleton International Airport	P-N	270,633
Eau Claire	EAU	EAU	KEAU	Chippewa Valley Regional Airport	P-N	21,304
Green Bay	GRB	GRB	KGRB	Green Bay–Austin Straubel International Airport	P-N	292,868
La Crosse	LSE	LSE	KLSE	La Crosse Regional Airport	P-N	94,047
Madison	MSN	MSN	KMSN	Dane County Regional Airport (Truax Field)	P-S	903,155
Milwaukee	MKE	MKE	KMKE	General Mitchell International Airport	P-M	3,327,536
Mosinee	CWA	CWA	KCWA	Central Wisconsin Airport	P-N	119,222
Rhinelander	RHI	RHI	KRHI	Rhinelander-Oneida County Airport	P-N	20,414

FIGURE 14-2: The Wikipedia page of Wisconsin airports, with major airports selected.

Then read the data into R:

```
wisc.airports <- read.csv("clipboard", header=FALSE, sep = "\t")
```

Next, keep the columns for City, FAA Abbreviation, Airport Name, and Enplanements:

```
wisc.airports <- wisc.airports[,c(1,2,5,7)]
```

and then name them, like this:

```
colnames(wisc.airports) <- c("city","faa","airport","enplanements")
```

Here's a glimpse at the data:

```
> glimpse(wisc.airports,60)
Observations: 8
Variables: 4
$ city         <fctr> Appleton, Eau Claire, Green Bay, ...
$ faa          <fctr> ATW, EAU, GRB, LSE, MSN, MKE, CWA...
$ airport      <fctr> Appleton International Airport, C...
$ enplanements <fctr> 270,633, 21,304, 292,868, 94,047,...
```

Each column is a factor. For what I show you how to do later, you have to turn the first three into character columns and the last one into a number. The first three are easy:

```
wisc.airports$city <- as.character(wisc.airports$city)
wisc.airports$faa <- as.character(wisc.airports$faa)
wisc.airports$airport <- as.character(wisc.airports$airport)
```

The last one is a bit more complicated. You first have to use the `gsub()` function to remove the comma from each entry (actually, to replace it with nothing) and then turn the entry into a number:

```
wisc.airports$enplanements <- as.numeric(gsub(",","",wisc.
   airports$enplanements))
```

To plot the airports, you have to get the latitude and longitude for each one. A `ggmaps` function called `geocode()` gets this done. Give it a place name and it returns the latitude and longitude: For example,

```
> geocode("Statue of Liberty")
       lon      lat
1 -74.0445 40.68925
```

Pretty slick, right? (The function also returns the URL of the web page that the information comes from; I left that out of the example.)

So, to apply this function to `wisc.airports$airport`:

```
airport.info <-geocode(wisc.airports$airport)
```

An error message indicates that the function failed on the airport name for Green Bay ("Green Bay-Austin Straubel International Airport"), so `airport.info` looks like this:

```
> airport.info
        lon      lat
1 -88.51119 44.26029
2 -91.48222 44.86223
3        NA       NA
4 -91.26390 43.87526
5 -89.33641 43.13907
6 -87.89665 42.94755
7 -89.67268 44.78420
8 -89.46387 45.62621
```

To fill in the gaps, try a different name for the Green Bay Airport:

```
GB <- geocode("Green Bay Airport")
```

```
> GB
        lon      lat
1 -88.13439 44.48336
```

And now, this code fills in the blanks:

```
airport.info[3,] <- GB[1,]
```

The final step is to bind `airport.info` to `wisc.airports`:

```
wisc.airports <- cbind(wisc.airports,airport.info)
```

Here's the result (without column 3 so that it fits neatly on the page):

```
> wisc.airports[,-3]
         city faa enplanements       lon      lat
1    Appleton ATW       270633 -88.51119 44.26029
2  Eau Claire EAU        21304 -91.48222 44.86223
3   Green Bay GRB       292868 -88.13439 44.48336
4   La Crosse LSE        94047 -91.26390 43.87526
5     Madison MSN       903155 -89.33641 43.13907
6   Milwaukee MKE      3327536 -87.89665 42.94755
7     Mosinee CWA       119222 -89.67268 44.78420
8 Rhinelander RHI        20414 -89.46387 45.62621
```

Plotting the airports on the state map

Now you can use `Wisconsin` and `wisc.airports` to plot the map in Figure 14-1.

Begin with `ggplot()`:

```
ggplot(data = Wisconsin, aes(x=long,y=lat)) +
```

The first argument is the geographic data that enables you to plot the map of Wisconsin, and the second is the aesthetic mappings of longitude to the *x*-axis and latitude to the *y*-axis.

The next line plots the map as a polygon with a black border and white fill:

```
geom_polygon(color = "black", fill="white") +
```

The next three lines add the points, the city names of the cities, and the FAA airport abbreviations. The data source for each of these is the `wisc.airports` data frame. For these points

```
geom_point(data=wisc.airports,aes(x=lon, y=lat, size=enplanements)) +
```

you should note that longitude in this data frame is `lon` rather than `long` as in the `Wisconsin` data frame.

For the city names and the FAA abbreviations:

```
geom_text(data=wisc.airports, aes(x=lon +.40, y=lat, label=city))+
geom_text(data=wisc.airports, aes(x=lon +.40, y=lat-.15, label=faa))
```

REMEMBER

The positioning numbers are the result of trying different values. Your ideal numbers might be different, depending on your screen resolution.

Here's the entire code snippet that produces Figure 14-1:

```
ggplot(data = Wisconsin, aes(x=long,y=lat)) +
  geom_polygon(color = "black", fill="white") +
  geom_point(data=wisc.airports,aes(x=lon, y=lat, size=enplanements)) +
  geom_text(data=wisc.airports, aes(x=lon +.40, y=lat, label=city)) +
  geom_text(data=wisc.airports, aes(x=lon +.40, y=lat-.15, label=faa))
```

Quick Suggested Project: Another source of airport geographic info

You use the `geocode()` function to find the latitude and longitude of each airport. Can you think of another way to get that information? Perhaps from a data frame you might have read about in Chapter 13? And maybe use `merge()`?

Suggested Project 1: Map Your State

What state do you live in? How about a map of the airports in your state, just like the one I show you how to do for Wisconsin?

TIP

That data frame from the `maps` package has no latitudes and longitudes for the 49th and 50th states. So, if you live in Alaska or Hawaii, adopt another state temporarily.

Use the `map_data()` function along with `subset()` to map your state. You'll need the Wikipedia information about airports in your state, and `geocode()` to get the airport latitudes and longitudes. Then try your hand with `ggplot()`.

If you live in New York, Virginia, Michigan, Massachusetts, North Carolina, or Washington state, read the next Suggested Project before you begin.

Suggested Project 2: Map the Country

Earlier, I mention that this code

```
states <- map_data("state")
```

is the foundation for mapping the contiguous USA. This project does just that.

First, the USA map. Based on what I already showed you, this should be pretty straightforward, right? This code produces Figure 14-3:

```
ggplot(data = states, aes(long,y=lat)) +
  geom_polygon(color = "black", fill="white")
```

Though it's true that this land was made for you and me, what's with all those crisscross lines from California to the New York island, and from the Redwood Forest to the Gulfstream waters? And more?

The `geom_polygon()` function uses all the latitude and longitude information to draw one big polygon.

But the US is not just one big shape with a single border running all the way around it. New Yorkers know that New York City (except for the Bronx) is not connected by land to the rest of the state. Virginians, Michiganders, Massachusettsans (yes, that's a word), North Carolinians, and Washingtonians know that their state geographies can't be captured using a single border line — otherwise, poor Martha's Vineyard would be left out in the cold.

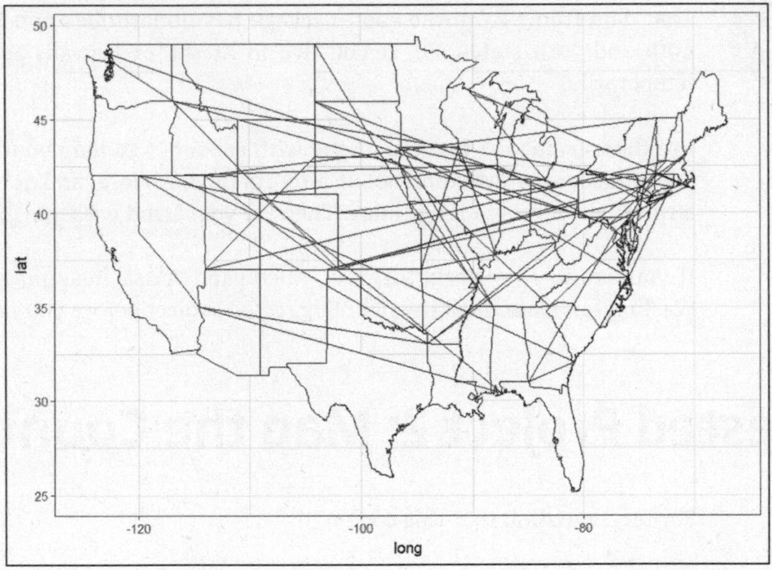

FIGURE 14-3: The contiguous 48 states, with some unwanted extras.

So a state (and, of course, the country) can consist of more than one group. The `group` column in `states` captures this. New York has four of them. How many are in the contiguous United States?

```
> length(unique(states$group))
[1] 63
```

Okay, 63 it is. How many are in your state?

The extra lines shown in Figure 14-3 connect all the points into one big polygon, irrespective of what group they happen to be in. To draw all 63 groups as separate groups, you have to supply a group aesthetic to geom_polygon():

```
geom_polygon(color = "black", fill="white",group=states$group)
```

This code draws the map properly, as Figure 14-4 shows:

```
ggplot(data = states, aes(long,y=lat)) +
  geom_polygon(color = "black", fill="white",group=states$group)
```

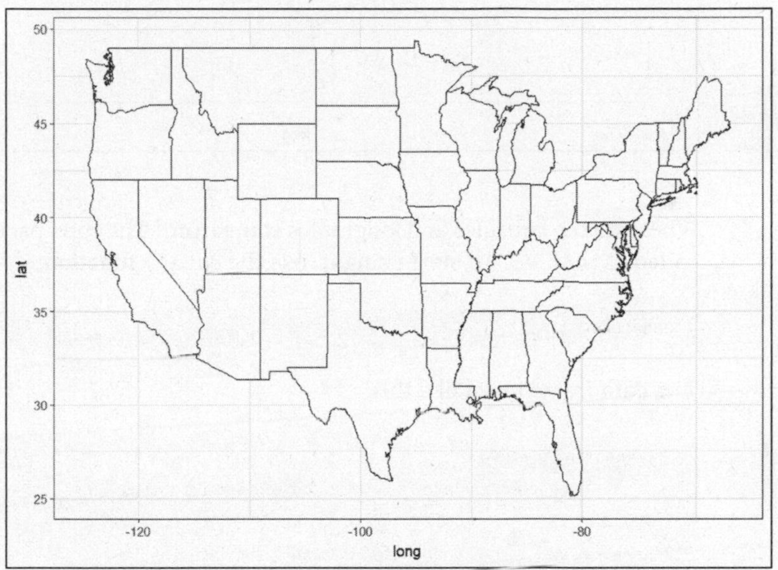

FIGURE 14-4: The contiguous 48 states of the USA.

Plotting the state capitals

The finished product for this map looks like Figure 14-5. The points show the locations of the state capitals, and the size of each point represents the population.

In the screen resolution I have to use to create figures, this one looks pretty squished. To make it less so, I removed the legend that explains the size of the points. You won't have to do that, because the figure will probably look better on your screen.

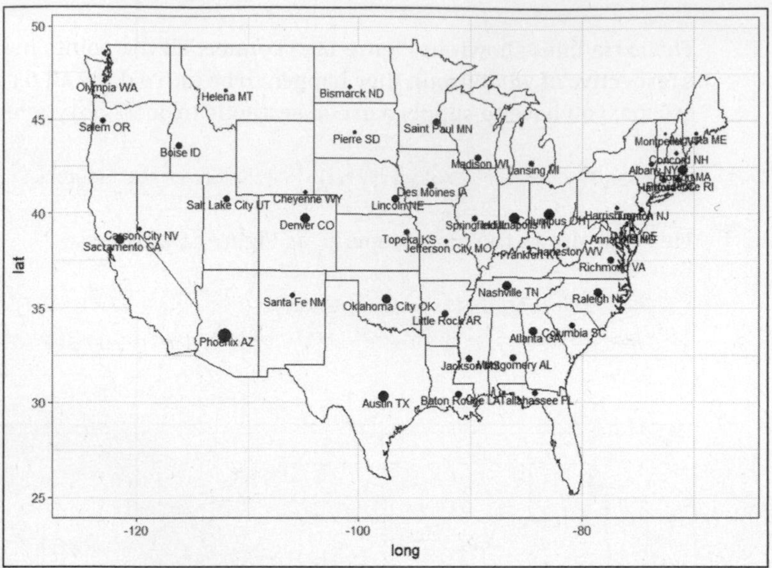

FIGURE 14-5: The state capitals of the USA.

Where do the latitudes and longitudes come from? The `maps` package has a data set called `us.cities`. To start using it, use the `data()` function:

```
data(us.cities)
```

The data frame looks like this:

```
> head(us.cities)
        name country.etc    pop   lat    long capital
1 Abilene TX          TX 113888 32.45  -99.74       0
2   Akron OH          OH 206634 41.08  -81.52       0
3 Alameda CA          CA  70069 37.77 -122.26       0
4  Albany GA          GA  75510 31.58  -84.18       0
5  Albany NY          NY  93576 42.67  -73.80       2
6  Albany OR          OR  45535 44.62 -123.09       0
```

A value of 2 in the `capital` column represents a state capital, as is the case for Albany, New York. Use that indicator to create a subset of state capitals. When you do, eliminate the two that are not in the contiguous 48 states.

Take it from here.

Plotting the airports

Figure 14-6 shows the finished map for this one. It plots the locations of the airports in the contiguous 48 states. Adding the FAA abbreviations and other info would just clutter it up, but you can give it a try, if you like. (Don't bother with enplanements.)

Where will you get the latitudes and longitudes? If you've thought through the earlier Quick Suggested Project, you know that the answer comes from Chapter 13.

Also, you have to create a subset of the data that falls within the contiguous 48 states. Limits on latitude and longitude will do this for you. What are those limits? Figure 14-6 helps you find them. Use the bottom border of the figure to determine the easternmost longitude and the westernmost longitude. Then use the left border to determine the northernmost latitude and the southernmost latitude.

Good luck!

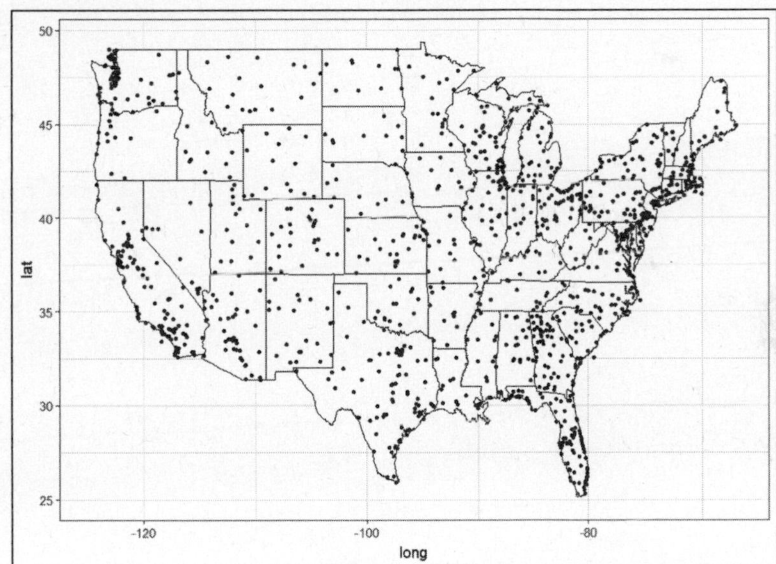

FIGURE 14-6: Airport locations in the contiguous United States.

IN THIS CHAPTER

» Exploring the magick package

» Transforming images

» Working with animated images

» Combining stationary images and animations

Chapter 15
Fun with Pictures

R is not known as a language for image processing, but its capabilities in that arena, as in others, are expanding all the time. To get you started with image processing, I take you through the magick package for manipulating, modifying, and combining pictures.

Polishing a Picture: It's magick!

The magick package is a recent development in R, designed to make life easier for anyone who wants to process images. On the Packages tab, click Install to open the Install Packages dialog box. In the dialog box, type **magick** and click the Install button. When the package finishes downloading, select its check box on the Packages tab.

Here's a good place to find an image to work with www.connectmyapps.com/Dummies: This URL links to the web page that looks something like Figure 15-1.

I say "something like" because your screen's resolution is undoubtedly higher than the resolution I have to use to create screen shots. The web page will look better on your screen.

Anyway, that Dummies Man logo is the image I work with, so here's how to download it. Right-click on the logo (not on the picture of the book) and select Save Image As from the pop-up menu that appears. I save it in my Documents folder, which is also my working directory for R. The image is called dummiesman02, and it's in PNG (Portable Network Graphics) format.

FIGURE 15-1: Part of www.connectmyapps.com/Dummies.

Reading the image

You begin by reading the image into R and turning it into a magick object called dummy:

```
dummy <- image_read("dummiesman02.png")
```

What's in the object?

```
> print(dummy)
  format width height colorspace filesize
1    PNG   827   1097       sRGB    46040
```

Figure 15-2 shows that, in addition to this image information, the image appears on the Viewer tab.

Obviously, it's way too big to use for much of anything. To resize it, use image_resize():

```
dummy <-image_resize(dummy, "206x274")
```

The print(dummy) function now produces what you see in Figure 15-3:

FIGURE 15-2: The `magick` object `dummy` on the RStudio Viewer tab.

FIGURE 15-3: The resized `dummy`.

Rotating, flipping, and flopping

Now that you have a `magick` object, you can transform it in several ways.

Figure 15-4 show the result of rotating the image 45 degrees:

```
image_rotate(dummy, 45)
```

rotating it on a horizontal axis (also known as *flipping*):

```
image_flip(dummy)
```

and rotating it on a vertical axis (also known as *flopping*):

```
image_flop(dummy)
```

FIGURE 15-4: Rotating, flipping, and flopping an image.

Annotating

You can add text to an image in a couple of ways. The following code results in what you see on the left side of Figure 15-5:

```
image_annotate(dummy, "I'm smart", size = 50, gravity = "southwest", color =
   "gray80")
```

The right side of Figure 15-5 shows the product of this code:

```
image_annotate(dummy, "The magick of R", size = 20, color = "gray40",
               boxcolor = "gray90", degrees = 40, location = "+40+150")
```

Note that the coordinates of `location` (the starting point of the text box) are in a string. This is called a *geometry string*.

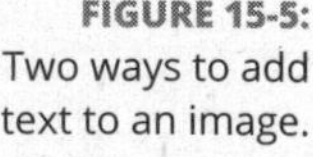

FIGURE 15-5: Two ways to add text to an image.

Combining transformations

In this section, I flop the image, rotate it, give it a light gray background, and then give it a darker gray border. `magick` provides two ways of combining these transformations.

The first (chaining) works like this:

```
chained.dummy <- image_flop(dummy)
chained.dummy <- image_rotate(chained.dummy,90)
chained.dummy <- image_background(chained.dummy, "gray90", flatten = TRUE)
chained.dummy <- image_border(chained.dummy, "gray50", "10x10"
```

The second (piping) uses `%>%` (the *pipe* operator), which I describe how to use in Chapter 13. With the `tidyverse` package loaded, here's what the code looks like:

```
piped.dummy <- image_flop(dummy) %>%
  image_rotate(90) %>%
  image_background("gray90", flatten = TRUE) %>%
  image_border("gray50", "10x10")
```

The second way seems a bit easier to follow.

In both of them, you use `flatten = TRUE`. What's that all about? Each image, the Dummies Man and the background, is in a layer. Flattening combines them into a single image that has the size of the first image.

Either way you code it, the result is shown in Figure 15-6.

FIGURE 15-6: Combining image transformations.

Quick suggested project: Three F's

You have to love the terminology: First you flopped, and then you flattened. What does the whole thing look like if you flip, flop, and flatten? Try to envision, and then verify.

Combining images

In addition to combining transformations, `magick` can combine images. Figure 15-7 shows the Dummies Man pointing to the `iris` data set I describe how to use in many of the preceding chapters.

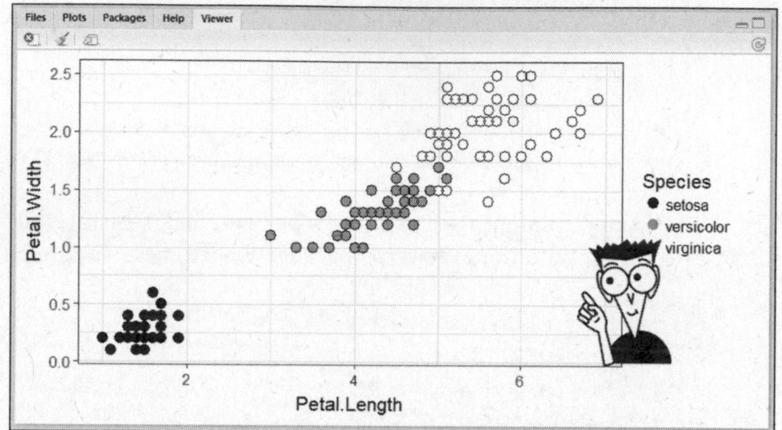

FIGURE 15-7: The Dummies Man, pointing to the `iris` data set.

To make this happen, you need a smaller Dummies Man image:

```
little.dummy <- image_resize(dummy, "103x186")
```

Next, you need an image of the plot of the iris data set. Just as a refresher, it's four measurements of 150 irises, with 50 of each of three species. The measurements are the length and width of sepals and petals, and the plot in Figure 15-7 shows petal width and petal length.

Here's how to save an image of the plot:

```
ggplot(iris, aes(x=Petal.Length,y=Petal.Width, color=Species))+
  geom_point(size=4)+
  scale_color_manual(values=c("grey0","grey65","grey100"))+
  geom_point(shape=1,size=4,color="black")+
  ggsave("irisplot",device="png",scale=.8)
```

In a sidebar in Chapter 10 ("Plotting the irises"), I explain the first four lines. The only new line here is the fifth one: the `ggsave()` function saves the plot in a PNG file called `iris.plot`, at 80 percent of the original plot size.

You refer to the plot as background and use image_backgroud() to do it:

```
background <- image_background(iris_plot, "white")
```

You use the magick function image.composite() to put the background together with the little.dummy and produce Figure 15-7:

```
image_composite(image=background, composite_image=image_flop(little.dummy),
   offset = "+615+200")
```

The offset argument positions the flopped little.dummy. The positioning information is in a geometric string. Think of the upper left corner as the origin (0,0). Rightward (the first coordinate) is positive, and downward is positive, too. So this is 615 pixels to the right and 200 pixels down from the upper left corner.

Animating

Stationary images aren't the only kind that magick deals with. Animation, in fact, is a big part of this package. Figure 15-8 shows a gyroscope. When it opens in the viewer, it's spinning.

FIGURE 15-8: This gyroscope GIF spins whenever it opens on the Viewer tab.

The image comes from this URL:

```
https://commons.wikimedia.org/wiki/File:Gyroscope_precession.
  gif - /media/File:Gyroscope_precession.gif
```

Right-click the image, select Save Image As from the pop-up menu that appears, and save it in your Documents folder under its given name: Gyroscopic_precession. This code makes it a magick object:

```
gyroscope <- image_read("Gyroscope_precession.gif")
```

This command

```
print(gyroscope)
```

puts it in the viewer and prints 30 rows in the Console window, indicating that this gif consists of 30 frames. Each frame, of course, is a .gif image with a slightly different view of the gyroscope. Putting each frame onscreen in rapid succession gives the illusion of animation.

This command

```
rev(gyroscope)
```

reverses the direction of the rotation.

Making your own morphs

You can create your own animations. One possibility is to make one image appear to gradually become another. This is called *morphing*, and the magick function that does this is called image_morph().

A good example is a shrinking Dummies Man:

```
shrinking.dummy <- image_morph(c(dummy,little.dummy), frames=20)
```

The first argument is a vector of two images. The first will morph into the second. The second argument is the number of frames between the two images. The function creates those frames for you. (How does it do this? Well . . . magickly.)

The image_animate() function puts the animation in the Viewer window:

```
image_animate(shrinking.dummy, loop = 10)
```

The loop argument specifies how many times to show the animation. Without that argument, it just goes on and on.

I can't show you the morphing in a figure, of course. You'll just have to try it for yourself!

Project: Two Legends in Search of a Legend

I've shown you images, animated images, and combined stationary images. This project walks you through the next step: Combine an image with an animated image.

Figure 15-9 shows the end product — the plot of the `iris` data set with comedy icons Laurel and Hardy positioned in front of the plot legend. When you open this combined image in the Viewer, you see Stan and Ollie dancing their little derbies off. (The derbies don't actually come off in the animation, but I think you catch my drift.)

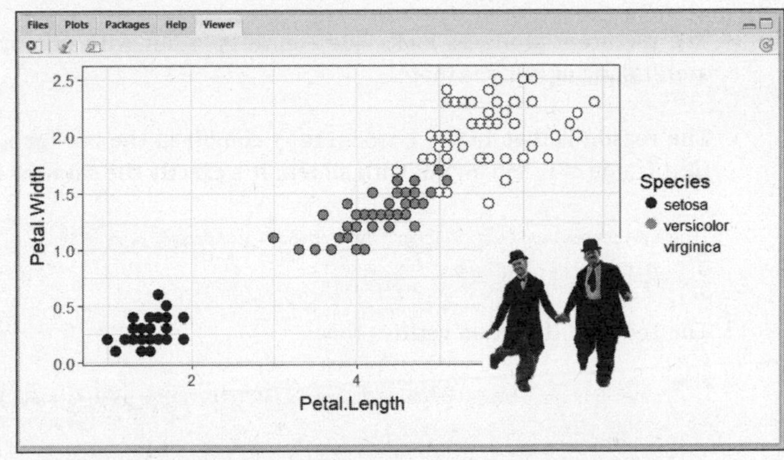

FIGURE 15-9: Laurel and Hardy, dancing in front of the legend in the `iris` plot.

Getting Stan and Ollie

The Laurel and Hardy GIF lives at `www.animatedimages.org/img-animated-dancing-image-0243-79244.htm`. Right-click the image and select Save Image As from the pop-up menu that appears. Save it as `animated-dancing-image-0243` in your `Documents` folder.

Then read it into R:

```
l_and_h <- image_read("animated-dancing-image-0243.gif")
```

Applying the `length()` function to `l_and_h`

```
> length(l_and_h)
[1] 10
```

indicates that this GIF consists of ten frames.

TIP

To add a coolness factor, make the background of the GIF transparent before `image_read()` works with it. The free online image editor at `www.online-image-editor.com` does the job quite nicely.

Combining the boys with the background

If you use the image combination technique from the preceding section, the code looks like this:

```
image_composite(image=background, composite_image=l_and_h, offset = "+510+200")
```

The picture it produces looks like Figure 15-9 but with one problem: The boys aren't dancing. Why is that?

The reason is that `image_composite()` combined the `background` with just the first frame of `l_and_h`, not with all ten. It's exactly the same as if you had run

```
image_composite(image=background, composite_image=l_and_h[1],
                offset = "+510+200")
```

The `length()` function verifies this:

```
> length(image_composite(image=background, composite_image=l_and_h,
        offset = "+510+200"))
[1] 1
```

If all ten frames were involved, the `length()` function would have returned 10.

To get this done properly, you have to use a `magick` function called `image_apply()`, which I tell you about next.

Explaining image_apply()

So that you fully understand how this important function works, I digress for a moment and describe an analogous function called `lapply()`.

If you want to apply a function (like `mean()`) to the variables of a data frame, like `iris`, one way to do that is with a `for` loop: Start with the first column and calculate its mean, go to the next column and calculate its mean, and so on until you calculate all the column means.

For technical reasons, it's faster and more efficient to use `lapply()` to apply `mean()` to all the variables:

```
> lapply(iris, mean)
$Sepal.Length
[1] 5.843333

$Sepal.Width
[1] 3.057333

$Petal.Length
[1] 3.758

$Petal.Width
[1] 1.199333

$Species
[1] NA
```

A warning message comes with that last one, but that's okay.

Another way to write `lapply(iris, mean)` is `lapply(iris, function(x) {mean(x)})`.

This second way comes in handy when the function becomes more complicated. If, for some reason, you want to square the value of each score in the data set and then multiply the result by three, and then calculate the mean of each column, here's how to code it:

```
lapply(iris, function(x){mean(3*(x^2))})
```

In a similar way, `image_apply()` applies a function to every frame in an animated GIF. In this project, the function that gets applied to every frame is `image_composite()`:

```
function(frame){image_composite(image=background, composite_image=frame,
  offset = "+510+200")}
```

So, within `image_apply()`, that's

```
frames <- image_apply(image=l_and_h, function(frame) {
  image_composite(image=background, composite_image=frame, offset = "+510+200")
})
```

After you run that code, `length(frames)` verifies the ten frames:

```
> length(frames)
[1] 10
```

Getting back to the animation

The `image_animate()` function puts it all in motion at ten frames per second:

```
animation <- image_animate(frames, fps = 10)
```

To put the show on the screen, it's

```
print(animation)
```

All together now:

```
l_and_h <- image_read("animated-dancing-image-0243.gif")
background <- image_background(iris_plot, "white")

frames <- image_apply(image=l_and_h, function(frame) {
  image_composite(image=background, composite_image=frame, offset = "+510+200")
})

animation <- image_animate(frames, fps = 10)
print(animation)
```

And that's the code for Figure 15-9.

One more thing. The `image_write()` function saves the animation as a handy little reusable GIF:

```
image_write(animation, "LHirises.gif")
```

Suggested Project: Combine an Animation with a Plot

This suggested project is to replicate the previous project but with a different background and a different animated GIF. Which plot? Which GIF? You decide.

One possibility is to use a map from Chapter 14 as the background. (Perhaps it's a map you developed in Chapter 14's "Suggested Project" section.) Then search the web for an animated GIF. Because most of the Chapter 14 maps deal with airports, you might look for a GIF of a plane and put that one on your map. You'll find a lot of animated planes here (scroll to the bottom of the web page):

```
http://bestanimations.com/Transport/Aircraft/Aircraft.html
```

Finally, use the `magick` functions to put your background together with your animation, and then use `image_write()` to save it as a GIF.

If you decide to use the Wisconsin airport map as the background and `Jumbo-05-june.gif` from `bestanimations.com`, and then save your work as GIF, it just might look like Figure 15-10.

Good luck!

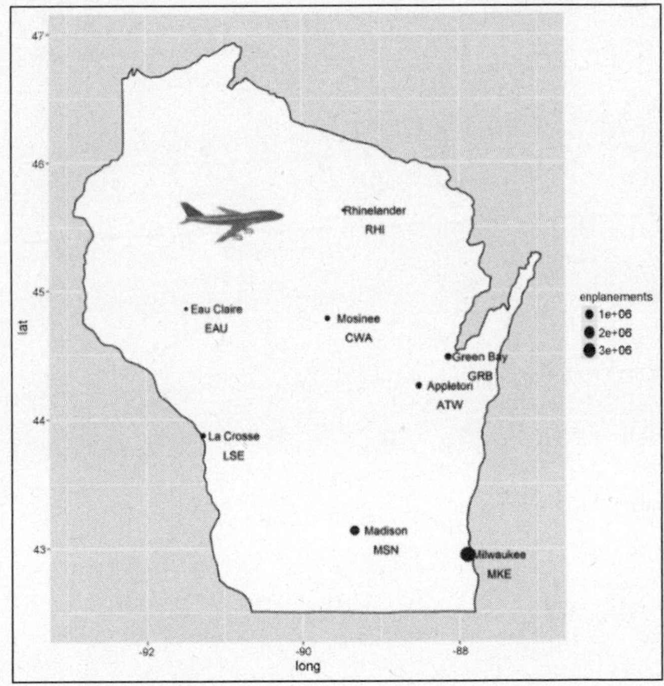

FIGURE 15-10: The airports of Wisconsin, with an animated plane.PE and bw: We eliminate this following caption thing, right?

6

The Part of Tens

IN THIS PART . . .

Discover useful R packages for your projects

Learn about books and websites for further information

IN THIS CHAPTER

» Machine learning packages

» Database packages

» Packages for maps and images

» Text analysis packages

Chapter 16

More Than Ten Packages for Your R Projects

The projects I walk you through in this book are vehicles for sharpening your R skill set. These projects depend on R packages specialized for the topics I cover. In this chapter, I tell you about some packages that can serve as the foundation for additional projects, and for further honing your R skills.

These packages address subject areas I cover in this book, and one area that I don't.

Machine Learning

The goal of the `caret` package is to make it easy for you to work with machine learning. Consistent with R formula notation, its simple syntax connects with a huge array of machine learning methods. Additionally, the package offers a number of data sets to try them out on. If I were writing a book about the gamut of machine learning, I'd include this package. (In fact, it might cover *only* this package.)

As its name implies, the `neuralnet` package is all about neural networks. It goes beyond `nnet` (the package that `Rattle` interfaces with) in allowing more than one hidden layer and providing a built-in function to visualize the trained network.

Speaking of `Rattle`, it's worth your time to take a second look at one of the packages it interfaces with. The `e1071` package, which `rattle` uses for support vector machines (see Chapter 9), provides a number of functions for other kinds of machine learning, including several types of cluster analysis.

Databases

If you're going to work with large data sets, (say, around 100GB in RAM) the `data.table` package is for you. Its syntax is designed to minimize coding time for operations like subsetting, selecting, joining, and more.

The `gdata` package has a variety of functions for manipulating data, from medical unit conversion to pulling out components of date-and-time objects. You'll also find functions for manipulating text strings, working with Excel spreadsheets, and joining data frames. And I've just scratched the surface.

Maps

If you progress into mapping beyond Chapter 14, consider the `GEOmap` package. This package's functions perform some pretty advanced topographic and geological mapping. You can also test your large-data manipulation skills (and perhaps use `data.table`) on its `EHB.LLZ` data frame, which provides the latitude, longitude, and depth of 119,000 earthquakes.

How does `GEOmap` work? Very well, thank you. Although its subject matter is advanced, its syntax is straightforward. For a map of, oh, the whole world, here's what you do:

```
data(worldmap)
plotworldmap(worldmap)
```

The result is shown in Figure 16-1. Those numbers at the bottom will most likely look better on your screen.

To superimpose topography and geology, GEOmap functions work with data from the geomapdata package.

Okay, so topography and geology might not be your cup of tea. Instead, you're interested in plotting maps that show the geographic distribution of a particular attribute, like rainfall, dental care, or car ownership. In that case, consider the tmap package. Similar in operation to ggplot, its functions enable you to create colorful, informative thematic maps. Just for starters, Figure 16-2 shows how the tmap function qtm() maps the world:

```
data(World)
qtm(World)
```

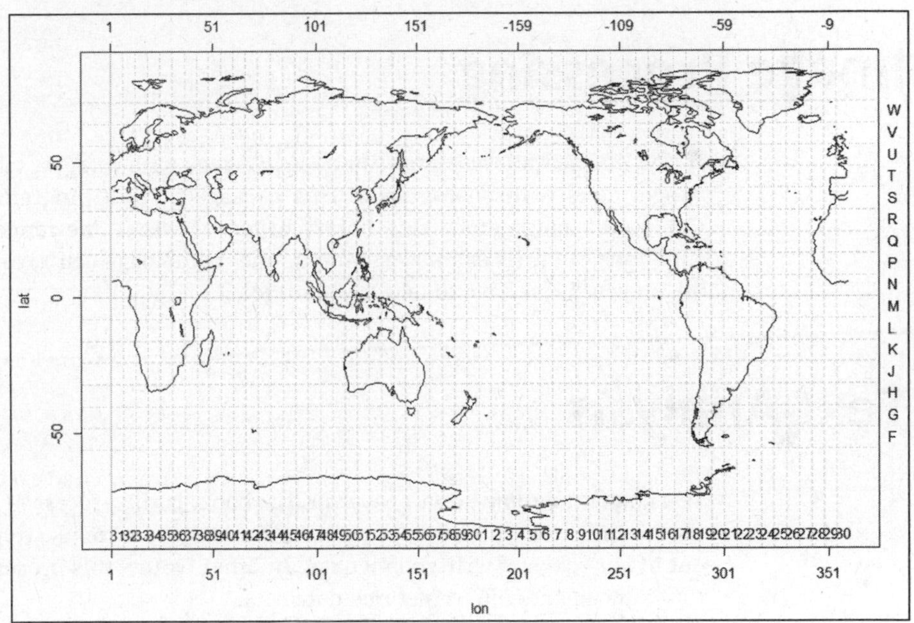

FIGURE 16-1: The world, as mapped by the GEOmap function plotworldmap().

If you're looking for map-related data to plot, you'll find quite a bit of it in the maps package. One data set has latitude, longitude, and population for Canadian cities. In Chapter 14, you might recall, I use the analogous maps data set for US cities. Another data set in this package has the info for cities throughout the world. Still other data sets provide information on ozone concentration in 41 US cities and on unemployment in US counties.

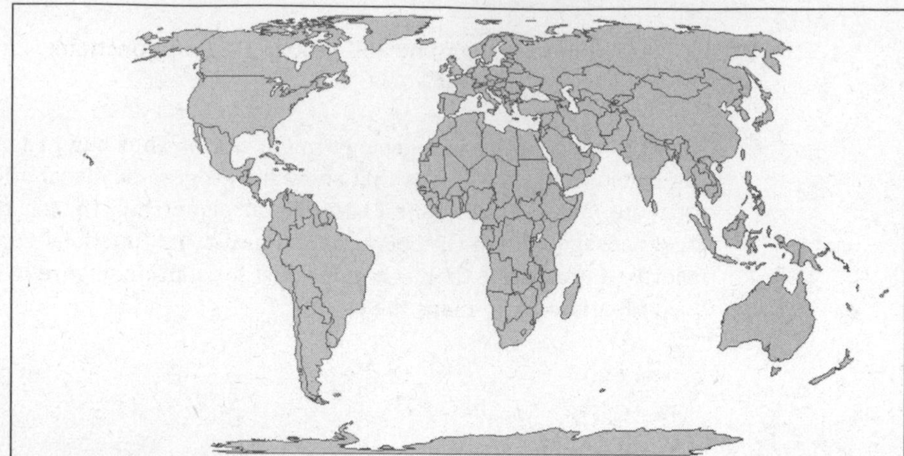

FIGURE 16-2: The world, as mapped by the tmap function qtm().

Image Processing

If you enjoyed all the things that magick does with images, take a look at what imager does with photographs. This package gives R programmers access to a C++-based image processing library called CImage. The range of what imager functions can do is extensive. A black-and-white page can't really do justice to it all, so you'll just have to take my word for it.

Text Analysis

Text analysis, a topic I don't cover in this book, is the process of extracting information from text that a computer can process. It's sort of like trying to make order out of the chaos of written language. In other words, this process turns unstructured documents into structured data sets.

Like maps and image processing, R isn't known as a language for text analysis. But like those two areas, R's capabilities in this field are constantly expanding. Here are two packages that are fueling the expansion:

- koRpus: This package can analyze a text's readability, its word *frequencies* (how many times each word occurs in the text), and its *lexical* diversity (how many unique words are in it). The first thing a text analyzer has to do is called *tokenizing* the text. This is the process of identifying each word and its part of speech (noun, verb, and so on.), which then enables statistical analysis of the text. To tokenize properly, you have to install additional (non-R) software. If all you want to do is distinguish between words and numbers, koRplus has a built-in tokenize() function.

» `SentimentAnalysis`: *Sentiment analysis* takes text analysis one step further: This type of analysis extracts attitudes and emotions from text. The aptly named `SentimentAnalysis` package provides functions for doing just that. Its functions use built-in dictionaries to decide whether a text is positive or negative.

Here's an example to show you how text analysis works. I copied this from `www.dummies.com`.

> People are becoming more aware of R every day as major institutions are adopting it as a standard. Part of its appeal is that it's a free tool that's taking the place of costly statistical software packages that sometimes take an inordinate amount of time to learn. Plus, R enables a user to carry out complex statistical analyses by simply entering a few commands, making sophisticated analyses available and understandable to a wide audience.

This passage comes from promotional material for a book. If I recall correctly, the book is entitled *Statistical Analysis with R For Dummies*, but my memory might be a bit hazy on this.

I store the `www.dummies.com` sentences as a vector of three strings in an object called `statrfd`. Next, I use the `analyzeSentiment()` function to do the analysis:

```
sentiment <- analyzeSentiment(statrfd)
```

The result is a list with a number of properties. The `$SentimentGI` property shows this:

```
> sentiment$SentimentGI
[1] 0.3333333 0.1176471 0.1764706
```

The three positive numbers indicate that each sentence expresses positive sentiment. Just to confirm:

```
> convertToDirection(sentiment$SentimentGI)
[1] positive positive positive
Levels: negative neutral positive
```

Try this one on some sentences of your own!

TIP

Developers continually add new packages to the Comprehensive R Archive Network (CRAN). To search CRAN for packages that might interest you, point your browser to `www.rdocumentation.org/`.

IN THIS CHAPTER

» Shiny-related resources

» Books and websites on machine learning

» Resources for databases, maps, and images

Chapter 17 More than Ten Useful Resources

In this chapter, I tell you about books and websites that help you learn more about the areas I cover in this book. Rather than split the information between websites and books, I thought it best to organize by topic.

Without further ado . . .

Interacting with Users

If you want to delve deeper into R applications that interact with users, start with this tutorial by `shiny` guiding force Garrett Grolemund:

```
https://shiny.rstudio.com/tutorial
```

For a helpful book on the subject, consider Chris Beeley's *Web Application Development with R Using Shiny*, 2nd Edition (Packt Publishing, 2016).

Machine Learning

For the lowdown on all things `Rattle`, go directly to the source: `Rattle` creator Graham Williams has written *Data Mining with Rattle and R: The Art of Excavating Data for Knowledge Discovery* (Springer, 2011). The companion website is here:

```
https://rattle.togaware.com
```

The University of California-Irvine Machine Learning Repository plays such a huge role in the book you're reading (see Chapters 6–12) that I thought I should mention it again. Here's how its creator prefers that I tell you about it:

> Lichman, M. (2013). UCI Machine Learning Repository [`http://archive.ics.uci.edu/ml`]. Irvine, CA: University of California, School of Information and Computer Science.

Thank you, UCI Anteaters!

If machine learning interests you, take a comprehensive look at the field (under its other name, "statistical learning"): Gareth James, Daniela Witten, Trevor Hastie, and Robert Tibshirani's *An Introduction to Statistical Learning with Applications in R* (Springer, 2017).

An Introduction to Neural Networks, by Ben Krose and Patrick van der Smagt, is a little dated, but you can get it for the low, low price of nothing:

```
www.infor.uva.es/~teodoro/neuro-intro.pdf
```

TIP

After you download a large PDF, it's a good idea to upload it into an ebook app, like Google Play Books. That turns the PDF into an ebook and makes it easier to navigate on a tablet.

Databases

The R-bloggers website has a nice article on working with databases. Check it out here:

```
www.r-bloggers.com/working-with-databases-in-r
```

Of course, R-bloggers has terrific articles on a lot of R-related topics!

I learned quite a bit about RFM (Recency Frequency Money) analysis and customer segmentation at `www.putler.com/rfm-analysis`.

I have a feeling you will, too.

Maps and Images

The area of maps is a fascinating one. In Chapter 14, I show you the easiest way to get started. You might be interested in something at a higher level. If so, read *Introduction to visualising spatial data in R* by Robin Lovelace, James Cheshire, Rachel Oldroyd (and others). You'll find it at

```
https://cran.r-project.org/doc/contrib/intro-spatial-rl.pdf
```

David Kahle and Hadley Wickham's *ggmap: Spatial Visualization with ggplot2* is also at a higher level than Chapter 14 of this book. Point your browser here:

```
https://journal.r-project.org/archive/2013-1/kahle-wickham.pdf
```

Fascinated by `magick`? The best place to go is the primary source:

```
https://cran.r-project.org/web/packages/magick/vignettes/intro.
  html - drawing_and_graphics
```

Index

Symbols

A

B

C

D

E

H

I

K

L

M

Q

R

T

U

V

W

X

Y

Z

About the Author

Joseph Schmuller, PhD is a veteran of academia and corporate Information Technology. He is the author of several books on computing, including the three editions of *Teach Yourself UML in 24 Hours* (SAMS), the four editions of *Statistical Analysis with Excel For Dummies* (Wiley), and *Statistical Analysis with R For Dummies* (Wiley). He has created online coursework for Lynda.com, and he has written numerous articles on advanced technology. From 1991 through 1997, he was Editor-in-Chief of *PC AI* magazine.

He is a former member of the American Statistical Association, and he has taught statistics at the undergraduate and graduate levels. He holds a B.S. from Brooklyn College, an M.A. from the University of Missouri-Kansas City, and a Ph.D. from the University of Wisconsin, all in psychology. He and his family live in Jacksonville, Florida, where he is a Research Scholar at the University of North Florida.

Dedication

For my awesome MA thesis mentor, Jerry Sheridan — who taught me a thing or two about projects a long time ago . . .

Author's Acknowledgments

So I keep writing these *For Dummies* titles, and the fun just keeps increasing. I had a total blast with this one. I explored some new areas, expanded my horizons, and best of all, I get to tell you all about it.

No author can write a book without a great team, and Wiley always provides one. Acquisitions Editor Katie Mohr started the ball rolling. My continuing compadre Project Editor Paul Levesque monitored my writing, and kept all the moving parts in motion. Coordinating all the necessary components in a book like this is way harder than it sounds, and not nearly as easy as Paul makes it look. Copy Editor Becky Whitney tightened my prose and made it easier to read. Technical Editor Russ Mullen made sure the code and the technical aspects were correct. I am the owner and sole proprietor of any errors that remain.

Speaking of indispensable individuals, my thanks to David Fugate of Launchbooks.com for representing me in this effort.

My mentors in statistics in college and graduate school shaped my knowledge, and thus influenced the book you're holding: Mitch Grossberg (Brooklyn College); Al Hillix, Jerry Sheridan, the late Mort Goldman, and the late Larry Simkins (University of Missouri–Kansas City); and Cliff Gillman, and the late John Theios (University of Wisconsin–Madison). I hope my books are an appropriate testament to my mentors who have passed on.

As always, my thanks to Kathy for her inspiration, her patience, her support, and her love.

Publisher's Acknowledgments

Acquisitions Editor: Katie Mohr
Senior Project Editor: Paul Levesque
Copy Editor: Becky Whitney
Technical Editor: Russ Mullen
Editorial Assistant: Matthew Lowe
Sr. Editorial Assistant: Cherie Case

Production Editor: G. Vasanth Koilraj
Cover Image: © whiteMocca/Shutterstock